Country Lawyer

Books by Bellamy Partridge

SIR BILLY HOWE: *Life of the Gay Revolutionary General*
AMUNDSEN: *The Splendid Norseman*
THE ROOSEVELT FAMILY IN AMERICA: *An Imperial Saga*

The Country Lawyer Goes to Church

COUNTRY LAWYER

by
BELLAMY PARTRIDGE

Illustrated by
STEPHEN J. VOORHIES

Whittlesey House

McGRAW-HILL BOOK COMPANY, INC.
NEW YORK · LONDON

PUBLISHED BY WHITTLESEY HOUSE
A division of the McGraw-Hill Book Company, Inc.

Printed in the United States of America by The Maple Press Co., York, Pa.

TO THE MEMORY OF MY FATHER

Samuel Selden Partridge

Contents

Contents

Country Lawyer

By Way of Introduction

VILLAGE life in America was at its best when, in the late sixties, my father opened a law office in Phelps, New York. The spirit of family solidarity—that priceless importation of the Pilgrim Fathers, worth far more than all the tables and chairs, real and imaginary, brought over in the *Mayflower*—was still alive in the land. A son of the small town might go off to college in quest of an education, but once he had been graduated he would come home and go into business with his father or open a store or office of his own across the street. The daughter was content to marry the boy next door and set up housekeeping just around the corner. The days of the bond salesman and filling station were happily far beyond the horizon. If a boy went off to the city to live, people used to feel sorry for him because there seemed to be no place for him in the home town.

Phelps was a serene and gracious example of what the small town could be before the coming of the automobile. From end to end the main street was lined by tall elms and maples, with here and there a gnarled locust or a shedding chestnut tree to relieve the monotony. My father's first shingle was hung from the limb of a tree outside his office window. At that time there were shade trees in front of nearly every place of business in the village. Many of these grizzled giants had been there when the street was still an Indian trail; but, alas, they fell before the unsparing ax of progress and were replaced by tie rails and hitching posts at which long rows of horses stood stamping and switching in the summer sun or shivering before the searching blast of a winter's gale.

The town was for the greater part built along a single street. There were, of course, some back streets, but they were known only to the people who lived on them, and the tax assessor. The life of the town was along the main thoroughfare, and had been since the days when the old stagecoaches came rumbling in from the last leg of the Albany run and changed horses for the first leg of the run to Buffalo.

John Decker Robinson, a gentleman in fringed coat and buckskin moccasins, said to be the first settler, is reputed to have arrived by canoe in 1789. He had pushed through the lands of the Onondagas well up into the hunting grounds of the Senecas by way of the Oswego River and the outlet of Canandaigua Lake. The council fires of the Eries and the Niagaras were smoldering off to the west of him, and the tepees of the Irondequoits were scattered along the shores of Lake Ontario only a score of miles to the north. But the intrepid John was not afraid of the Indians; he had come to trade with them—as well as to clear himself a homestead on their fertile acres, now that Sullivan's Raid had demonstrated to the redskins the advantage of being polite to white settlers.

John had pitched his first camp not far from the ford where the Indian trail crossed the stony bed of a creek. And he had chosen the place wisely, for not long afterward the State Survey came through and laid out a highway which crossed the creek at this selfsame ford. Other settlers came in on horseback and by covered wagon, and soon the population began to feel that the place should have a name. Like

4

the simple woodsmen that they were, they chose the name from nature, and because of the vast number of hammer-headed birds which congregated thereabouts they called the place Woodpecker Village.

As the town grew, however, the name began to seem inadequate. With Syracuse, Geneva, Aurelius, Marcellus, Brutus, Cato, Sempronius, and Venice dotting the neighboring landscape, it was inevitable that a high-sounding name should be adopted. The choice finally fell on one of the great continental capitals of Europe, and while stumps were still standing in the middle of Main Street the name was officially changed to Vienna.

For a time this name satisfied the craving for elegance, though a little local flavor was added by pronouncing the name "Vy-enna." But eventually the owners of the great Phelps and Gorham Purchase, by which a huge slab of what is now the western end of New York state was bought from Massachusetts, began to take a hand in the naming of the lands they had bought and arbitrarily christened the township Phelps. In time the village reluctantly followed suit, and the name of the gay continental capital gave way to the drab and colorless name of a real estate operator.

For more than half a century my father practiced there as a country lawyer, occupying the same office and using the same furniture for forty consecutive years. During the last decade of his life I was his law partner and closest associate. He was a great storyteller, and many of the incidents in this volume have been related just as I heard them from him. Others were found in his files, some by chance and some by dusty research at the prompting of my own recollection or that of some aged inhabitant who had been a juryman or perhaps a spectator at a trial.

The source material to which I am most deeply indebted, however, is a little black notebook in which my father had jotted down curious incidents of his practice, of which no other record was ever found. Some of the entries sketched the outline of an incident; others gave pages of dialogue and even bits of description. It was obviously material from which he intended to write some of the story of a country lawyer—an ambition which was never fulfilled and which I have long desired to attempt.

About this informal record of his my father had maintained the strictest secrecy, for in all the years I spent around his office I didn't know of its existence until quite by accident I came upon it, woolly with dust, in an unused compartment of an old desk.

Although the incidents related in this volume are without exception taken from actual cases from my father's practice, I have in most instances used fictitious names in order to keep in strict confidence the privacy of his clients, even though many of them have moved on to that happy state where privacy no longer greatly matters.

The fact that these incidents have been taken from the practice of a single country lawyer in an upstate New York town should not be accepted as a reason for regarding either the town or the lawyer as regional. The setting could well have been duplicated in any of five thousand small towns scattered over the American landscape; and the country lawyer might as easily have sprung from Kansas or Kentucky origin as from a Vermont-born father and a mother of native New York stock.

The period of my father's practice as a country lawyer— the half century of comparatively peaceful times between Appomattox and Sarajevo—seems from the viewpoint of today to have been the golden age of the country town and the country lawyer. I do not mean to say that life was better then or fuller: merely that, more secluded and less regimented than life today, it gave greater scope to the development of the individual and of the flavor of the locality.

1. A Place to Hang His Shingle

MY REMEMBRANCE of my father as a country lawyer dates from the time when I first saw him standing in the light of the evening lamp removing the tape by which the pages of a legal paper were bound together. Having removed the tape, he shuffled the pages and went around the dining-room table, distributing them among the members of the family, who sat with pens in their hands and inkwells before them, ready for an evening of copying.

This was back in the eighties before the typewriter had come into general use. It had been patented in the sixties, but the inventors were still busy trying to make it work, and all legal papers had to be written out by hand.

This particular occasion must have been the first evening that I had been allowed to help with the copying. I had been training for the event for some time; one had to be a fast and accurate penman. The thought of copying papers does not seem so attractive to me now, but then it was the most desirable thing in life, for it meant that I could sit up until ten o'clock, when the rest of the family went to bed. We were eight children—and a lawyer's children were expected to help with the copying of legal papers just as a farmer's children were expected to help to get in the crops.

7

We used to gather around the table as soon as the supper dishes had been cleared away, and evening after evening we would sit there and write until it was time to go to bed. For a lawyer with a good practice the means of having papers quickly and accurately copied was a matter of great importance. Sometimes a long complaint in a real estate action with complicated descriptions of "all that tract or parcel of land" would run out to twenty or more pages, and quite often there would be more than a dozen defendants. Of course, a complete copy would have to be written out for each—and that was where we children could be useful.

After the various pages had been distributed around the circle, our method was to copy a page and pass it to the right. By the time each one of us had had all the pages the task would be finished. If there were eight of us at work there would be eight complete copies of the document, though no two would be in the same handwriting.

While we copied, my father usually sat at his desk in the library, bending over his calf-bound tomes and making notes on a large yellow pad. He was a man of medium height with a high, square forehead and snapping black eyes. He had a bold, almost a fearless chin, though nearly all his life it was hidden behind a beard. His hair what was left of it at this time was wavy and sprinkled with gray, and he was beginning to take on a little weight. Though habitually slow in his movements, he could on occasion move with the speed of lightning. In framing his legal papers he composed rapidly and seldom made any considerable changes afterward, and when it came to copying he could easily outdistance us all. Occasionally he would get up and come out to see how we were getting along; and sometimes when he was concentrating on his work he would forget what he had come for and would turn around and go back to his desk without knowing that he had been near us. Sometimes my mother would copy, too, though she was usually busy darning innumerable stockings or cutting down clothes to fit the coming generation.

We lived in a house large enough to be a hotel. It was three stories high, with an unbeautiful mansard roof. I have heard my father describe it as a packing-box type of house. There were four large rooms on the ground floor with a hallway through the middle. The library and dining room were at the left of the front door, and the parlor and back parlor at the right. Double doors connected the four rooms, and when these were all open we had a fine place to dance.

An addition at the back housed ample kitchens, pantries, and storerooms and provided a number of small sleeping rooms on the second floor. The master bedrooms in the main part of the house were always referred to as "chambers." There were the front chamber, the east chamber, the blue chamber. No crowding was necessary in order to find space for the eight children, a grandmother, an aunt or two, and an occasional cousin who would come for a week and stay all summer.

Our lot covered an acre of ground, with a lawn that always seemed unnecessarily large to me, and a garden that, when I had a certain number of rows to hoe on a summer day and there happened to be a ball game, looked bigger than the Great Plains.

We were, I imagine, a rather noisy family when we were not at work on a copying assignment. Nearly all of us could play some musical instrument, and there was endless practicing. Music for dancing could be furnished at almost any time, and, with a nucleus of eight to start with, our house was a magnet for the children of the neighborhood.

The copying of papers that I have been describing was not an isolated occurrence. Sometimes we would work every evening for a week, and a fortnight rarely went by when some of us were not called upon to help out by making copies of this or that. My father had a regular copyist

9

besides. Lawyers had *copyists* in those days—not stenographers or secretaries. He used to pay Libby Weston fifteen cents an hour for her work, and she was very glad to get it. She was accurate, but she was slow, and if father was in a hurry to get things finished he used to bring them home with him at night and turn them over to members of the family.

Libby did a good part of her work at home, though she was usually willing to come and sit in the office with her copying while father was away at court, as he was quite a good deal of the time. He was always in the Surrogate's Court on Mondays with some probate matter, and he rarely missed going on Saturday to the Special Term, the court for motions. And while he was gone, Libby was in charge.

She would sit at the flat-top desk in the front office, with a background of dusty pigeonholes, and smile brightly at anyone who entered the door, though she obviously did not belong there. This was a man's office with masculinity sticking out all over it. A man's old hat and rubber raincoat hung from an iron rack in one corner, and a man's galoshes and umbrella gathered dust underneath. The place reeked of cigar smoke, and there were usually several partially smoked cigars lying on the edge of a desk or bookshelf, cold and clammy, looking like dead mice. Libby always acted as much afraid of these extinct cheroots as if they really were dead mice.

Pigeonhole cabinets crammed with faded papers ran halfway to the ceiling, and a potbellied stove hugged the inner wall between the two rooms. The chairs were heavy, sturdy, uncomfortable—all except one, a low rocker intended for women clients. For thirty years my father tripped over the rockers of that chair almost daily, but never once was he known to sit down in it.

The rear office, my father's study, looked out on the hospitable doorway of a livery stable before which interesting transactions in the horse world were frequently taking place. In the center of this room was a large flat-top table piled with bundles of papers tied with faded pink tapes. These were the papers that were currently active. Behind the table was a stand-up desk at which my father used to work when he was tired of sitting and wanted to rest. A gloomy-looking safe stood in one corner and a mahogany commode in another, and on all sides, the crowded bookshelves reached to the ceiling. There was a large rug in this room, and a scattering of the same sturdy, uncomfortable chairs.

The tradition of the law hung like a cloud over the entire place, which had been built for a law office in the eighteen twenties and had never been used for another purpose. My father had taken a fancy to the place the first time he saw it. He had to wait ten years before it was available, but when he finally got possession he dug in and stayed for nearly half a century.

My father was not a native of Phelps. He had come there from Rochester upon his admission to the bar shortly after the Civil War. There was even at that time a current belief that the cities were overcrowded, and a young man's best chance for advancement was in going to a small place and, in the oft-repeated words of the distinguished journalist, growing up with the country. On that one point my father agreed with Mr. Greeley; and in addition to that he had a strong desire for country life. Though city-born, he had spent much of his boyhood on a farm and had acquired a love of the soil that stayed with him through life. Even before he was admitted to the bar he had been married. One of the eight children had already arrived and another was on the way before he had heard of what was said to be a very good place to hang out his shingle.

When he told my mother about it she got out the map and spread it on the table. Phelps township, green and symmetrical, lay in the northeast corner of Ontario County. The village was a tiny dot in almost the exact center of the township. My father marked a piece of paper and scaled the distance to near-by towns. Geneva lay eight miles to the south and Canandaigua, the county seat, fifteen miles to the west. Waterloo, across the line in Seneca County, was twelve miles east. And to the north, in Wayne County, were Lyons, scaled at ten miles distant, and Newark, at seven. According to the scale Phelps was only thirty miles from Rochester, though, as they learned afterward, the windings of the railroad which meandered this way and that to reach a town or dodge an obstruction of nature added a mile of side drift to every three miles of dead reckoning. So the distance was more nearly forty miles by rail.

My mother and father were elated over the prospects of their future home, whispering about it half the night because they were too excited to sleep. The next morning my father caught the early train and went down to look over the place.

As the train came to a stop before the little station he had a strange feeling that he was coming home. He felt even more at home after the train had pulled out and left him standing where he could smell the fragrance of new-cut hay drying in the sun. He fell into conversation with the station agent and learned from him that the last census of the village had shown a population of close to twelve hundred, though there were over five thousand in the township. He also learned that the place had been a change station on the old post road between Syracuse and Rochester.

"Is there a lawyer in the town?" my father asked.

The station agent smiled. "Well, sort of—in a way. Charley Hobson has an office here. You'll see it as you go along the street." He then went on to explain that Charley was old and in ill health and that he was so well-to-do that he didn't need to work any longer anyway.

"Do you think there's an opening here for a young law-yer?" my father asked.

"Ought to be," the station agent answered promptly. "Old Charley always made a good living here. Why don't you go talk to him? Lives in the big brick house on the corner about forty rods below the Town Hall."

"I'll do that," said my father. "How do you get to the Town Hall?"

"You can't miss it. It's on Main Street right in the middle of the town—acrost from the Inn. Just walk along Church Street until you come to Main."

My father found Church Street a pleasant thoroughfare lined on either side by tall elms and maples. The houses were not large, but they were well kept and comfortable-looking. Halfway through the block he passed a small stone church

and saw just beyond it a compact one-story building with pillars in front. He recognized at a glance that it was a replica in miniature of the county courthouse in Canandaigua —itself a copy of a Greek temple. Then he noticed a small sign hanging from a large tree outside the plank sidewalk. It read:

C. E. HOBSON
ATTY AT LAW
Notary Public with Seal

He tried the door but found it locked. Evidently this was not one of the days when Mr. Hobson was at his post. He peered through the window to get an idea of the size of the rooms; then he walked off a few paces and stood looking over the building. What a place that would be to start his career as a lawyer! With one last look and the hope that the office was for rent, he went on to the principal business center, which he found clustered around the intersection where Church Street came into Main.

It was, as the station agent had told him, a one-street town. Everything that was not on Main Street was just off. And the business buildings, all twenty of them of frame construction except the Woodpecker Inn and the Town Hall, nestled back under the giant shade trees which lined both sides of the street. Many of the business signs were nailed to the trees or hung suspended between a tree and the front of a building. Before the Inn, a brick building three stories in height, the largest in town, was a low horse block some fifteen feet long at which the stagecoaches had formerly stopped; and in a hitching shed at the rear the battered remains of an ancient stagecoach stood rotting with disuse. The street was unpaved, spacious, and almost free from traffic, though long lines of teams were tied to the posts and hitching rails along the dusty gutters dug deep by many years of stamping hoofs.

14

As my father stood there looking up and down the street, filling his lungs with the clean country air, he caught a sudden whiff of newly split wood. A moment later he became conscious of the jingle of trace chains and the creak of harness leather. Even the clumping of the farmers' boots on the planks of the walks sounded familiar and good to him. Here was what he wanted—a life that was close to growing things, people of the soil around him, neighbors who would be friends. With every breath he drew he was feeling more and more at home.

In a fork of the street a hundred paces to the left of the corner stood a circular bandstand with a high-pointed roof topped by a flagstaff from which the colors were displayed on days when there was to be an evening concert. Across from the bandstand, set well back from the street, was the empty hulk of the Old Globe Hotel, its doors and windows boarded up but its painted sign still plainly visible, though the building had been vacant for many years. It was, he was told, a relic which marked the passing of the stagecoach, and it had put up its shutters a few years after the coming of the railroad.

Between the Old Globe and the bandstand Main Street dipped and at the bottom of a short hill followed a stone bridge across a brawling stream. My father caught a glimpse of a carriage factory and a stone mill and, beyond the mill, the soft glow of the forge through the open doors of a blacksmith shop. Looking in the other direction along Main Street, he could see the more pretentious houses of the town and the steeple of a church thrusting up above the deep green of the towering shade trees. Down this way, he recalled, old Mr. Hobson lived; but he thought that before seeing him he had better call on some of the businessmen of the town.

On the corner behind him the bank door stood invitingly open, and he went in and introduced himself. Jim Hoyt, the banker, received him with encouragement. There was work in town for a lawyer to do, he said, and certainly old Charley was not doing it. Leman Hoskins, the banker across the street, was not so encouraging. He shook his head dubiously. A young lawyer, he opined, might pick up a living, but he would never get rich here. Why not go where there was a little more wealth running around loose? My father learned afterwards that Mr. Hoskins had a son then away at school who, he hoped, would be interested in the law and build up a practice in Phelps. It was a hope which was never fulfilled; the son turned out to be more interested in fast horses and fast women. The aversion that my father felt toward Mr. Hoskins on this first meeting he never had reason to change. The merchants and townspeople, however, were friendly and cordial. Most of them agreed that there was a splendid opening for a young lawyer, and some went so far as to promise him their law business—if they ever had any.

This was very heartening to my father, but he kept telling himself that he must not make up his mind until after he had talked with Mr. Hobson, that the old lawyer's attitude might change everything. He completely forgot to eat lunch, and early in the afternoon he opened the gate before the spacious grounds of the Hobson place and walked nervously up to the front door. It was old Mr. Hobson himself who answered a jerky pull at the doorbell.

He was a small man with bandy legs, and as he opened the door a crack and peered out over the tops of his glasses he looked both inquisitive and fierce. When my father explained the purpose of his call, Mr. Hobson threw wide the door and swept him inside with a motion of the hand. The gusto with which he was received only added to my father's nervousness; he thought that Mr. Hobson was altogether too glad to see him. But he needn't have worried. Mr. Hobson's enthusiasm was real. He was pleased at the prospect of having another lawyer in town so that people would not keep bothering him with their legal troubles.

"They come down here at night and ask me to draw papers for them," he grumbled. "They even stop outside the fence and fire their legal questions at me while I'm working in my garden. It was all right as long as Rockwell lived; I used to send them to him and he'd take care of them. But since he died they've been bothering the life out of me."

My father had not talked with Mr. Hobson for more than five minutes before his mind was made up; he was going to settle in Phelps. The next thing was to find an office. He was, of course, disappointed when Mr. Hobson refused to rent him the little office building on Church Street. The old lawyer assured him that he had no intention of practicing law there and only wanted a place where he could putter around. Good office space above almost any of the store buildings in town, he said, could be had for a song. My father's real trouble was going to be in finding a place to live.

This proved to be only too true. My father had no difficulty in leasing two large rooms over the drugstore; but when he did eventually get a home he found it necessary to buy one. And such a home! What he really needed was a little cottage with five or six rooms; what he bought was a mansion with sixteen. It was the only house on East Main Street that was for sale. He didn't know what he would ever do with all that room, but that was because he had no idea of what the future had in store for him.

This big place cost him $3,500. He paid $1,000 down—all the money he had—and secured the balance by a purchase money mortgage. When his estate came to be settled after he had lived there for some fifty years, the place brought just what he had paid for it, $3,500.

My father had so concentrated his attention on his quest of an office and a house that he missed the last train for Rochester and was compelled to stay in town overnight. He

17

was disappointed, of course, but the station agent spoke so highly of Woodpecker Inn that he decided to give the place a trial. He sent a telegram from the station to explain his delay—there were no telephones at the time—and walked over to the Inn. It was, he reflected as he went along, about the only place he had not visited while he was making his calls.

He found the proprietor, John Tickner, familiarly known as Old Tick, in his shirt sleeves and carpet slippers, seated in an easy chair, reading aloud to all who cared to listen a dispatch in a morning paper.

Old Tick stopped as my father entered and glanced at him over the top of his paper. "Somep'm I can do for you, sir?" he asked in his high, querulous voice.

"I find that I've missed the last train for Rochester, and I'd like to get accommodations for the night."

"You live in Rochester?" Old Tick lowered his paper and eyed him suspiciously. Well-dressed strangers were always an object of his distrust.

"Yes. I came here today to look over—"

"Whereabouts in Rochester do you live?"

"On Ely Street."

"Never heared of it. Ain't no such street there 't I know of."

"It's near Main—up above Clinton."

"I know all about Clinton, and I know all about Main." Old Tick shook his head. "But I never heared nuthin' about no Ely Street."

"It is rather secluded."

Old Tick folded up his newspaper. "Must be. Say—" He began to look around the room. "Where's your baggage? Ain't you got no grip or nuthin'?"

"Well, no, I haven't. You see, I didn't intend to stay when I left home this morning. As I told you, I missed my train."

18

"Folks around here don't usually miss trains."

My father smiled. "I'll try not to let it happen again. Now how about a room?"

Old Tick weighed the situation. It did not look too good. Young feller giving a fake address. Still, he had on good clothes—and fifty cents was fifty cents. "It'll cost you half a dollar—in advance," he said finally. "And you can't take no women up there neither."

Old Tick squinted at the register after my father had signed his name. "S. S. Partridge," he read slowly. "That's your name, is it?"

"That's right."

"And you live in Rochester?"

"Correct."

"That'll be half a dollar."

As my father laid the money on the counter he noticed a large brass gong hanging on a nail driven in the wall. Old Tick intercepted the look.

"That there's my cymbal." He struck it lightly with a fingernail. "When you hear it you'll know that supper's ready."

The supper hour was approaching when my father saw Old Tick take down the cymbal and make ready to beat it with a padded stick. The innkeeper took out a large silver watch as thick as his wrist and laid it on the counter. Then, with the stick poised for action, he watched the second hand until it was on the tick of the hour; whereupon he began to belabor the cymbal, which was nearly two feet across, until the windows rattled with the unendurable clatter. Still beating it, the old fellow made a wide circle of the office, passed through the barroom, then along the hallway, where he paused for a time at the foot of the stairs, hammering lustily, though my father was the only guest in the house. After that he stepped out on the front veranda, from which he gave the approaching night a rousing salute.

19

"When you hear this in the mornin'," he said, "it'll be six o'clock. Train goes at seven."

My father nodded. "I'll be ready. I won't miss it again."

When he did hear the gong again it seemed to him that he had just closed his eyes. The place was pitch-dark. And after he had lighted the kerosene lamp his watch told him that the hour was only a little after midnight. Still, he could smell coffee brewing and the appetizing aroma of food cooking; so he dressed and went down to the office. Old Tick gaped at him as if he were seeing a ghost.

"Jees Cri!" he wheezed. "I fergot all about you. 'Tain't breakfast time yet. I was just poundin' on the cymbal to tell the folks acrost the street that their supper is ready. They're havin' a dance up there." He scowled at my father. "You'd oughta knowed that yourself. Didn't you hear the music?"

"Well, yes, I did hear distant music, but my room's on the other side of the house."

"Don't make no difference. It's your own fault. You shoulda knowed better'n to get dressed and come down at this time of night." And Old Tick turned and shuffled out toward the kitchen.

As my father used to tell the story, he let Old Tick get away with this and went back to bed without a word of protest. He said that he did not want to begin life in his future home town by quarreling with the innkeeper. This may have been true, but my father was a man of violent temper in his younger days, and what he must have been thinking about Old Tick as he trudged back upstairs to go to bed would not look well in print.

It was, however, the beginning of a friendship that was to last for many, many years.

2. The First Case

AT THE time my father was admitted to the bar his knowledge of the law was entirely theoretical. He had never drawn a deed, he had never framed a complaint or an answer; indeed, he had never even filled out a summons or a subpoena. He realized, of course, that although he was a member of the bar he was not yet equipped to render very valuable legal services to the public, and to make up for his deficiency he spent a few intensive weeks in one of the busiest offices in Rochester trying to grasp something of the practical machinery of the law business. Here he learned to draw simple wills as well as contracts and conveyances, how to start actions and serve papers. He sat in on trials and arguments, but at the time when he hung out his shingle and opened his office in Phelps he had tried only one case in his life—a little skirmish in police court in which he defended a janitor who was facing a charge of petty larceny.

Preparation for the bar in the sixties was much simpler than it is today. Academic requirements were practically nil. Nor were there formal examiners who made it a business to tangle up and trip, if possible, any youth who fondly imagined that he wanted to be a lawyer. Some local jurist was told off to examine a group of candidates, and he examined them according to his own fitness and his own ideas. If he happened to be a probate lawyer they were in for a severe quizzing on the law of wills, whereas if he was a criminal lawyer the questions were more likely to veer toward the distinction between manslaughter and murder, or the theory of reasonable doubt. And there were oral as well as written questions to test the candidate's fitness.

There was little or no supervision of the reading of a law clerk in those old days. The student was expected to read the commentaries of Kent and Blackstone and to familiarize himself with the works of Coke, Chitty, and Story, but there was no prescribed course of study such as is furnished by the law schools of today.

If my father had done a little less reading and a little more of the actual work of a going law office he would have had much less grief over some of the early clients who came to him with questions which puzzled him and which really should have been matters of ordinary routine. For example, the proper way to describe a cow in a chattel mortgage caused him no end of trouble, and the effect of hortatory words written on the outside of a will after it had been properly signed and witnessed had him digging into his books for half the night.

Business began coming to him from old Charley Hobson before my father had chairs enough in his office for the clients to sit down on. And within a week he had been retained as defense counsel in what turned out to be one of the locally famous cases of the season, though it never went further than the justice court. This case was the outgrowth of a desire on the part of the youth of the town to give the advent of the Fourth of July a suitable welcome.

For many years the arrival of the Fourth had been heralded by the lighting of a huge street bonfire on the bank corner. The preceding year, however, the boys had thoughtlessly built their fire so close to the curb that the heat from

22

The country lawyer and his wife
at the time of their marriage.

it had cracked a plate-glass window in the bank, and the Village Fathers had passed an ordinance forbidding all fires in the streets except for the burning of leaves and grass. The Solons had also taken the precaution of warning the merchants and storekeepers that if they should furnish the boys with the materials for a bonfire they would be held accountable for any damages that might result.

But, as was to have been expected, the youth of the town did not propose to have their patriotic zeal curbed by the ukase of Four Old Men, and as soon as night had fallen on the evening of the third they began to scout around for materials that would make a good bonfire. When they found the usual supply missing from the back doors of the stores, they enlarged the scope of their quest, with the result that when, on the stroke of twelve, the match was applied, the astonished villagers beheld on the bank corner a beacon fire, the like of which, both in brilliance and in aftereffects, had not been seen within the memory of the oldest inhabitant. It was such a bonfire as Chic Sales' "specialist" would have appreciated and enjoyed, for it was composed almost entirely of the small though useful structures of which that talented fabricator in wood was an acknowledged master builder.

Whoops of delight arose from the spectators as the flames went crackling upward through the well-seasoned wood which ignited with the speed of tinder boxes and burned with the roar of a forest fire.

Some of the buildings, as they burned, were neatly outlined, the doors, the oddly cut windows, the little wooden chimneys boldly etched in flame. High on top of the pile was a tidy red building with yellow trimmings which matched in color and architecture the barn of the Village President. Before the flames had reached this brilliant red-and-yellow apex of the pile, murmurings of regret were heard that it should have been given so important a position, only to be turned upside down. When, however, it became well ignited and the beholders saw how it burned in three tall pillars of fire reaching far into the sky—two large and one small—their lamentations died on their lips, and a laughter that was Jovian indeed burst in great tumult upon the midnight air.

As a bonfire it was a decided success, but there were, as I have intimated, reverberations. The Village Fathers were outraged, incensed, and insulted. They turned the minions of the law out with instructions to "get" the culprits, and before the end of the week there were arrests. Five young men, four of them scions of the best families, were arraigned before Lysander Redman, a local justice of the peace, charged with malicious mischief and violation of an ordinance—and my father was retained to defend them.

He entered a plea of not guilty for his clients and called for a jury. This required an adjournment, and he took the youths and their fathers to his office for a conference. When the case came on for trial a week later, the Village Fathers showed how much in earnest they were by appearing in court with a prosecutor from Geneva and twenty witnesses. Some of the most indignant of the witnesses were those who had laughed the most loudly on the night of the fire.

The arraignment had been in Justice Redman's office, but the trial was held in the Town Hall. Several times a day my father had passed the rather plain stone building with a wooden portico reaching all the way across the sidewalk, but he had never been inside it before. The entrance to the hall was in the middle of the building, with the town clerk's office on one side and a shoe store on the other. A broad stairway led to the second floor, which was completely occupied by a large barnlike room with recessed windows. Above the stairway a stepped gallery extended all the way up to the raftered ceiling. Across the end of the room opposite the gallery was a sturdy fence. Beyond the fence were two large tables, a number of chairs for the litigants and their lawyers, and a straight-backed bench for the jury. There were a few benches along the walls outside the fence, but for the main part of the crowd, aside from those seated on the hard wooden steps of the gallery, there were no seating accommodations at all.

As the presiding justice walked in with the two lawyers, followed by the five defendants and their fathers, the crowd fell back to let them inside the enclosure. Then the gate was shut, and a constable was put in charge. The justice opened his docket book and called the name of a juryman. A man from the crowd came forward and was admitted through the gate. If he was accepted he remained, but if he was rejected he was led out through the gate. A satisfactory jury was soon found and sworn in, and, after a brief opening by the prosecutor, the examination of witnesses began.

The prosecution had no trouble in proving that all the defendants were on the scene on the night of the fire. Some of them were recognized as persons who had helped to draw the light wagon by which the fuel was brought to the location of the fire. Others were pointed out as members of the party who had piled up the materials in preparation for the conflagration. And one defendant was positively identified by an enraged citizen as the person who had sat on his chest to hold him down while the other boys had carried away certain inflammable parts of his freehold. No evidence was introduced, however, to show who had applied the match.

It was on this ground that my father moved for a dismissal of the complaint. Motion denied. Exception. He then announced that he would call no witnesses and was ready to present his case to the jury.

Though there had been some moments of hilarity during the trial, my father chose to regard his summary to the jury as a momentous occasion. It was his first opportunity to show his new friends and future clients what he was made of.

He felt conscious of his youth and inexperience as he stood up before them; but he was unafraid, and he could not have been more serious if he had been addressing the Supreme Court of the United States. If people had come there expecting coarse jokes and broad humor they were doomed to disappointment. Never once did he refer even indirectly to the fuel of which the bonfire had been built. He confined himself strictly to the safe if humorless subject of patriotism. Were these young men to be punished, were they to have their records blackened and their characters besmirched because of a crime which was nothing more than excess of patriotism?

For a full hour he made the eagle scream. This was really no great effort on his part, since he still had fresh in his mind a Fourth of July oration that he had delivered in the little town of Irondequoit only a few days before, and he let the judge and the jury have the whole of it. Packed to suffocation, the Town Hall rang to the rafters with applause when he had finished.

The prosecutor had taken the case as the average lawyer takes justice court litigation. He regarded it as trivial and had made no particular preparation for it. He must have been somewhat surprised at the flight of eloquence displayed by his youthful opponent; but he disregarded it entirely and shouted with indignation over the uncontested evidence in the case. The good men and true, however, were not interested in uncontested evidence. Patriotism was much more important to them than a miscellaneous lot of carpenter's masterpieces, and after all the shouting was over they brought in a verdict of not guilty.

With fifty dollars in his pocket—ten from each defendant —my father walked home, feeling very much on top of the world. He laid the money on the table before my mother where they could both look at it and enjoy it—the first real money he had ever earned at his profession. There was never any other money like it. He remarked that it would pay for the new baby. It did, several months later, with twenty-five dollars left over.

The trial of this case brought my father welcome publicity, but it also brought him a nickname that was not quite so welcome. As he was going out of his front gate the next morning, two of the neighborhood boys went past. They touched their caps respectfully—a little too respectfully, he thought—and said, "Good morning, Judge." My father smiled as he returned their greeting. But he did not smile when the clerk in the post office said, "Well, Judge, I see you won your case."

My father did not look up from his mail. "Better be careful what you put on your bonfires in the future," he said and turned and walked out.

He resented the use of the title, since he felt sure that it was based on a desire to tease him. He hoped that the little joke would soon be forgotten. Perhaps it was. But the title stuck. There were little variations, of course. In time it became "the Judge" and after a good many years, "the Old Judge." And, ironically enough, at no time in his life was he actually a judge.

The trial of the bonfire case brought him something more important than a high-sounding nickname, however, and that was a realization of how abysmally ignorant he was about conducting a case in court. He realized, as he looked back on the trial, how fortunate he had been to have the Irondequoit speech to fall back on, and he shuddered as he recalled how awkward and ill at ease he had been in his questioning of both jurors and witnesses. The difference between doing a thing himself and watching somebody else do it became painfully apparent. And it was plain to him that he would have been floundering hopelessly had it not been for the example of his opponent, who was a lawyer of experience.

27

It was at this time that he recalled the oft-repeated advice of the old judge in whose office he had read law. "The justice court is the natural training ground for the young lawyer," he used to say. "It's the cheapest place there is to buy your experience. And if you can't try a small case well you can't try a big one any better." My father had thought that the old jurist was harping too much on the importance of justice court training, but after a single experience he could see that there had not been harping enough.

The lesson had gone home in no uncertain way, and it was my father's boast that for the next ten years he did not lose a single opportunity to try a case in justice court. Indeed, he never lost his relish for a keen bout before a justice of the peace.

"Have you got ten dollars?" I once heard him ask a prospective client with a cause pending in justice court.

"No."

"Have you got five?"

"No."

"Have you got any money at all?"

The fellow shook his head. "No—just a little change."

"Then how do you expect to pay your witnesses their fees?"

"They've promised to come anyway."

"All right, I'll take the case. Only, of course, I'll want to talk to those witnesses before they go on the stand."

During his first few years in practice he tried literally hundreds of these minor cases, some of them involving a total amount of no more than fifteen dollars. From the standpoint of cash it was not remunerative business, but in the matter of imponderables it was priceless. All the time he was schooling himself in the selection of jurors, the examination of witnesses, the tactful handling of the court, and the parrying with difficult counsel. It is well known among lawyers that the pettifogger is at his best in the minor courts. He has, indeed, almost ceased to exist in the courts of record. The lower courts in the larger cities are still infested with attorneys of a low order who wrangle and connive, coach witnesses, and even suborn if they dare, but as the bench improves and the bar tightens its regulations, they are being crowded out, or at least kept in hand.

In justice court, however, there is no way to cope with them. Anyone may practice there, and in almost every community there is a shrewd old codger, possibly an ex-justice, who, though not a member of the bar, knows all the tricks and pitfalls of justice court practice. A justice of the peace can make his rulings on the admission of evidence but cannot enforce them. The pettifogger knows this, and over the objection of opposing counsel and the ruling of the court he goes right ahead and introduces any evidence that he thinks will help him win the case. To meet one of the gentry on his own ground, an attorney must be alert and more than ordinarily resourceful. My father's method of fighting the pettifogger was to turn his own weapons against him if possible.

He was once called upon to prosecute a case of hog stealing in a distant corner of the county, far from the beaten track and miles from the railroad. After a long, muddy drive he found himself confronted by a fat, shifty-eyed old pettifogger and knew that he was in for trouble. Theft is never too easy to prove. Thieves are seldom caught in the act, and to prove them guilty, circumstantial evidence is nearly always necessary. My father had a strong case, however, and in spite of the most determined and exasperating opposition, aided and abetted in every possible way by the court, which favored the defense at every opportunity, he drove home his evidence.

After both sides had rested, the defendant's lawyer got to his feet and solemnly intoned to the six-man jury of farmers one Latin quotation after another. "*Nulli est homini perpetuum*

29

bonum. Qui desiderat pacem praeparet bellum. O quam cito transit gloria mundi!"

The counsel for the defense rolled these under his tongue with relish, and the jury seemed much impressed. Then in a low, almost an injured tone he began a discussion of the "ridiculously inadequate" evidence that had been offered against his client. As he went on he gathered force and soon was shouting so that he could have been heard blocks away. But at the end he lowered his voice and fell once more into Latin. *"Ego cogito, ergo sum."*

After the defense counsel had seated himself my father rose and stood silent before the jury for a time. Then he began to intone in imitation of his opponent all the most common Latin phrases which came readily to mind.

"Sic semper tyrannus . . . multum in parvo . . . tempus fugit . . . e pluribus unum . . . "

He paused, looking earnestly from one member of the jury to another. "That, gentlemen of the jury, is Latin. *But,"* he shouted in a thunderous voice, "what has *Latin* got to do with it? This man was arrested for *stealing hogs*—!"

An outburst of laughter greeted this sally, and after that it was all over but the shouting. The defendant was held for the grand jury and eventually sent to Auburn, where he had a long time to reflect upon the maxims quoted by his learned counsel.

All the justices of the peace in a township have concurrent jurisdiction, and it is a favorite trick of the pettifogger to bring his suit before the justice least accessible to the defendant. The more isolated the place the better the pettifogger seems to like it. In an early case of my father's involving the sale of a threshing machine the defendant was summoned to appear before Justice Smith, a delightful old farmer who used to hold court in his own parlor among the framed mottoes on the wall and the wax flowers under glass. The stool of an Esty organ was used as the witness stand, and the opposing counsel sat at opposite ends of a sewing table. My father had brought with him a dozen or more threshing hands who were to be called as witnesses, but there was no room for them in the house, and they stood in the dooryard and listened to the testimony through the open windows.

When dinner time came the justice excused himself and retired to his own dining room to eat, leaving lawyers, litigants, and witnesses to sit in the parlor, where they could smell the tantalizing aroma of roasting meat, the pungent scent of pies baking in the oven. The case had not been completed at six o'clock, and the torture was repeated. There was no place within miles where they could go to eat; so they sat and suffered. The famished jurymen did not get the case until nearly nine o'clock, and at one minute after nine they were back with a verdict. My father never could remember which side won the case. That little detail was apparently not important enough to remain in his memory. But there was one thing he never could forget: the only person foresighted enough to bring his lunch was the pettifogger who brought the case.

During the early years of my father's practice there was hardly a week when he did not have horse cases to try. At that time the entire burden of rural transportation fell to old Dobbin. He pulled the plow and the farm machinery; he drew the crops to market; he hauled the buggies and carriages as well as the hacks and stages. Where a car or a tractor stands today there stood at that time a horse, or perhaps a team of horses.

A good horse, sound and well-broken, could be bought in those days for $100. For $50 a fair horse for work or general utility could be had. Usually these $50 nags were more than eight years old. After a horse has passed eight summers the condition of his teeth ceases to be an indication of his age. All that can be told is that he is more than eight years old. Nothing short of a high-blooded stepper would bring as much as $150. A good Morgan or a Hambletonian could be bought for that figure, and the books are full of cases in which a very ordinary critter would be sold as blooded stock. In almost every horse case the question of warranty would come up, a warranty as to age, breeding, disposition, or soundness.

With the passing of the horse, the justice court lost much of its color as well as its revenue; for swapping automobiles, even the kind that has the "heaves" and is knee-sprung, brings very little litigation into the justice court.

There was a famous old horse lawyer in Wayne County who had formerly been a Methodist minister but had fallen from grace and gone into law. He was a tall man, bald as an egg, with a long, bulbous nose that he used to stroke diligently whenever he was angry or perplexed. It was well to look out for yourself when old Luke Horton began to pull his nose. The old fellow was absolutely without ethics or principles, and he had a diabolical faculty for finding holes in the law through which a slimy malefactor could slip to safety.

When the ex-parson was around, no warranty, however ironclad, was safe unless it was in writing and nailed down. Old Luke's speech, which always had a strong nasal twang, was quick and jerky. In cross-examining he counted on confusing the witness by his speed, and he used to fire his questions with the rapidity and confusion of a corn popper. His summing up sounded like a mixture of prayer and Billingsgate. At times it was hard to tell whether he was addressing his remarks to the Squire or the Deity.

My father remarked once during a trial that he hardly knew whether to make his objections to this court or the one behind the Gates of Jasper.

"Either of 'em, Counselor," the parson snapped back. "One is as likely to give you hell as the other."

While he was acquiring the technique of pleading horse cases my father took some severe drubbings from Old Luke.

But the time came when he could meet the old horse wrangler on his own ground at even money. After that the news of a horse case between them would bring the whole countryside into town. Both were good entertainers, and in addition to a sharply tried lawsuit the spectators were sure of some good laughs. As a result of his experience with horse cases my father became a real expert on the diseases of horses. Veterinarians dreaded to be cross-examined by him, for he could question a man on a simple ailment like spavin for two hours without repeating himself. He once completely nullified by his cross-examination of a noted horse trainer testimony that might otherwise have cost his client the loss of a race horse worth several thousand dollars.

There were those who made a business of horse cases, but to my father they were simply part of the day's work. He took them whenever they came along, just as he took every other kind of case. And at the end of five or six years of training in justice court he had rounded into a very competent trial lawyer, at ease in court, with a gift in the selection of juries that amounted almost to clairvoyance and an aptitude for handling witnesses that kept his cases unusually free from the exceptions that so often wreck an otherwise watertight verdict.

3. He Surveys the Possibilities

EVER since my father's boyhood in the country he had wanted to grow things, and now he had his chance. With an acre of ground a man can keep himself pretty well occupied during his spare time. Always an early riser, my father was now up with the first twitterings of the earliest bird. He was at work in his garden long before the sun came up above the distant rim of the world. Here he worked silently for an hour or two before he came to the house and tapped on the stovepipe of the kitchen stove to wake up the hired girl who slept in the room directly above. He would shake down the stove and open the drafts, and by the time she was downstairs there would be enough fire to start the breakfast.

A large rising bell stood on a little corner shelf at the foot of the back stairs. Promptly at seven o'clock in summer and at seven-thirty in winter, this bell was rung lustily, first at the back stairs and then at the front. Breakfast was half an hour later.

Of course, before we children could sit down to breakfast we had to "go on the carpet"—that is, we had to pass a fairly rigid inspection by my mother. Faces, hands, ears, and necks must stand scrutiny. Collars must be clean, clothes in good order, and shoes properly polished. We used to line up in a row after racing down the stairs, for this was a case of first come, first served. We always hoped to skim through, but, alas, there was hardly a day when one of us did not have to go back to repair some oversight—perhaps a broken shoestring or a button off a blouse, though more often the offense was dirty fingernails or a hole in a stocking. Even today it is painful to recall that my sisters were almost never sent back—but they were older. Probably that is the explanation.

We used to grumble somewhat about the severity of the rules, but with so large a family, discipline had to be rather severe.

As the boys became old enough, they were expected to take care of the work around the place. In summer we cut the lawn and performed regular tasks assigned to us in the garden, and in winter there was snow to shovel from the walks and numerous heating stoves to take care of. The girls had their work, too. They looked after their rooms, and, though we usually had kitchen help—when we could get it —my sisters were supposed to set the table and, if they had no company, to help out with the dishes.

There were large maple trees in front of the place when my father bought it, but on the entire acre of land there were only two fruit trees. My father soon remedied this—he planted thirty. He also started an asparagus bed, set out grapes and berries and currants, and laid out an extensive garden. A garden is not so much trouble until it begins to come up. Once it is above ground, however, it shouts for attention, and my father found that it was more than he could take care of single-handed. For a good many years he worked in it for an hour or two every morning before going to the office and for another hour or two in the evening be- fore darkness, together, doubtless, with mosquitoes, finally drove him inside; but to keep the weeds down throughout the growing season he had to hire a man for at least two days a week.

With nobody around to watch them, these occasional workmen did plenty of loafing, and a great deal of hiring and firing went on for several seasons before my father finally found a gardener to his liking. This man, Jerry Billings, was a cantankerous fellow in his thirties, hard to get along with, always complaining about something; but he was so competent a gardener and so faithful a workman that my father put up with him in spite of his faults. There were plenty of people who did not like Jerry and would not have him around, but in time my father became quite attached to him and was more amused than annoyed by his whining. In fact, the arrangement worked out so well that Jerry stayed on year after year until his gardening activities were brought to an end by a catastrophe which made a startling change in his life and let my father in for one of the most difficult cases of his career, as we shall see later on.

Meanwhile, my father had been applying himself to the building up of a practice. One of the results of Mr. Hobson's lackadaisical attention to his legal work had been to drive many of his most desirable clients to out-of-town attorneys. Some of the business went to Geneva; some drifted to Lyons or Newark or other of the near-by towns, but the greater part went straight to Canandaigua, the county seat, which, in spite of its limited population, then about four thousand, had always been noted for its distinguished bar.

It was some little time before my father discovered to how great an extent his townspeople were taking their legal work to these other places. He did not know quite what to do about it and asked the advice of the old judge in whose office he had studied law. The jurist did not help him much. He warned him against soliciting business from people and gave him a sound talking to on the subject of professional ethics. The only solution, he said, was to make the people see that it was to their advantage to consult the home lawyer. Roughly speaking, it was the old mousetrap advice,

36

though not put quite so neatly as Emerson phrased it—if he did.

All the way home on the train my father kept thinking about it. If he was going to get that business he would have to be as good a lawyer as those the people were already consulting. In Geneva that meant George Hemiup, Dwight Backenstose, and Charley Rose; in Canandaigua he would have to measure up to Tom Bennett, Frank Rice, and Bradley Wynkoop; in Waterloo there was Colonel Manning; in Lyons, John Camp and old Judge Collins; and in Newark, Marvin Greenwood and Steve Williams. Most of these men were no older and no better lawyers than he was. Surely his mousetrap would be as good as theirs. It was the older men who worried him, men like Senator Lapham, Gideon Granger, and old Judge Folger, just back from a brief sojourn on the Court of Appeals bench. These were distinguished men; he could not hope to compete with them. Perhaps in his old age he might stand up to them, but in the meantime he had his living to make.

He began to analyze the business possibilities of the town very much as an advertising firm of today analyses a prospective market. Farming still predominated in the neighborhood. Manufacturing was small and unimportant. There was some milling on the large streams, but the flour produced was only enough for the local consumption. People still worked with their hands, and by working hard and saving their money they would get ahead and buy a farm or start a small business. Actions arising from personal injury were almost unknown at this time, and it soon became plain to my father that the greater part of his legal work would have to come out of the wealth of the community, which was largely real estate. This meant that his practice would have to be built on probate work and the settlement of estates, with an occasional mortgage foreclosure, partition, or some other proceeding concerning the title to land.

37

For a time he puzzled over the best way to build up a probate practice. He remembered the old lawyer in Canandaigua who was reputed to attend funerals all over the county, even though he was not acquainted with the deceased, in the hope that the family would see him there and give him the estate to settle. How well the old fellow fared he did not know, though he was quite certain he had succeeded in earning the contempt of all the lawyers in the county and lowering the dignity of a noble profession. Following the hearse, as it was called, did not appeal to my father at all. He had a much better idea: if he could get enough people to have him draw their wills—and could keep the originals in his safe—he would eventually, if he lived long enough, have a probate business. He reasoned that if people had to come to him to get the will they were very likely to give him the work of settling the estate.

It was a good idea. The only catch was to get people interested in having their wills drawn. He was still pondering over the question when one day, as he was passing the Inn, Old Tick called to him from his chair on the veranda.

"Hey, Judge! Come up here a minute. Got a little matter I want to talk over with you."

Old Tick led him into an inner room behind the office and set out a bottle and two glasses. "It's about makin' a new will," he said. "I've come into a little property back east, and now I gotta change my will." He poured out a drink. "Jees Cri! I can't go to Can'daigua to change no will. Can't go up there in these goddarned carpet slippers anyway—and I ain't been able to git my feet into a pair of shoes in five years. Frank Rice—he drawed a will for me when I first come here. Charged me five dollars for it. What do you charge for a will?"

My father did some fast thinking. If he should make his price low enough he might stir up a little business; perhaps that would be the quickest way to get some wills in the safe.

38

The regular price for drawing a deed or a mortgage was a dollar. Why not the same for a will?

"Those fellows in the bigger towns have to charge a little more," he finally said "My price is one dollar."

Old Tick threw up both hands. "Jees Cri! No reason for a man to die untestate when he can get a will for a dollar!"

Evidently the news got around, for soon afterward people began to ask my father if it was true that he would draw a will for a dollar. Within a month he had several wills tucked away in his safe, and as time went on he kept drawing more and more. They were mostly simple wills, with only a few bequests and no complicated provisions. He always kept the original and gave a copy to the maker containing an endorsement that the original was on file in his office.

I have no way of knowing the greatest number of wills he may have had there at any one time, but when, some years later, I came into his office as a partner I found in the safe a bundle containing more than one hundred wills of people who were still living. In addition to this little nest egg, there were at that time some thirty estates in his office in the various stages of settlement. Some of the estates, of course, would be settled in a few months, but others would hang on for years. One of his dollar wills brought him an estate from which he drew fees for over twenty years. He could not, as the old jurist had said, ask people to let him draw their wills, but he had found a way to reach them.

Another idea that added a number of wills to the bundle in the safe was a practice he made when drawing a deed of reminding both parties of the effect that the conveyance of real estate might have on any existing will. This would precipitate a discussion and often would lead to the drawing of a new will or the change of an old one by the addition of a codicil—and as often as not the will would end up in his safe.

In his early efforts to build up a practice my father never entered very seriously into the business of being a "joiner."

Though this is one of the accepted ways of widening one's circle of acquaintances in the city, it is of little use in a small town, where everybody knows everybody else without joining anything at all. My father did make a point, especially when he first came to town of getting acquainted with all the people he could, both in the village and in the surrounding country, and to a certain extent he cultivated the propertied people from whom his practice must necessarily come.

He had not been there very long before he heard of a certain Phineas Dodd, who was said to be the richest man in town. He asked Mr. Hobson if he had ever done any work for Phineas. Mr. Hobson answered with a grunt and asked if my father had met him, and when he was assured of the negative he muttered that he did not think my father would like him. He added, a little cautiously, my father thought, that Phineas had his legal work done in Canandaigua. Jim Hoyt, the banker, was a little more articulate on the subject. He did not hesitate to say that Phineas was a damned old usurer who made a specialty of robbing widows and orphans and that he had foreclosed more mortgages than any savings bank in Rochester. Jim also volunteered the information that Phineas could not look at a dollar without having his yellow eyes glisten like gold pieces and that it was common gossip among his hired men that at night his eyes would glow in the dark like the eyes of a cat.

My father smiled when he heard the story, but when, a few days later, Phineas walked into his office for a notarial acknowledgement on satisfaction of mortgage, my father was ready to believe all that he had heard.

As Phineas first came in the door my father took him for a vagabond. He was a short man, well knit, but dressed in the seediest kind of clothes. His beard was untrimmed, his nails uncut, and his hands, coarse and clawlike, were scabby with dirt. But it was his eyes which compelled attention. They were, as Jim Hoyt had said, yellow, and they did have a peculiar glow; and, as my father learned later, when Phineas was angry his eyes could become as savage as those of a wolf. There was, of course, no charge for the acknowledgment; my father never charged for notary fees. And when Phineas found this out he came back for more. Then he began to stop in occasionally to have a lease or a land contract drawn. So far as the money went his business was trifling, but my father felt that he was winning the money lender's confidence and might eventually get some of his worth-while business, which he had reason to believe must be quite extensive.

However, time dragged along for three or four years with no development of importance, and then one day Phineas came stamping into the office in an angry mood and asked my father to represent him in a justice court case.

My father was jubilant—not because this particular case was important in itself but because it indicated that he had really made some progress with the richest man in town. There was, as a matter of fact, only twenty dollars in money involved, but Phineas was angry all the way through and determined to show the blankety-blank so-and-so what was what.

The difficulty had arisen over the sale of a cow by Phineas to Clint Cameron, who was one of the town's most accomplished dead beats. Clint had made a part payment and had given a chattel mortgage for the balance, but when the debt fell due and Phineas went around to collect the money Clint had denied the entire transaction and ordered him off the place, whereupon Phineas had "slapped a summons on him."

To my father it looked like a plain case. The chattel mortgage had been properly filed in the town clerk's office, and there was no prior lien. Unless the defendant could disprove the signature or establish fraud in the transaction he did not see how Phineas could fail to win. The defendant

41

was already in court when they arrived, and though he had no lawyer he said he was ready to go on.

In justice court the complaint may be verbal, and my father started proceedings by stating that the action against the defendant was for the recovery of a cow secured by chattel mortgage and wrongfully detained after default. Clint's answer was a verbal denial. After these preliminaries had been noted by the justice my father had Phineas sworn as a witness. He identified the chattel mortgage, testified that he had drawn it himself and had seen the defendant sign and deliver it. The instrument itself was then put in evidence and marked exhibit A.

"Now, Mr. Dodd," said my father, "will you tell the court what was said and done on the occasion when the chattel mortgage was given?"

"Well," said Phineas, "Clint come to me to buy a cow. I told him he could have the pick of the herd for forty dollars. So he picked out a cow and paid me twenty dollars down and give that there chattel on the cow for security of the balance. I give him a rope and he went off leadin' the critter."

"Then what?"

"Well, when the chattel come due last Wednesday and I went around to get my money or the cow, he wouldn't give me neither one. He claimed I didn't have no chattel on this cow, and he ordered me off the place in pretty rough language."

"Then what happened?"

"I come down here and slapped a summons on him."

"That's all," said my father. He turned to Clint. "Any questions?"

Clint shook his bullet head. "Nope. Ain't nuthin' I want to ask him."

"Very well," said my father. "That's our case. We rest."

The justice turned to Clint. "Any witnesses?" he asked.

"Nope. Just myself."

The justice administered the oath and told him to go ahead.

Clint scratched his head. "Well, Judge, it was like this, I did go over there to buy a cow, and he told me I could have the pick of the herd for forty dollars. So I picked a cow, and I asked him how much milk she give at a milkin', and he told me she give from six to eight quarts. I said that was fine, I'd take her, but I only had twenty dollars, and he said he'd take a chattel for the balance. So I paid him twenty, and he wrote out a chattel, and I signed it. And I did take that cow home. But when I come to milk her I found she wasn't as represented. She only give about four quarts. So first thing next mornin' I took her back and told him he couldn't pull that kinda stuff on me, that the cow was no good. I told him if he'd come down off that porch I'd take it out of his hide."

"Well," asked the justice, "did he come down?"

"He certainly did not. He stayed there on that porch and give me a big argument. I thought I'd have to go right up on his own porch and fight him, but he finally come around and told me I could return that cow and have my pick of the rest of 'em. So I turned that one loose and took another one —and that's all there is to it."

My father pointed to the chattel mortgage lying on the desk. "Is that the paper you signed?"

Clint picked it up and examined it. "Sure. That's my signature."

"In that case," said my father, "I ask a verdict for the plaintiff."

Clint began to laugh. "But that chattel ain't no good. That deal didn't go through."

"What do you mean, it didn't go through?" roared Phineas. "You got the cow, didn't you?"

"Not the cow described in that there paper!" Clint cried jubilantly. He took up the chattel mortgage and ran his

43

finger along the line as he read. "This calls for one red cow four years old named Bessie—and I ain't got no red cow named Bessie. All I got is a black and white cow named Jennie, and there ain't no chattel on her and never was."

That was when my father saw the look of a wolf in the eyes of Phineas Dodd. Judgment was, of course, for the defendant, and although Phineas had nobody but himself to blame for not making a new mortgage when the cows were exchanged, he never recovered from the humiliation of being outwitted by a small-time dead beat like Clint Cameron, and he took his resentment out on my father by never coming into his office again. Phineas did not even pay him for trying the case.

The probability is that if my father had shown a belligerent attitude and sued Phineas for his fee the old usurer would have had more respect for him; for though a miser may hate a man who wrings money out of his hide, he has little respect for a man with a valid claim against him who fails to enforce it. It was no lack of courage on my father's

part that kept him from collecting his fee; it was, on the contrary, a nauseating distaste for the old money lender and all his ways. He felt that it was worth ten dollars to be rid of the unsavory penny pincher. And, in addition, my father's ego may have been slightly inflated at the time, for he had just been retained by an affiliate of the Pennsylvania Railroad to clear and pass all titles for a right of way they were buying for a short line to Lake Ontario which was to pass across the western end of the township.

This railroad work kept him busy for nearly two years and enabled him to make many friends along the right of way which he succeeded in clearing without a single condemnation suit.

It was while he was working on the railroad right of way that he inherited the fine law library of his uncle in Rochester. Until this time his law books had been few and battered; he had a set of the revised statutes, several form books, and a few text books on the law of real estate and wills. When a question came up which required research he had been compelled to go to the county library. Now, however, with one of the best libraries in the county in his own office and about all the work he could handle, he began to feel that he was really on his way.

4. To Sue—or Not to Sue

ONE of the early questions which caused my father some perplexity was whether litigated work in a small town did not make him as many enemies as friends. Nearly always the opposing party—any person involved in a lawsuit is a party—would be an acquaintance and often a person he would have liked to have for a friend. He felt that he must not let up on the opposition for that reason, however; that if he took a case he should fight it to a finish, though he did make a special effort not to let his hostility in court make a difference in his personal contacts outside the arena. For example, in the Cosad will case he raked Fred Hogan fore and aft every day for a week, though he never failed to go into Fred's store and purchase his groceries, usually from Fred himself, every evening after returning from court. He thought he was handling the matter with great tact and astuteness, but when Fred's mother died a few months later and left a nice little estate to settle it was the other lawyer who got the business.

In horse cases it worked just the other way. A man he had fought to a standstill and had flayed before a jury as a liar, a cheat, and an imposter would in all probability come straight to my father the next time he was mixed up in a lawsuit over the sale or trade of a bit of horseflesh. However, these horse traders, as he soon found out, were in a class by themselves. They did not mind being regarded as shrewd and sharp and sly; they did not particularly object to being called cheats or frauds so long as they had the satisfaction of beating the other fellow. Horse trading was a game of wits, and to beat a shrewd trader and then make the deal stand up in a court of law was a real accomplishment.

As time went on my father became firmly convinced that the best course in the long run was to try his cases hard and clean, to win if it was humanly possible, and then to trust to luck that his opponents would believe that they had been beaten by a better man—or if they did not happen to be beaten, that they would know they had been in a real fight.

There was at that time no public prosecutor for lesser crimes in the country districts served by the justices of the peace. If a farmer caught a thief stealing his chickens he could not merely call in an officer and let the law take its course. He had to carry the matter before a justice and "swear out" a warrant. And if the culprit was found and arrested, the farmer had to become the complaining witness and furnish sufficient evidence for a conviction. If it so happened that the defendant came into court with a lawyer, it was up to the complainant to hire a lawyer for himself unless he wanted to be hopelessly outclassed and perhaps be beaten on a technicality. Of course, in the more serious crimes such as homicide, robbery, and crimes of moral turpitude the district attorney of the county would take charge; but in anything less than an indictable crime the entire burden would fall on the complaining witness.

My father had both prosecuted and defended many cases involving these lesser crimes, and he used to wonder why it was that the defendants, though ruthlessly prosecuted, seldom held any resentment against him, whereas the complaintants, if my father happened to be on the other side and freed his man, were very likely to hold it against him for a long time to come. But of all the various kinds of case that he tried first and last, he found that the will contest was likely to arouse the greatest bitterness and maintain it the most stubbornly.

He liked best to prosecute suits against large outside corporations such as the railroad or one of the big insurance companies. These suits created no hard feelings on either side, and if he won a verdict he was very likely to be able to collect it. And he had noticed that winning a certain kind of case often brought him other cases of the same kind. His victory in an insurance case where there was a suspicion of incendiarism had brought him two other cases where the insurance company was reluctant to pay for a fire loss.

The town had inadequate fire protection at this time, and insurance rates were high, as my father found out when he applied for insurance on his house. Will Morton, the local agent, smiled dubiously as he told my father about the two volunteer fire companies which, he said, were very active in the matter of parades and minstrel shows, though they were not so much interested in putting out fires. After his talk with the agent my father walked over to take a look at the fire equipment, which he found to consist of a fancy high-wheeled hose reel, a hook-and-ladder truck hung with many rubber buckets, and "Old Ocean," a huge hand-power pump of the period.

The pump was a really handsome piece of equipment. The mechanism itself was concealed within an ornate body mounted on four large, impressive wheels with gleaming brass-covered hub caps. To provide the operating power there were handrails on each side long enough to accommodate six or even eight men. When forcibly thrust down, these handles furnished a power stroke to a large piston hidden somewhere inside. As one handle went down the other

48

went up, and the water came spouting out of a pipe on the front from which it was conveyed by hose to a position from which it could be squirted on the fire.

From the rear of the pump a large rubber hose went down into the water supply. The water was usually taken from the nearest well or cistern, though in the center of the town a large reservoir had been built underneath the main street. This reservoir was filled by the drainage of rain water from the roofs of the surrounding buildings.

The current boast was that Old Ocean was capable of throwing a stream over the top of any building in town. But my father found the statement misleading. If there was only a short length of hose, the pump successfully sent the water onto the roof of a three-story building, but if the water had to be carried any distance from the source of supply, the pressure was greatly reduced and the range correspondingly lessened.

A sturdy wagon tongue fitted with brass grips and a long rope provided a handhold for hauling the engine to fires, though my father soon discovered that the members of the fire department were not noticeably enthusiastic about pulling this heavy piece of apparatus. They were quick to get out with their light hose reel or the hook-and-ladder truck, which was not so light, but they were quite willing to have the humble citizenry of the town drag Old Ocean to the scene of a fire, especially if it was at a distance. Once the big machine was there, however, the fire laddies immediately took charge and relegated the yeomanry to the humble task of carrying removable effects from the burning buildings and protecting adjacent property by means of the lowly bucket brigade. Then, if the two companies did not get into a fight over the position of the engine or the choice of pump handles, they would divide into teams with the Hose Company on one handle and the Hooks on the other and try to pump each other to exhaustion.

This was not often possible; the water supply would run out or the building would burn down before either side would be anywhere near collapse. But the rivalry between the companies was bitter. At the first fire my father attended, the firemen got into a fight which occupied them until nothing was left of the building but a bed of coals in the cellar. What the fire companies really longed for was an occasion when both fire and the water would last long enough for them to pump out their differences to a finish and prove which was really the better crew. The opportunity was a long time in coming, but come it did, and when it had passed it left both companies looking a little ridiculous.

The summer had been long and dry, and in the fall fires became quite frequent, though they were for the most part unimportant. They began with insignificant brush fires that would destroy a patch of shrubbery or perhaps a few rods of board fence, and though my father had been wondering how it happened that these fires always started at night, nobody seemed to have thought of incendiarism until haystacks began to burn. Until this time there had been no haystack fire for several years. It suddenly dawned on people that a haystack was being burned almost every Saturday night.

That was the beginning of actual nervousness on the part of people, for it was quite obvious that these fires were being set by somebody who liked to see a haystack aflame. My father had never realized what a thrilling sight a fire could be until one night when, driving in from the country, he saw a haystack flare up in a field not a thousand feet away.

Well-dried hay ignites almost as fast as gunpowder, and the flames from a stack go up in a pillar of fire that reaches to an unbelievable height, especially after dark, when every little tongue of flame is visible. The snow came early that year and put an end to the stack burning, for incendiaries have scruples against leaving footprints by which they may be traced. For a month or two the incendiary took a much-needed vacation, after which he moved into the village and set fire to two buildings on the same night.

The first of these was a coal shed, which burned slowly, with great clouds of smoke and not much flame. As my father stood watching it and thinking that it must have been a disappointment to a really enthusiastic pyromaniac, the sky was suddenly lighted by the flames arising from an old cider mill, also near the railroad but at the other end of the town. The well-seasoned timbers of this ancient building made a very brilliant blaze. When, however, the flames ignited an old pile of dried pomace standing near by, an aroma was loosed that drove all onlookers to cover and must have spoiled much of the incendiary's pleasure.

By this time the town was becoming very jumpy—so much so that a fire started in a woodpile against the side of a dwelling in the eastern part of the village was discovered and extinguished with only slight damage, though it occurred in the middle of the night. My father heard the cry of fire and reached the scene before the alarm had begun to ring and, with the aid of other neighbors, scattered the woodpile—which had been drenched with kerosene—and beat out the flames before the apparatus had even left the firehouse.

The incendiary must have been forewarned by this alertness, for he restrained himself until the winter was nearly gone. When, however, he did touch off another blaze he took plenty of precautions to make a success of it. Not only did he select for his conflagration a large empty house on the top of the schoolhouse hill, but he iced the hill to prevent the firemen from getting their apparatus near enough to do any effective fire fighting. This was accomplished by the simple expedient of diverting the overflow of the watering trough which stood near the top of the hill and letting the water run down the roadway until it was a glare of ice.

When the cordon of public-spirited citizens who were hauling the apparatus at a smart clip struck this treacherous bit of
ice they went sprawling in all directions. One piece of
apparatus came crashing back into another, and before
anyone had time to block the wheels, the hose reel, the
hook-and-ladder truck, and Old Ocean, inextricably inter-
mingled, came sliding down the hill and landed with a crash
in the ditch at the bottom, where the confused mass of
damaged apparatus lay useless until the coming of the morning. Meanwhile, the fire had burned itself out quite unmolested and almost unattended. And my father limped
home on a sprained ankle.

This icing of the hill brought quick action from the Village Fathers. They immediately assigned a night watchman
to patrol the streets. The incident also brought quick action
from the insurance companies, which canceled some policies
outright and raised the rate on others. By this time the
townspeople had become thoroughly aroused. Guns loaded
with buckshot stood in a convenient corner of a number of
the homes my father went into, and it became very risky to
cut across a neighbor's lawn after dark.

My father thought that it might be an opportune time to
bring up the subject of a village water supply. For some time
past he had been considering this question. It was a project
that he felt the town would have to face sooner or later.
Surrounded as it was by towns with an adequate water
system, he was convinced that business could never go ahead
so long as the town remained dependent for its water on
wells and cisterns. And he had not entirely forgotten the
matter of personal comfort; for in those days before
the invention of the pressure tank, unless there were pipes
in the street to furnish pressure there could be no household
plumbing.

He made a hasty tour of the neighboring towns which had
installed water systems and assembled some figures. These

were, of course, approximate, but they gave a rough idea of the probable cost. He then stirred up the interest of a few influential citizens who were among the largest taxpayers, and at a meeting of the Village Board he walked in with his backers and asked for the passage of a resolution that would have brought the question of a village water system before the taxpayers in the form of a bond election.

He had intended the application as a surprise, but the news leaked out, and the retired farmers of the town, always ready to repel anything in the way of an improvement that looked like an invasion of their pocketbooks, were there in a body to start a robust chorus of noes to every proposal of the water party. Always a man to whom opposition was an encouragement, my father began to let loose a flood of oratory on the pressing need of a water supply at just that time. He made no specific mention of the specter of incendiarism stalking in their midst, but he enumerated a long list of costly fires which, he said, might easily have been extinguished with a proper water supply. He also went into the subject of insurance and pointed out the high price they were paying in comparison with towns with adequate fire protection, and he commented on the reluctance of some of the insurance companies to pay their losses even after the imposition of exorbitant premiums.

But the opposition were too strong for him. By the time he had finished speaking, their scouts had filled the hall with their henchmen, who overwhelmed the meeting with their continual chorus of noes.

All this negation must have sounded very heartening to the Village Fathers, who were rendered quite breathless by the proposal to bond the village for a staggering sum that would probably reach some fifty thousand, and they quickly voted to table the resolution. After quiet had been restored, they brought up a proposal of their own to insure better fire protection. The chief cause of the failure to extinguish fires, they said, was the slowness of getting the apparatus to the scene. So they proposed to set up a standing offer of ten dollars for drawing the heavy engine to the fire, to be paid to the first person bringing a team to the fire house after the sounding of the alarm.

The retired farmers were heartily in favor of this proposal, and the board quickly passed it and adjourned.

My father was disappointed. He felt that an opportunity had been lost. But he had learned his lesson. Never again would he try to surprise the Village Board.

The next day John Erlish, one of the local cartmen, stopped my father on the street and asked him what constituted a team. Old John was an incorrigible joker, and the two frequently exchanged badinage. My father answered promptly that if John was contemplating exemption from execution the courts had frequently held that a single horse and vehicle were as much a team as a coach and four.

"But what," asked John, "is a team within the meaning of the ordinance passed last night? Old Charley here," he pointed to his broad-backed buckskin horse, "is around town as much as any of 'em, and if he's a team he might pick up a ten spot the next time the firebell rings."

"You think old Charley can pull the engine?" my father asked.

John laughed heartily, his fat belly shaking, his yellow teeth gleaming beneath his great rope of a mustache. "That remains to be seen."

A little later, as the town clock was striking twelve, my father saw the buckskin starting for home alone. Old Charley was impatient of his master's irregular hours, and if John happened to be roistering in a saloon when the town clock struck the hour of noon he was very likely to have to walk home, for Charley would start off without him and plod patiently down the center of the street, turn into his own driveway, and come to a stop in the shed where he

54

knew that his mid-day meal would be waiting for him. And oftener than not John's little black dog, Kaiser, would be sitting on the seat of the dray as if in full charge of the performance.

As he saw the old dray horse starting down the street, my father could not help smiling, for he knew how annoyed John would be when he found that he had to walk home. In his mind he pictured John as somewhere blowing the foam from a large glass of beer; but as he passed the office of the local paper he saw George Busby, the editor, letting himself very quietly out of the door. George raised a cautionary finger, then pointed to his office.

"This time I've got one on old John," he said. "He came in to collect a freight bill and dropped off to sleep in his chair. When he wakes up he'll find that I've gone home to dinner!" The newspaper man had difficulty in suppressing his laughter.

My father smiled. That was the way things went around here. Everybody was always trying to play a joke on old John. He thought no more of the matter until he was on his way back to his office after he had eaten his dinner. As he was passing the newspaper office he glanced inside and saw that John was still sitting where Busby had left him. His hands were hanging over the arms of the chair, his head drooping forward on his chest. Then suddenly he noticed that the old drayman's eyes were wide open. He stepped quickly inside and took hold of his hand. It was cold.

This was one time when the joke was not on old John.

Charley never did get his chance to earn the ten-dollar award by drawing the fire apparatus—which he probably would not have been able to pull. He did not survive his former master by more than a month and was, indeed, in his grave before the incendiary felt the urge to enjoy another fire.

5. The Lawyer Loses His Books

IT WAS the middle of April when the incendiary struck again. My father was in the Town Hall trying a case before Justice Sayre when the alarm sounded. He was engaged in cross-examining a witness at the time and had just succeeded in getting him nicely tangled when the hoarse, unmusical clamor came pealing down into the room from a small tower on the roof. The first sound of that bell was always a shock. It stunned people—it stopped whatever they were doing.

My father had asked what he considered a very pertinent question, but the witness did not answer. Instead he cocked an ear aloft. The crowd, too, was in a listening attitude, perfectly motionless for a time. Then my father saw the mass of people swing slowly toward the door with the movement of a receding wave.

The rumble of their footfalls on the stairs was too much for Ben Guilford, the constable in attendance. He jammed his hat on his head and said he guessed he'd go out and see where the fire was. The justice followed, declaring a recess over his shoulder just as he went out the door. Half the jury were already gone, and the rest now followed on a run. My father did not happen to see his witness decamp, but the chair was empty, and soon he was alone with his client, a horseman named Ichabod Lord.

56

"Get your hat," said Ichabod. "Let's go outside. We may not see much of a fire, but we ought to see a pretty good horse race."

"The last fire I went to was more like a dog fight."

"But have you forgotten the race to earn that ten dollars? There's been a pool up on it ever since the ordinance was passed. Most of the teamsters are off plowing gardens today, but there isn't one of them who won't make a try for the money."

My father glanced around as they reached the street. "Wonder where the fire is."

Ichabod sniffed. "I don't smell smoke, but we'll soon find out."

That did not, however, prove to be the case. Nobody seemed to be interested in the fire, and, instead of making the usual rush for the apparatus, the people were gathered in the street before the firehouse, craning their necks and peering into the distance at two teams of horses which were thundering up the highway in a terrific cloud of dust— minus their wagons—a rider on one horse of each team and the race apparently neck and neck.

Keen-eyed horsemen said that the blacks on the left belonged to Dick Burnell and that Windy Jim's grays were on the right. My father noticed that excited tradesmen were now pouring out of their stores and places of business, the cobbler in his leathern apron, the butcher in bloody smock and rattan cuffs, the grocer in his shirt sleeves. They had come to find out about the fire but were almost immediately absorbed by the excitement over the race.

Suddenly a third contender came swinging in from a side street. He was slightly ahead of the others but was hampered by his wagon, in which he stood up like a chariot driver, lashing his steeds with a whip.

"That's Jack Ruberry in the wagon!" somebody shouted. "Pretty smart the way he cut in front."

57

My father thought so, too. "I guess it's all over but the shouting," he said to Ichabod.

"Don't be too sure about that," said Ichabod. "Remember his nags are pulling half a ton of wagon."

Ichabod was right, for a moment later the mounted horses were abreast of Ruberry's team. For a short distance none of the three had any advantage, and then the two mounted teams drew ahead, leaving Ruberry in a cloud of dust. There was little choice between the two teams as they entered the home stretch, except that Windy Jim was on the side toward the firehouse, which seemed to give him a slight edge.

My father could see that both teams were badly winded. They were slowing down perceptibly and were puffing hard. Dick's off horse was bothered by a tug that had come loose and was dangling around its feet. But Dick was still lacing his team with the end of the reins in an effort to get around Windy Jim and cut into the driveway ahead of him. Windy was apparently aware of this, for he did not slacken his pace until he was almost ready for the turn.

Cries of "Dead heat!" went up from the crowd as the two teams came clattering to a halt in the broad driveway of the firehouse just beyond the Inn, where the members of the two fire companies had gathered and were waiting for them.

"Better run it over again!" bellowed somebody with a lusty guffaw.

My father caught Ichabod by the arm. "Here's where the trouble begins," he said. "There never was a better setup for a fight between those two fire companies."

"Guess that's right," said Ichabod. "Dick belongs to the Hooks—and Windy got there first. Ought to be a good recipe for trouble."

At first the fracas, though rough and violent, seemed good-natured. Then suddenly tempers flared, fists struck

58

out, and in another tick of the clock the approach to the firehouse was filled with a writhing mass of fighting men and plunging horses.

Fighters were up—then down—then up again. Some of those who went down stayed down. A few stayed up and were still on their feet at the end. In the heat of battle most of the participants forgot what they were fighting about. It was just a matter of Hooks against Hose Company.

In the confusion the horses tried to bolt and were caught by spectators—but the firemen fought on. My father saw Old Tick come shuffling out on the veranda of the Inn but did not realize what he was about until his cymbal set up an unearthly clangor which brought the battle to an almost immediate end. Always that cymbal seemed to set people right.

At the sound, fighters backed away from each other and dropped their guard. Those who were sitting astride fallen adversaries arose and walked away, dusting off their hands or feeling of their jaws or noses. The underdogs sat up, struggled quickly to their feet, and began sheepishly to brush off their clothes. All were up who were able to get up by the time that Old Tick had ceased pounding on his big brass gong and had begun screaming in his high-pitched voice.

"Jees Cri! Be you goddamn fools gonna keep on a-fightin' while the goddamn town burns down!" He brandished his drumstick hysterically. "I can see from my back windows it's already burned Gus Decker's house damn near to the ground—and now it's catchin' the back of Joe Cooley's store!" Again he began brandishing the drumstick. "What the hell y'standin' there fer? Git a-goin'! Y'think I want this here hotel to burn down over my head!"

When the firemen turned toward the firehouse, they became aware that the engine was no longer there. Jack Ruberry had driven his team up the alley and hauled it out the back door while the fight was going on. And a moment later he came driving it into the street.

"Hey, Ezra!" he called to the fire chief. "Where do you want I should take this?"

The chief stopped nursing a black eye and pulled himself together. "Back her up there to the big cistern." Ezra indicated with a movement of his head the large metal manhole cover at the junction of Main and Church Streets. "Head her north—we'll want the front end that way."

Ezra bellowed out some further orders, and the hose reel and hook-and-ladder truck came rolling out. My father, though not a fireman, gave a hand on the rope of the hook-and-ladder truck, and as the apparatus reached Joe Cooley's store he saw Joe come hurrying out of the door with his account books under one arm and a black tin money box under the other.

"It's goin' like hell in back there!" Joe shouted to the firemen as he passed. "Whole damn town'll go if you don't get some water on it pretty quick!"

That was the moment when it first occurred to my father that his own office might be in danger. He dropped the rope and ran around behind the buildings which had been obstructing the view to see how much of a start the fire had really made. He found the back of Joe's store roaring like a blast furnace, with the flames already pouring out of the windows of the stores on both sides. He knew at a glance that the drugstore was doomed—and his priceless library was directly above.

As he started on a run for his office he bumped into Jerry Billings, just turning into the alley. "Come with me, Jerry!" he panted. "We've got to get some things out of my office—"

They found the office thick with smoke as they rushed inside. My father pointed out some books to Jerry. "Begin there," he said, "and carry all you can."

He slammed the doors of the safe and gave the combination a whirl. Then he snatched up from the desk all the papers he could hold in his arms and led the way out of the door and along the smoke-filled corridor. They could feel the heat under the stairway as they went down, and before they could carry what they had to safety and come back for more, the interior of the building was an inferno.

My father stood in the street and looked helplessly around. Long lines of citizens wound in and out of the various stores in the path of the fire, carrying out the stock and even fixtures. The stores with insurance were not so anxious to be salvaged; but some of the merchants who had refused to pay the high premiums were without any coverage at all, and, of course, they wanted to save everything they could. At first my father thought that he would help with the salvage work, and then it occurred to him that he might be more useful on the pump. So he went up and stood where he would be available when needed.

He saw the hose clapped on Old Ocean, and the pump handles, manned on one side by the Hooks and on the other by the Hose Company, begin to go slowly up and down. After a few strokes the hose rounded out and straightened some of its kinks. A few more, and a fitful stream came sputtering from the nozzle. Gradually the pressure grew stronger as the pumpmen speeded up their stroke, and a sizable stream began pouring into the second-story windows above Joe Cooley's store.

But they were too late. As my father stood watching, he could see the flames beginning to come through the roof, and the neighboring buildings were being showered with sparks and embers. Ladders were quickly brought, and men went up to protect the roofs, though there was little that they could do. Dozens of small fires were starting all around them, and the chief decided to raise the pressure and give the roofs a good wetting. This meant that the speed of the pump would have to be increased.

The band leader, a small man named Myron Fuller, climbed to the top of the engine and began to count in a stentorian voice as he kept time with his hands, "One-two! One-two!" The pump handles went faster and faster, and at last my father saw the stream from the hose break over the roof tops.

"There we are!" shouted the chief. "Now hold it!"

Fuller nodded. "One-two! One-two!"

At this fast stroke, pumpmen began to drop away from the handles, but as quickly as they dropped others stepped in to take their places. No man could stand such speed for any length of time, and substitutions were frequent. As my father stood in line, peering ahead at the pumpers, he discovered that ordinary citizens were mixed in with the firemen on both pump handles, and it came to him that the showdown for which the Hooks and the Hose Company had fought for years had come—and gone—and nobody had even noticed which had outlasted the other.

The line ahead of my father melted away rapidly. Suddenly he discovered that there were only three between him and the pump—then two—then only one—then he was next. Very much on the alert, he saw a man drop and leaped for the opening. The handle nearly tore his arms off when he first caught hold of it, but he clung to it, and after he had found his equilibrium he began to give that handle all the power he had. How long he was there he did not know. All sense of time had gone from him. He could see nothing, feel nothing but that flailing handle, and he stayed with it until his arms were numb and his head reeling before he fell back to make room for a substitute. After a rest he went back in again, first on one handle and later on the other. In fact, he was still with the pump when the cistern ran dry and

"Old Ocean" out for a practice pump.

people began carrying water from private wells in the neighborhood.

Meanwhile, the fire had swept everything before it until it came to the solid brick fire wall of the Inn. There it stopped and eventually burned itself out.

When my father finally reached home he was black with smoke, his hat was ruined, and several holes had been burned in his clothing by falling sparks. It was his best beaver hat and his second-best broadcloth coat, and he had no insurance on either.

My mother's eyes opened wide when she saw him. "Am I to understand that you were actually pumping that old engine with a beaver hat on?"

He nodded wearily. "There were plenty of beavers on both handles after the firemen gave out. People weren't thinking about what they had on—they were trying to keep the town from burning up."

The town was in a sullen mood the day after the fire. My father noticed the drawn lips and narrowed eyes of the men, and it seemed to him that the gestures of the women were nervous, almost furtive, as they stood talking in their dooryards. He did not need to be told that they were talking about the incendiary and the fact that he had been bold enough to strike in broad daylight. By this time the origin of the fire had been pretty well worked out. When they were discovered the flames were leaping up through the roof of a tool shed on the back of Gus Decker's house. It was well known around town that the whole Decker family had gone away for the day to attend the funeral of a relative in Port Gibson, and, since the tool shed was unlocked, the incendiary had only to walk inside, lay his fire, and apply the match.

My father went around and looked over the burned premises. It was plain to him that the fire had spread from the Decker house to a shed in the rear of Cooley's store and had leaped from the shed across the driveway and caught the rather flimsy one-story addition at the rear of the store. He thought it quite obvious that the fire could have been confined to the shed if the firemen had not been otherwise engaged in a highly competitive pursuit. However, he passed no remarks on that phase of the subject and went about the gloomy task of hunting up a new office. Plenty of black eyes and swollen lips were visible on the streets; but everybody was now treating the fight at the firehouse rather lightly. That seemed to be the best way to handle it.

Justice Sayre stopped my father on the street and asked what had become of the case they were trying the day before. My father smilingly replied that further proceedings seemed to have been prevented by an act of God and suggested an adjournment *nunc pro tunc* until the following week.

In his quest for an office my father's first move was to call on old Mr. Hobson to see if perhaps—by reason of the emergency—the building on Church Street might have become available. Mr. Hobson was a little apologetic about it, but he still felt that he must have an office where he could putter around. Finding no better place, my father rented a little triangular room over the Hoyt bank on the corner. Since the bank itself was too small for an inside stairway, access to the room was by means of gaudy iron stairs scaling the outside wall of the building. For his furniture my father hunted up a table and two chairs. His library was the armful of books that Jerry Billings had carried out for him. The handful of papers that he had snatched from his desk were all the records he had left, for his files were a complete loss. His safe was still lying over in the ashes where the drugstore had stood. Nobody seemed to know when it would be cool enough to open.

After my father had been in the new office for a few days he called in Elder Woodruff and had him measure the place for a desk. The elder said he had some fine butternut that he had been saving a long time for just such a job, which he thought he could finish in about a month. My father had a high regard for the elder's ability to make either a prayer or a desk and told him to go ahead.

A week passed. The safe was hauled out of the cellar and its contents found intact. Several large shade trees, ruined by the fire, were cut down, and the broad street looked vacant and lopsided without them. People were making a conscious effort to talk about something besides the fire. Then one day the town was thrown into a frenzy of excitement when an undercover man from an insurance company walked into Justice Redman's office, dragging behind him a prisoner in handcuffs, and announced that he had caught the incendiary.

Five minutes later a boy came scrambling up the iron stairs leading to my father's office and said that my father was wanted right away over at Squire Redman's office. "They've caught the firebug!" the lad cried excitedly.

"Who is it?" my father asked. "Anybody you know?"

"Sure I know him—so do you—it's *Jerry Billings!*"

6. The Perfect Miscarriage of Justice

LEFT to themselves, the townspeople would probably never have found any reason for directing their suspicions toward Jerry Billings. Jerry was a good worker. He always paid his debts. He was crotchety and difficult to get along with, though nobody had ever suspected him of having criminal instincts. It took the undercover man from the insurance company to do that.

This man had been around town for weeks, though nobody thought that he was connected with an insurance company. He had worked as a handy man in a saloon and as a roustabout in a livery stable. He was strong and willing, and whenever anybody needed an extra man he could usually be found. Everybody took him to be just another common laborer drifting around looking for a steady job.

In going over the ground after the big fire, this inspector had noticed some shavings near a back corner of Gus Decker's garden where somebody appeared to have been whittling. He picked up some of the shavings and saw that they were of seasoned pine. With this as a start, he searched the premises thoroughly and found two small pine splinters whittled in such a way that most of the shavings adhered to them. These were lying in the deep grass where nobody had noticed them. Just outside the fence he found a pop bottle containing a trace of kerosene oil. He put these things away and went on looking.

At this time Jerry was working two days a week in my father's garden. He preferred gardening to any other employment but could not always find enough of it to keep him busy. At such times he would take any work he could get; and it was his occupation as man of all work that led to his downfall. He had been hired to rake up and burn some rubbish that had gathered in the rear of the Town Hall where there was an open space between the rear wall of the building and the livery stable next door. Some of the rubbish which was inflammable had been seen from a rear window and immediately translated into a fire hazard.

Jerry had finished raking it up and was trying to set fire to it with some pieces of newspaper; but it had rained the night before, and both the rubbish and the newspapers were wet. After using several matches unsuccessfully, Jerry had given up and had gone cross-lots to his home, which was only a short distance away. When he came back he was carrying a few sticks of dry pine wood and a pop bottle of kerosene oil. He stood there beside the pile of rubbish and whittled the sticks in such a way that the shavings were left adhering to them. Then he piled up the kindling, poured on the kerosene oil, and tossed the bottle aside. He had paid no attention to the roughly dressed fellow who had been loitering by the corner of the stable. He had seen the man around but did not know who he was. Jerry had not even noticed that the stranger had picked up the bottle and carried it inside the barn, and he was taken entirely by surprise when, a few moments later, the fellow walked up to him and quickly snapped a handcuff on his wrist. In another moment Jerry had found himself shackled to the wheel of a near-by wagon while the stranger was kicking the bonfire to pieces.

The fragments of kindling that the undercover man was able to save corresponded exactly with those found near the scene of the Decker fire, and the bottle was identical—a pop bottle from the Forgham Bottling Works. That was all the real evidence there was, though the district attorney tried to conjure up some motive on the part of Jerry against Gus Decker. He found people to testify that some fifteen years previous it had been common talk around town that Jerry and Gus were sweet on the same girl and Gus had married her. The girl herself was unable to testify, since she had died some years before. The district attorney also dug up another story bearing on the question of motive. This had to do with a quarrel between the two men over a load of manure from the sheds of the Presbyterian Church.

Jerry, according to the report, had raked it up to use for fertilizer on his garden, and while he went to hunt up a teamster Gus had come along with his wagon and hauled it away. Jerry was said to have been very angry when he came back with his teamster and found the manure gone. He had demanded that it be returned, but Gus had refused. He said that it was as much his as anybody's. There was a rather wordy quarrel, but since Gus was twice Jerry's size and as strong as a bull there was no fight. And Jerry had finally gone away, muttering threats about getting even.

Gus laughed about it. So did everybody else. They thought it quite a joke and did not realize that the time would ever come when they would shake their heads over it and regard it as significant.

My father's defense of Jerry was his first big case. He had tried cases in the Supreme Court before this, and though they had been difficult and bitterly fought, they had lacked the human interest, the sentimental elements of Jerry's case. These burnings had been going on for months. They had aroused the whole county and the neighboring counties as well, and to accuse a man of so monstrous a series of crimes

68

was to brand him as no less than a fiend. Never for even a moment did my father doubt Jerry's innocence, and his first words to Squire Redman on reaching his office the day of the arrest were, "You've made a mistake here—you've got the wrong man."

To him Jerry was a simple man of the soil, a man who loved growing things and had a way with them. It was impossible that he could be a fiend, unthinkable that he should go around burning down men's homes because they had crossed him fifteen years before. That was something that he could not and would not believe. In his defense he was not merely fighting for a client, he was defending a retainer and friend—and aside from my father Jerry had nobody that he could really call a friend. He had never taken the trouble to make any. All his life his attitude had been that he did not give a damn what people thought of him—and now he was fighting with his back to the wall while the hysterical townspeople, after the long torment they had been through, were in full cry for a victim.

If my father ever was influenced by the unpopularity of the cause he was defending he never admitted it. He threw himself into the fight with all his power and spared no expense, even though the money came out of his own pocket. He went so far as to pay his own expenses to a small town in Ohio to investigate the private life of the undercover man, who was to be the principal witness of the prosecution, and he had the satisfaction of tearing the fellow to ribbons on his cross-examination.

He called more than twenty witnesses in an attempt to clear up the revenge motive from the alleged love affair, and he called almost as many witnesses in connection with the little incident at the church sheds. But he was not the only one who was putting everything he had into the case. The district attorney, who was to come up for re-election the following year, seemed to sense in the hysteria of the villagers a fertile field for votes, and he left no stone unturned to bring what he called "the perpetrator of these vile and inhuman outrages" to the bar of justice.

In those days the newspapers had not yet invaded the courtroom with their news hawks and photographers, but they followed this case with an avid interest; and from the day the trial opened crowds overflowed the courtroom and filled the corridors with curiosity seekers. As the case drew to a close, the crowds became larger and larger, and my father must have felt a very great sense of responsibility as he stood up in court on that final day to begin his summary to the jury.

At the defense table sat Jerry Billings alone, his face expressionless, his unruly hair in disarray. My father glanced around the packed courtroom, from the high walls of which a whole gallery of his illustrious predecessors looked down on him inscrutably from their heavy gilded frames. By raising his eyes to the window he could have seen across the courthouse square the little office once occupied by Stephen A. Douglas when he was a struggling young lawyer. Over the top of the judge's desk the shiny bald head of ponderous Judge Grover was barely visible. At the prosecutor's table were hawk-eyed District Attorney Rice and the crippled associate who always sat at his elbow during the trial of a case.

Judge Grover gave his steel-rimmed spectacles a hitch and nodded. "You may proceed."

My father nodded in return. "If the court please—gentlemen of the jury: On the day of the fire when I suddenly became aware that the flames had reached the back of the building in which my office was located, I started for the stairway in the hope that I might be able to salvage some of the valuable law library that had only recently been placed in my office. These books were the accumulation of a lifetime of an eminent jurist who has, unhappily for us, passed

70

to his reward. You have been told how I encountered the defendant running to the fire and requested him to help me carry out some of my books and how the flames devoured the building so rapidly that he was able to carry out only a single armful. In that armful was a small volume which I hold in my hand, and as I look at it I am moved to wonder whether it was not Providence which placed this particular book in that particular spot. It is called *Famous Cases of Circumstantial Evidence*. The cases reported in this little book are indeed famous. There are ten in all. In every case the defendant was found guilty on circumstantial evidence, and in every case, by some newly discovered evidence, the accused was subsequently proved to have been innocent."

"Has this book been offered in evidence?" asked the district attorney irritably.

My father turned on him. "Have the law books on your table been offered in evidence?"

"What is the purpose of this?" asked the court.

"Merely to cite from an old and reliable authority," replied my father.

"You may proceed."

A few excerpts were then read from the little book as a prelude to my father's attack on the circumstantial aspects of the case. He had introduced in evidence more than fifty Forgham pop bottles found in various parts of the village to show how common they were thereabouts; and he had produced in court kindling wood from half the woodsheds in town, any piece of which could have passed for the wood found on Jerry's premises. All these exhibits were in bushel baskets before the jury as he talked, and from time to time he would brandish a bottle or kick a basket of firewood for emphasis.

He hooted to high heaven the implications in the alleged love affair of a decade and a half before and had the courtroom roaring with laughter over the incident of the load of

manure on which the prosecution was basing its allegation of revenge. But when he came to the lonely life led by his simple tiller of the soil, the dreary shack where he lived in solitude without kith or kin, his single-handed defense of his liberty without the help of a living being he could call friend, my father turned on all the sentiment he had. It is not wholly for oratorical effect that a lawyer tries to make a jury laugh and cry; the theory is that this working over melts their emotions to a jellylike substance that can be molded as the counsel wishes by a final appeal to pure reason. This jury both laughed and cried copiously, and my father was spent and as limp as a rag when he ended his appeal with a demand that Jerry be allowed to walk out of the door a free man to resume his solitary tilling of the soil he loved.

The district attorney was an able lawyer, and after he had nailed down his facts to his complete satisfaction he flayed the very hide from the defendant, painting him as a lone wolf, a fiend and a destroyer, a dastardly sneak who hoed in men's gardens by day only that he might burn their houses over their heads at night. He wound up his summary with the dramatic declaration that if the truth were to appear blazoned in letters of fire on yonder wall the words would read, "*This is the man!*"

The jury received the case just at nightfall, but the crowd lingered in the courtroom until nine o'clock, the hour when the building was customarily cleared of spectators. When, at midnight, my father dragged himself wearily out of the judge's chambers to go over to the hotel for some sleep, people were still milling around outside the courthouse doors. And in the morning when he went over for the opening of court a way had to be cleared for him by a brace of deputies from the sheriff's office. Nothing, however, had come from the jury, though the watchman outside the door had heard acrimonious arguments far into the night.

As soon as he had convened court, Judge Grover sent for the jury and asked if they wished any further instruction or desired to have any of the evidence read over to them. The jurymen shook their heads and were sent back. All day they remained in the jury room, with waiting crowds filling the corridors and even the streets outside. It was nearly five o'clock when a loud pounding was heard on the door of the jury room, and the attendant rushed into court with the news that the jury had agreed.

Judge Grover recessed the jury then occupying the box, listening to a drowsy case of trover, involving the fate of sixty tons of hay. He asked them to step down while he received the verdict in the arson case. As soon as the jury box was empty the Billings jury filed in, haggard and unshaved, and took their places. At almost the same moment Jerry was led in by two jailers and placed in the prisoners' dock.

"Gentlemen of the jury," said the judge, "have you agreed upon a verdict?"

The foreman stood up. "We have."

"How do you find?"

"We find the defendant guilty as charged."

"So say you every one?"

"We do."

"The clerk will poll the jury and enter the verdict upon the records of the court."

As soon as the poll was completed and the jury discharged, my father leaped to his feet with a fiery motion to set aside the verdict and grant a new trial. To allow the verdict to stand, he said, would constitute a gross miscarriage of justice. Judge Grover entertained the motion, which was argued with great animation and citation of authorities a week or two later—and then he denied it and sentenced Jerry to ten years of hard labor at Auburn Prison.

My father was so convinced of the erroneousness of the decision that he appealed the case at his own expense. It was argued at the General Term, as the appellate division was then called, and the verdict of the lower court unanimously affirmed. There was a painful scene in our garden when my father went out to break the news to Jerry, who all this time had been out on bail provided by my father. My father began with some general remarks about the widespread stupidity of people, how they would get an idea in their heads and could not get it out. They reasoned, he said, from prejudice instead of fact. They were able to make themselves believe whatever they wanted to believe. This

74

was not getting him quite where he wanted to go, but Jerry had caught the point.

"Heard anything from Rochester?" he asked.

"It's gone against us." My father mopped his face with his handkerchief. "Unanimous decision."

"Then I'll be—goin' down the road?"

"That's what it means."

"Well, you needn't feel so damn bad about it." Jerry sounded a little indignant as my father used to tell it. "Guess you done all you could—and a damn sight more'n I had any call to ask of you or anybody else."

"A miscarriage of justice if there ever was one."

"When do I get turned in?"

"The sheriff will probably be down this afternoon."

"You act as if you was goin' instead of me."

Jerry was taken away that afternoon, but it was a long time before my father could speak of the Billings case with equanimity. It was unlike any other lost cause in his career. Usually he could take a drubbing with as good grace as anybody. "When the law ceases to be an art and becomes an exact science," I have heard him say, "then a lawyer will be able to win all his cases."

Adelbert Moot, a famous trial lawyer of my father's day, once said to me soon after I was admitted to the bar, that when he first began to practice he never appealed a case unless he felt absolutely certain of winning and that during that period he won only fifty per cent of his appeals. The upper courts, he said, had a way of finding grounds to beat him that he had not thought of. They also found grounds for sustaining his appeals that he had not thought of. Later on in his practice he began to appeal every case—and his percentage of victories, though he was handling twice as many appeals and making a much larger income, was still around fifty.

How many times I have heard my father bemoan the loss of the Billings case I would hesitate to say. I used to think that he had the feeling that if he could only have put a little more into it he might have won it. Once when he mentioned the matter in the presence of Mr. Hobson, the old lawyer laughed and shook his head. "Aren't you ever going to forgive Frank Rice," he asked, "for sending that wonderful gardener of yours to jail?"

My father laughed heartily, but I have always felt that there was more than a vestige of truth in what Mr. Hobson said.

7. Act of God

IN A small town people have a way of taking things personally. Practically nobody in town would even speak to Jerry Billings while he was out on bail. People treated him about as cordially as they would have treated a polecat. Some of the women would cross over to the other side of the street if they saw him coming. But Jerry took it like a man. He never winced, and he never complained.

My father, too, felt a certain amount of resentment. He knew that people were criticizing him behind his back for taking Jerry's case, but he did not let it disturb him. He realized that any lawyer is likely to get an unpopular cause now and then, and he felt that the first time he took hold of a popular case all hard feelings would be forgotten. And fortunately a popular case came bobbing to the surface soon after Jerry had gone away for his long stay.

The case derived primarily from the dry weather of the summer before. For weeks on end not a drop of rain had fallen. Crops withered in the field. Wells went dry, and springs that had long been regarded as perpetual shrank to a tiny trickle. The situation was becoming rather serious when young Mr. Duncan McLeod, the new Presbyterian minister, took matters in hand and organized a huge movement for a collective prayer for rain. Mr. McLeod's idea was not merely to get the godly people of the town to pray in a union prayer meeting of the various churches. His idea was much more comprehensive; he wanted every person in the town, good and bad, to get down on his knees at twelve o'clock noon on a certain Saturday in August and join in one great big town-wide supplication for rain.

Of course, he started his organization with the churches. But as soon as the churches had come in he opened his campaign on the shops and business places of the town and exacted from nearly all of them a promise to suspend business for five minutes after the blowing of the noon whistles, to give every man, woman, and child at least an opportunity to pray for rain. Every person in every home was invited to cooperate. And so complete was his organization that even the saloons, then suspected of being the personal handiwork of the devil, joined in the pause.

There were only three whistles in town at the time—at the grass seeder factory, the tin shop where sprayers were made, and the plow works. Not many, but still enough to raise a very creditable din, and when the noise subsided on that hot August day the town stood stock still for five full minutes.

In the crowded churches the prayers of the clergy ascended heavenward in loud and fervent tones, and though in the places of business the prayer was mostly of the silent variety, there were occasional spots were some godly man would raise his hands for silence and lead his fellows in an audible prayer for rain. One such instance occurred in the hardware store where Elder Wheeler was buying Paris green to kill his potato bugs and another, in the post office where Eddie Brownell, leader of the Baptist choir, was laying a new floor and was already on his knees anyway.

It was everywhere felt that the effort had been a great success, which was probably true if one may judge by the

78

immediate results. By one o'clock there were small clouds in the sky; by two a gusty wind had begun to blow; by three the temperature had dropped almost twenty degrees; and by four a thunder storm of cyclonic proportions swept the township, drenching the parched countryside with nearly two inches of rainfall, washing out one highway bridge, seriously undermining the abutments of another—and igniting with a bolt of lightning the largest hay barn of Mr. Phineas Dodd, which burned to the ground with its contents, a total loss.

Phineas Dodd was the one person in town who had raised his voice against Mr. McLeod's idea. He was as anxious as anybody to have a good rain, but he was opposed on general principles to interfering in the affairs of the Almighty. Not that he was a reverent man; quite the opposite. His usual references to the Almighty were for emphasis only, and he was as likely to hurl them at a hog as at a human being. Mr. Dodd was willing enough to accept the benefit of the rain, but he was very angry over the loss of his barn, and when he heard that Mr. McLeod was accepting congratulations over the success of his idea he presented the Reverend gentleman, as well as the board of trustees of the Presbyterian Church, with a bill for $5,000 to cover the loss of his barn.

When Mr. McLeod and the board of trustees, acting on the advice of my father, refused to pay the bill, Mr. Dodd brought suit in the Supreme Court. My father joined issue by entering a general denial, and the case came on for trial before old Judge Rumsey at the October term.

For two days Phineas Dodd's attorney called a succession of witnesses to prove that Mr. McLeod was the organizer as well as the moving spirit of the great congress of prayer, and particular pains were taken to establish the fact that he had repeatedly accepted congratulations on the success of the outcome. Most of these witnesses my father passed without cross-examination, but when Phineas himself took the stand he could not resist the temptation to give the old fellow a little grilling.

He caused some merriment in court when he asked Phineas if he had joined in the prayer for rain. Phineas replied grumpily that he had not. My father then asked him if he believed in the efficacy of prayer. This was of more importance than appeared on the face of the question, for if Phineas had replied in the negative his answer would have implied his own disbelief in the allegations of his complaint. His attorney was on his feet in an instant with a storm of objections, but the question was allowed. Phineas, however, had caught the warning and answered in the affirmative. But this only led him into deeper water.

"How long since you have prayed, Mr. Dodd?"

"Don't recollect."

"Did you ever pray?"

"I can't remember."

"And still you believe in prayer?"

"Why, yes—it's all right for folks who want to pray."

"You mean that you believe in it for other people but not for yourself?"

"That's one way to put it."

"If you do believe in this great power, Mr. Dodd, can you explain how it happens that you never make use of it?"

"Couldn't say. Never thought of it, I guess."

"But don't you see that it gives other people an advantage over you?"

"An advantage? What do you mean by that?"

"Can you think of an easier way to get things than by praying for them?"

"I don't think folks get everything they pray for."

"Then you don't believe in the efficacy of all prayers?"

"Well, no, not all of 'em."

"Just the prayers for rain?"

"Some of 'em."

"You don't think all prayers for rain are answered?"

"No—not by a long shot."

"But what reason have you to believe that Mr. McLeod's prayer for rain was answered?"

"Well, in the first place, it wasn't no ordinary prayer; he got most of the people in town to back him. And in the next place, that storm begun to blow up right after they done the prayin'."

"Do you believe that the storm would not have come except for Mr. McLeod's prayers?"

"Well, I know it didn't come before, and it did come right after."

"Do you believe it would not have come except for his prayers? Answer the question yes or no."

"No, I don't believe it would."

"Do you know whether this rain was general or not?"

"Just what I read in the paper."

"What was that?"

"The paper said it covered considerable territory around there."

"Didn't it say that the storm covered the whole western part of the state?"

"Yes, I guess it did."

"Can you swear that it is your sincere belief that Mr. McLeod's prayers covered quite that much ground?"

"I wasn't interested in what ground they covered outside my own place."

"Did you have any insurance on the barn that burned?"

"Not on the barn. Just on the contents. The insurance on the barn had expired."

"How long ago?"

"Oh, a couple of days before the fire."

"How did that happen?"

"I didn't know it had run out, and the notice from the agent got delayed in the mail and didn't reach me until after the fire."

The examination went on for pages, frequently leaping back to the witness's belief in the efficacy of prayer, his belief in future rewards and punishments, his belief in present punishments for misdeeds, and a host of other matters that Phineas showed a great reluctance to discuss. After the cross-examination was concluded the plaintiff's attorney asked a few routine questions of redirect, just to take away the curse, and announced that the plaintiff rested. Whereupon my father produced a voluminous brief and began a vigorous argument for a nonsuit.

He had fortified his position with a formidable array of authorities, but it was when he had reached the point that the plaintiff had failed to produce any evidence whatever that the defendants had prayed for anything but *rain* and that the lightning was an entirely gratuitous gift from the Author of All Weather, in other words an act of God without the intercession of man—that old Judge Rumsey brought down his gavel with a bang.

"Nonsuit granted with costs," he said. "Findings may be presented for settlement at the Special Term at Rochester on the coming Saturday."

And since that time all the churches in town have felt quite secure in praying for rain whenever they thought that it was needed.

With Jerry Billings in prison, the resentment against him cooled down very rapidly, just as the public fury always cools down after a man is behind the bars. It is hard to keep a feeling of animosity nourished while the object of it is being submitted to a long-continued punishment. And any resentment against my father that may have been lingering in the public bosom was completely obliterated by the verdict in the Phineas Dodd case, which proved to be especially popular among the better element of the townspeople. But somehow my father never could seem to stay on the one side or the other very long, for soon afterward he allowed himself to be drawn into an amusing case when he took the job of defending quite a prominent figure among the local sporting men against a charge of disorderly conduct based on an allegation of reckless and careless driving of a horse and carriage on a public highway while intoxicated.

He could hardly have refused to take this case, for he had more than once called on Oswald for help in a difficult horse case and had never been refused. Then, too, he had a certain liking for Oswald, and my father was never one to turn down a friend in need.

Oswald Prince had all his life been addicted to spirited horses. He was an enthusiastic patron of the race tracks, though he never had any race horses of his own. He preferred to drive his horses up and down the street so that people could see how spirited they were and how well he could handle them. When sober, he was a fine horseman, but on occasions he was given to indulging in a little more alcoholic stimulant than was good for him, and at such times he had what amounted to a mania for showing off. Even when sober he found it hard to resist the temptation of providing thrills for a crowd; and when he was slightly intoxicated he found it impossible.

Saturday was market day. Farmers with their families kept drifting into town all day long, and by four o'clock in the afternoon the streets were pretty well crowded. There were no movies in those days, and after the trading was done the country folk would gather in little groups on the streets and in the stores and saloons and gossip. Any kind of diversion, such as a fight or a runaway, was always welcome, and it is not to be wondered at that with such an appreciative audience Oswald should give an exhibition of his very considerable prowess in horsemanship.

With all the spirited steeds he had owned, Oswald had never figured in more than one or two runaways, though some people were always hoping.

On the occasion of question Oswald was driving a new horse, that is, a comparatively new horse. He had not had it longer than a month. The animal was a very magnificent chestnut gelding with four white feet and a stripe on the nose. He was a rangy fellow, fully seventeen hands high, with an arching neck and magnificent knee action, but he had a way of showing the whites of his eyes in such a manner that those who knew horses were fairly sure he had an ugly streak in him.

Oswald denied this. He said the horse was as gentle as a baby, and one Saturday afternoon when his barroom cronies had been twitting him about being afraid of the horse, he offered to bet ten dollars that he could crawl under the horse and even between his legs without being hurt. A wager was placed, and Oswald won it. With the winnings, he proceeded to get a little more intoxicated than he was before, and in time he was warmed up to the point where he simply could not resist giving the villagers a driving exhibition. As it happened, my father did not see the exhibition, though he had heard of it soon after it was over. From all accounts it was the most spectacular exhibition Oswald had ever attempted.

He cut figure eights; he performed a huge spiral movement the entire length of the business section; he gave exhibitions of speed, of knee action, of rearing and plunging, and everything else he could think of.

The horse was never out of control, though often the crowd was, and in attempting to cross the street during one of the maneuvers the wife of the Village President, Mrs. Dan Richman, barely missed being trampled on. In her haste to get out of the path of the plunging beast she fell flat on the ground. By good luck she was uninjured, though her hands and her clothing were covered with mud and her dignity was deeply wounded. She was a woman of great force, a rather pretty woman of middle age with graying hair and black snapping eyes, and her first act after picking herself up was to report the incident to her husband, who took her angrily to Squire Redman and had her swear out a warrant for Oswald's arrest.

It so happened that no constable was on hand to make the arrest, and by the time a constable did appear Oswald had been warned and was nowhere to be found. His arrest was not effected until the following day, and by that time he was stone sober. When he was taken before the justice he demanded a jury trial and was released on his own recognizance; whereupon he came around and asked my father to defend him.

Inebriation was and is a difficult matter to prove. Facilities have improved somewhat, though the rules of evidence are pretty much the same. Mrs. Richman had no difficulty in recruiting an overwhelming number of witnesses—mostly women and children, who, from a safe place on the sidewalk, had seen the scandalous performances of the defendant on the seat of his skeleton wagon in the street and were quite ready to testify that he was thoroughly intoxicated. The only difficulty was that the law would not allow them to testify to inebriety at such long range. My father had fought this out with Squire Redman long before the trial had opened, and he had convinced the Squire that a witness could not be lawfully asked, "Was he drunk or sober at the time?" without some previous qualification. The law regards inebriation as a delicate question, a question that must be approached in one of three ways by the lay witness:

"Did you see him take a drink?"

"Did you smell his breath?"

"Did you see him stagger?"

Unless a witness could answer one of these three questions in the affirmative the law did not regard him as qualified to answer the question, "Was he drunk or sober?"

When the case was opened Mrs. Richman took the stand. She apparently set out to show her phalanx of witnesses the way the thing should be done; for she gave a vivid description of the streets on the Saturday afternoon in question. She described the crowds and the traffic and made particular mention of the number of women and children abroad. Then she told in some detail of the dangerous feats of horsemanship performed or attempted by the defendant and depicted his steed as a great wild, plunging, pawing beast, whipped and tortured by the driver, rolling its eyes in fear and fury and shaking the earth with the pounding of its iron-shod hoofs.

"And did you recognize the driver as the defendant in this case?"

"I did."

"And what, if anything, did you notice about his driving?"

"I noticed that he was driving very carelessly."

"The court will be the judge of that—just tell us what you saw—how he was holding his reins, and things like that."

"He was holding his reins very high—almost in front of his face—putting on airs."

Among the sporting men of the town this was as good as saying that Oswald was fairly tight; for the tighter he was the more style he put into his driving. But the Squire did not press the matter; he started off on something else.

"Did you observe his condition?"

"I most certainly did!"

My father stood up. "One moment, please." He opened a copy of Wait's *Law and Practice in Justice Court* which lay before him on the desk. "Before proceeding any further I should like to call the attention of the court to the rules of evidence which apply in a case where intoxication is sought to be proved." He read a paragraph or two. "Am I to understand that this is the law as interpreted in this court?"

The Squire cleared his throat. "That is correct."

"Very well," said my father. He laid the open book before the justice for his guidance. "Let's get on with the case."

The squire poked at his steel-rimmed glasses and ran his finger along the line. "Did you see the defendant take a drink?"

Mrs. Richman's eyebrows rose indignantly. "Most certainly not!"

"Did you smell his breath?" the Squire continued, without raising his eyes from the book.

"Of course I didn't smell his breath—not at *that* distance!" Bright red spots appeared on each of Mrs. Richman's cheeks.

"Did you see him stagger?" continued the justice imperturbably.

"How could I see him stagger when he was riding around in a high-wheeled wagon behind that terrible horse?" demanded Mrs. Richman angrily.

"Um—well—" the Squire cleared his throat, "I guess that disqualifies you from testifying whether in your opinion he was drunk or sober."

By this time Mrs. Richman's face was fiery red. "Do you mean to say that I can't tell you what I saw with my own eyes? That man was drunk, and I know it!"

"I'm afraid the witness doesn't quite understand the ruling of the court," said my father gently. "I think that last statement should be stricken out."

"Quite right," said the Squire.

"And you aren't going to let me tell what I know?"

The Squire shook his head. "What you know and what you can prove are two entirely different things in a court of law."

Dan Richman took a hand in proceedings. "According to your ruling nobody but the *bartender* would be able to testify that this man was drunk!" he shouted testily.

"Not a bad idea," said the Squire. "Do you want a subpoena for him—I see he's right here in court?"

My father turned quickly to Oswald. "What about this?" he asked.

"Let 'em put him on," said Oswald. "I was talkin' to him a little while ago. He's all set for 'em."

So they called the bartender, and the Squire questioned him.

"You've heard the testimony in this case and are familiar with the episode we are speaking of?"

"Yes, sir."

"Did you see the defendant take a drink that afternoon?"

"I certainly did."

"Did you smell liquor on his breath?"

"I certainly did."

"Did you see him stagger?"

The bartender shook his head. "No, I can't say that I did."

"How long before he gave this exhibition on the main street did you last see him?"

"Just before he started. I saw him getting his horse."

"It is the opinion of this court," said the Squire, "that this witness is properly qualified to testify as to the drunkenness or sobriety of the defendant on this occasion."

"The defendant is willing to concede that," said my father.

"Very well, sir," said the Squire. "Will the witness please tell us whether in his opinion the defendant was drunk or sober at the time?"

For a moment the bartender rubbed his chin with his hand. Then he said, "In my opinion the defendant was as sober as a judge!"

My father was always credited with this answer, though the truth was that he had nothing to do with it. But when the laughter had subsided the Squire asked if the complainant had any more witnesses she cared to call. She said that there was no use, since the judge would not let them tell what they had seen with their own eyes. So the Squire spared himself the responsibility of making a decision by submitting the case to the jury.

The jury retired, and after a rather hilarious discussion, brought in a verdict of acquittal.

8. The Elder Woodruff Desk

THE little triangular room over the bank, in spite of its commanding location, was not a very satisfactory office. To begin with, it was far too small, and by the time that my father had moved in some furniture and built bookshelves and pigeonholes along the wall, he found the place too crowded for comfort. In addition to this, being a single room, it lacked the privacy required for a law office, and if a second client happened to come in while a first one was there he had to be asked to wait outside, though my father sometimes got around this by excusing himself and taking the first client over to the post office across the street for a few private words in the lobby. Then, too, the location of this little office was a bit prominent. People do not always want others to know when they are consulting a lawyer, and there was absolutely no privacy about that outside iron stairway. Anybody climbing those ornamental cast-iron stairs was going to a law office—there was no other place to go.

These were all weighty though not compelling disadvantages. It was the fact that he could not get into the place the splendid butternut desk built by Elder Woodruff that finally induced my father to hunt up new offices. When the Elder had first taken the order, he had hoped to have the desk ready in a month. But he was poorly at the time and unable to work with any regularity, and several months had passed before he came tottering into the office and announced that the desk was ready.

My father went around to see it on his way home to lunch. It was a beautiful piece of cabinetwork with a surface rubbed to a soft, velvety finish that butternut will but rarely take. The width was right; the Elder's measurements had taken care of that. But the old cabinetmaker had failed to take into consideration the fact that the office door was very near the apex of the triangular-shaped office, and he had built the desk at least a foot too long to go through the door. My father realized this at a glance, though he took away none of the Elder's gratification from the excellence of his workmanship by telling him so. He assured the old craftsman of his delight with the desk but said that he would not take it for the present, since he was about to change to a larger office and did not care to submit so fine a piece of furniture to the risk of being moved twice.

It was the desk that spurred him into action, and within a week or two he had taken new offices on the ground floor of a frame building on Church Street. Gradually he was drawing nearer to his heart's desire, for this location was separated from Mr. Hobson's office by a single building—a structure with a business basement then occupied as an elite billiard parlor and living quarters on the parlor floor.

The new offices were more spacious than elegant. The private room in the rear looked out upon the side of a livery stable from the little windows of which a row of horses' heads could be seen poking out on any fine summer day. My father's safe, which he had been unable to get into the little office over the bank, and the new butternut desk were placed in the rear room together with a sizable bookshelf and a pigeonhole cabinet. I have heard my father say more than once that he won most of his cases at that desk.

It was a knee-hole desk with chastely paneled ends and eight roomy drawers in units of four on each side. There was a shallow center drawer cunningly let into the front of the desk in such a way that it appeared to be part of the molding. I had written scores of letters at that desk and had copied hundreds of pages there for my father before I discovered the existence of this drawer. If I had looked a little further at the time I might not have been quite so much surprised at some of the other things I found out about the desk later on.

It so happened, however, that my father did not long remain in these quarters; for he had been there only a few months when old Mr. Hobson died, and since young Mr. Hobson had no desire for an office in which to putter around he was glad to lease it to my father for an indefinite length of time.

A feeling of sadness came over my father as he took down Mr. Hobson's sign and hung up his own on the iron rod driven into the large tree in front. It seemed to him like the end of an epoch. He looked at the old sign, faded and weather-beaten, and reflected that when it was first hung there it had been new and bright—and Mr. Hobson had been a young man like himself, full of hope and enthusiasm. And the thought came to him that there would be a time— off somewhere in the future—when a younger man would take down the sign he had just hung up. He stood and wondered how much of a chance it would have to weather and season. But he need not have worried, for his sign hung there for nearly forty years.

I still remember quite distinctly the first time I ever went to see my father in the Hobson office. I don't believe I shall ever forget the strange man who was sitting there talking to him that day. He was a tall slim fellow with a cadaverous face and a small drooping mustache. What most attracted my attention, however, was the blue army cap he had on.

It had brass buttons on the sides, a shiny flat vizor, and a little round top. My father had worn just such a cap when he returned from the Civil War. At that moment it was hanging, slightly moth-eaten, together with his sword and sash and spurs, above the hatrack in our front hall.

The man's name, as I soon found out, was George Borison, though nobody ever called him anything but "Comrade." He had come to see my father about applying for a pension. During the Civil War Comrade had been wounded in the neck by a Minié ball which had left a scar on the outside and an unquenchable thirst on the inside. His life was one long uphill fight against that thirst. At rare intervals Comrade would seem to have the upper hand for a few weeks or even

a few months, though usually when he came to town he got very much the worst of the argument.

For some years after the war Comrade was never seen without his army cap. When one wore out another miraculously appeared. Where these caps came from nobody seemed to know. Later on he appeared in a G.A.R. hat with a wide brim, a cord, and a little gold wreath on the front.

People used to say that Comrade was crazy. Perhaps he was. He had a number of peculiarities, the most unusual of which was that whenever he went on a spree he used to get the idea that he had a squad of soldiers with him, and as he marched about he would march the imaginary men with him, keeping them in perfect formation and waving aside pedestrians who were forever getting in his way.

With a little encouragement he would put his men through their paces in an open space in the street in front of the Inn, with a crowd of urchins and idlers as an audience. It aroused an eerie sensation to see this erect and serious soldier drilling with the utmost precision a force of men visible only to himself. He used to reprimand them by name, and once he had a fellow he called Hank doing hayfoot-strawfoot for getting out of step.

Sometimes at the conclusion of an exhibition drill he would put his men through the manual of arms, barking out his commands rapidly and executing each order as if he himself had a musket in his hands.

One of the most striking features of Comrade's military performance was the perfect time he kept. All his movements were in rhythm with the beating of drums heard only by himself. He never missed a beat or lost a step, and when he was drilling his men before a crowd, as he sometimes did on a Saturday evening, the onlookers would soon find themselves keeping time by tapping on the ground with their feet as the invisible marchers went back and forth.

These martial drums were always beating in Comrade Borison's ears. If he was stopped on the street by an acquaintance, he would have to catch step with the music before going on. It was said, however, that all his marching was confined to the time when he was in town. My father, who had seen him on various farms where he had worked, insisted that while Comrade was at home—and sober—he was pursued by no military delusions.

When he marched along the street on one of his military sprees Comrade was alert to detect a salute, which he was a stickler about returning. Indeed, he was so much of a stickler that if an idler happened to raise his hand to scratch an ear while Comrade was passing, the movement was almost certain to be translated into a salute and smartly returned. We schoolboys were not backward about taking advantage of Comrade's weakness in this respect, and when we saw him coming we would string ourselves out in single file and keep him saluting steadily until the last one had passed.

In spite of his commanding presence and his piercing black eyes Comrade was always supposed to be harmless until one day when he ordered some little girls out of the open space in which he was drilling his men. The little girls giggled when he ran them out of his drill ground, slapping one of them paternally on the behind for emphasis. But when they went home and told their mothers what had happened, trouble began to brew. The mothers got their heads together and became very much excited over the episode. They set up a cry that old Comrade Borison was a dangerous lunatic—especially dangerous to little girls.

For a while their excitement went no further than talk, quite a good deal of talk. But it finally resulted in a movement. Somebody started a petition requesting the authorities to take proper steps to have Comrade adjudged insane and committed to an institution. Like most petitions this one was liberally signed by persons who had not taken the trouble to

95

read it. My father heard about the petition, but he paid little attention to it, for he thought the petitioners would not get very far with it. And then one day the news came to him that they had found two doctors who were willing to join the stampede to put the old fellow in custody.

When the hearing came on before the County Court the petitioners were somewhat surprised to find my father in court as Comrade's attorney, though they could not have been more surprised than Comrade himself. My father had brought with him as a witness a man named Hemingway Dilman, who had formerly employed Comrade as a farm hand. Dilman was at the time the Town Supervisor, a member of the school board, and an all-around substantial citizen, and when he testified that it was his opinion, based on long acquaintance and observation, that the bewildered condition of the alleged incompetent person was produced by overindulgence and offered to re-employ him, the case against Comrade collapsed. There were, however, certain repercussions that had not been anticipated.

Almost immediately the town found itself taking sides, not as to whether Comrade Borison was dangerous but as to whether the soldiers he had so long been drilling were wholly imaginary or only partly so. Plenty of persons told their friends confidentially that they had heard the mysterious foot beats of a considerable body of men during some of the exhibition drills. My father scoffed at this and insisted that the only foot beats they had heard were those of the spectators keeping time. Others immediately came forward to say that they had on occasion heard the muffled *tramp—tramp—tramp* of many feet when Comrade had passed them on the street—especially at about dusk. And Old Tick added fuel to the fire by spreading the story that one evening when Comrade was drilling his invisible host and the innkeeper was snoozing in his chair on the veranda, he had awakened suddenly from a doze to see the filmy outlines of men in blue

96

performing their evolutions at Comrade's command in front of the Inn.

The men in blue had vanished, to be sure, the moment Old Tick had become fully awake; but it was impossible to convince the fat innkeeper that he had not actually seen them. And when, late that night, Comrade was seized with a paralytic stroke and collapsed on the floor of the hotel office, Old Tick was convinced that what he had seen was a premonition.

Comrade was carried upstairs and put to bed, and a hurry call was sent for the doctor. There was, however, nothing for a doctor to do. Comrade's marching days were over. The old soldier never spoke again. He was completely paralyzed, and for a week he lay in a coma in the room on the second floor of the Inn to which he had been carried on the night of his stroke, his eyes closed, his body limp, his arms and legs inert and helpless. Then one morning at daybreak, just as Old Tick was coming out of the door of his room, he heard a shout that seemed to come from the room occupied by Comrade.

"The bugles—! Come on, boys—we're going in—!"

It was Comrade's voice. Old Tick could hear a commotion in the room as he hurried along the hall. At first it sounded like the shuffling of many feet—but as he came nearer the shuffling settled down to a *tramp—tramp—tramp*. But the sound of the marching feet receded as the fat innkeeper approached the door, and by the time he had entered the room it had died out in the distance.

A glance at the bed was enough to tell him that Comrade Borison was dead. But a strange thing had happened to him. His body was no longer limp, nor were his limbs inert and helpless. In death he lay as straight as an arrow, his left arm stiff at his side, and his right drawn up in a smart salute. His eyes were wide open and staring.

Old Tick staggered back, felt his way out of the door, and had started on a run down the hall when he saw the nurse coming. "Jees Cri!" he gasped. "So you heared 'em too, did you?"

"Heard what?" The nurse blinked at him. "What do you mean?"

"You know what I mean—them marchin' soldiers!"

"Soldiers? I heard no soldiers. I didn't hear anything—I was down in the kitchen heating some milk."

"But—but—but you must have heared him yell about them bugles!"

She shook her head. "I didn't hear a sound. I don't know what you're talking about."

"Well, Jees Cri! Where's your ears? I was just comin' outa my door when I heared him yell, 'The bugles—! Come on, boys—we're going in—!' I went on a run—but by the time I got to his door he was dead—and he was just the way he is *now!*"

"Dead!" She started hastily for Comrade's room. At the open door she paused. "But his arm—how did it get like that? *He* couldn't move it!"

"Don't ask me. That's the way it was when I found him."

As she started to go over to feel the patient's pulse Tick stopped her. "Don't you move that *arm!* You leave it just as it is. Nobody won't never believe it unless they see it for theirselves."

"But I must close his eyes."

"All right, close 'em if you wanta. But don't you touch that arm."

Nobody wanted to take the responsibility for moving Comrade's arm. The doctor looked at it and shook his head. He mumbled something about reflexes, but offered no adequate explanation. A number of other people—including my father—saw the body before it had even been touched by the undertaker. Old Tick had instructed his porter to call the doctor first and then to go right on and summon my father. And since Comrade had no family and the funeral was to be in charge of the G.A.R., the Commander of the Post was also called in for consultation. My father and the Commander reached the Inn at the same time and went in together.

Still wheezing with excitement, the innkeeper led them to the room where Comrade's body lay. "There he is—just the way I found him when I heared him yell and I come runnin' in here at daybreak! Ain't nobody touched him. I seen to that."

As Old Tick repeated once more the story of what had happened, the two visitors stood and regarded the body with great interest and not a little amazement.

"Well," demanded Old Tick impatiently, "ain't you got nuthin' to say about it?"

"It's a characteristic position," replied my father. "Probably it's the way old Comrade would like to have us remember him."

The Commander nodded his head slowly. "I think it's kinda nice."

"You mean—you mean you—you believe what I been tellin' you?" stammered the innkeeper.

My father nodded. "Certainly. I believe you found him just as he is."

"And you're gonna leave him that way?"

"What do you say about that, Commander?" asked my father.

"Well—it looks as if that was his own idear."

So they buried him that way. And nobody who looked into the casket thought there was anything out of the way about it. The episode would probably have passed quietly into history if it had not been for Old Tick's persistence in talking about the bugle call and the marching men. In Old Tick's earlier versions of the tale it was Comrade who had heard the bugles and translated them into a call to arms; but after a little the innkeeper began to believe that it was the clarion call of the ghostly bugle reechoing through the corridors of the Inn that had first aroused his attention.

Once the story had started to grow it rapidly assumed heroic proportions and soon was stretched to include the men in blue previously seen by Old Tick in front of the Inn. The tale would have been hard enough to believe even without the bugles or the marching men; and after these details had been added, and embroidered upon to some extent, people began to tap their heads with a forefinger whenever the old innkeeper's name was mentioned. Nor were they willing to let matters rest there, for they began to ask one another if it was a good thing for the town to have as the keeper of its principal tavern a man who "saw things."

There had actually been some talk of applying to the county authorities to have a commission appointed to examine into the old fellow's mental competency when my father thought the time had come for him to take the law into his own hands; so he took the innkeeper aside and told him what the townspeople were saying. At first Old Tick was very angry, but on reflection he followed my father's advice and began to treat the episode of the bugles and the marching men as more or less of a hoax. Not that Old Tick ever doubted the evidence of either his eyes or his ears on that momentous occasion, but my father convinced him that it might be good business to play the clown rather than the mystic.

9. The War of the Relatives

IN THE course of his long practice my father ran into a number of litigious families. It is well known among the members of the legal profession that nothing is quite so good for the lawyers as a spirited family fight. Unrelated individuals are often valiant fighters, but for malice and cruelty as well as resourcefulness and pertinacity nothing can come up to a contest between members of the same family. They know so well how to avoid each other's strength and get at the weakness.

This lesson had been brought home to my father very early in his career. A small estate involving not more than $2,000 had come into his office for settlement. When old Henry Sharp had died all was peace and harmony among his children. But when one of the daughters put in a large claim for supporting the old gentleman during his declining years the fat was in the fire. The other members of the family were enraged, and they declared that the daughter should never have a dollar of that claim even if it should take every cent of the estate to fight it. And that is exactly what happened. When the lawyers were through with their trials and arguments and rearguments and appeals, not a penny of the estate remained for the heirs. In fact, even the lawyers had to shade their bills on the final judicial settlement.

The Westfall estate was a much larger property. Old Jacobus had amassed quite a snug fortune from his distilling business. Even the members of the family did not realize how much it was until after his death. They evidently thought that there was enough to afford a good fight, for the hostilities started immediately after the funeral.

My father had drawn the will for old Jacobus, and on hearing of his death had notified the youngest son, Cordell, who was named as one of the executors, that the will was in his safe. Cordell had asked him to bring it to the house immediately after the funeral, and my father had driven the six miles into the country to the Westfall home for this express purpose. The formal reading of the will immediately after the funeral was a well-established custom in the country at the time. It was a ceremony that my father performed hundreds of times during the years of his practice. There was something impressive about going back to the home of the testator and there, in the midst of the descendants, reading to them the instructions left by the absent one concerning the disposition of his property. The custom had already begun to pass by the time that I was admitted to practice, and I did what I could to hasten its passing by charging ten dollars for reading a will—though I would still draw one for a dollar. But in spite of this charge I was called upon from time to time to go into the country and read a will in a musty parlor with the shades drawn and the family usually all in black, sitting expectantly around.

On the first of these occasions my father had warned me to be on the lookout for the decedent's chair. The custom of deferring to its vacancy was not always observed, he said, but when this happened, the family were greatly perturbed if anybody sat down in it.

The chair that was set apart was usually the favorite sitting place of the deceased, and I was advised to watch for any comfortable-looking chair placed temptingly beside either a

102

window or a table. The members of the family, being familiar with the chair, would, of course, stay out of it, though a mere lawyer just called in to read a will might, if he was not very careful, commit a most grievous breach of etiquette that would make the family quite unhappy.

At the Westfall mansion no such vacant chair was in evidence. The Westfalls knew each other too well to risk so obvious a cause of dissension. Some determined member of the family would have been sure to plump himself into it—

just to keep some other determined member of the family from doing the same thing. The moment my father entered the house he could feel the tension. There were only four children, two grown sons and two grown daughters, but they were all prolific. One daughter had ten children; I used to go to school with eight of them. Another had six. I am not sure about the families of the sons, who were both great hulking fellows well over six feet tall, gnarled and sturdy as oak trees. Both had plenty of posterity, and the house was literally overflowing with grandchildren as my father was led into the big sitting room, where he paid his respects to old Granny Westfall, now nominally the head of the clan.

The double doors into the half-darkened parlor were open, and my father could see a number of people seated there in funeral chairs. The sitting room was not so dark, though it was dark enough. Cordell ushered my father to a chair in the center of the room beside a small table. But my father did not sit down; he put his hat on the little table and took a large sealed envelope from his pocket.

"A little over five years ago," he said, "Jacobus Westfall came to me and said that he wanted to make his will. He told me that he had never made one before."

"He never had!" said Granny sharply in her high, piping voice. "I kep' at him and at him to make one before, but he never would."

My father nodded and went on. "He told me roughly what he wanted, and I made some notes. He came in again a few days later, and I showed him what I had written out. He made some corrections, and from that corrected draft I prepared the final will which was executed and witnessed a few days later. I am explaining this because I want you to understand that this will was drawn according to his ideas— not mine. After the will was signed it was sealed in his presence and put in my safe for keeping with instructions that the envelope was not to be opened until after his death. Now, if it is your wish, I will break the seals and read the will aloud."

In sealing a will for an occasion like this my father used plenty of wax, and the breaking of the seals was always a dramatic incident. The sealing wax flew in all directions as he tore open the flap. Then he inserted his fingers and drew out the will.

The Westfall will was a long one. It contained a trust, a complicated proviso for determining and setting apart Granny's dower, detailed instructions about continuing the business, and a number of other matters. It was written by hand on heavy foolscap paper, which crackled with importance as he handled it. But when he had unfolded it he saw that there was not enough light to read by, and he glanced around for the nearest window, intending to move in front of it and read the will there. Cordell anticipated his move and stepped to the window to throw back the curtains. Cordell was an outdoor man. If he had been throwing a tarpaulin over a haystack or shouldering a bag of grain he would have been in his element; but throwing back a curtain was too much for him—and with a single move he brought the hanging, fixture and all, down upon his head.

Some of the children started to giggle, but Granny let out a shrill cry. "Clumsy lout!" she screamed angrily. "Must you tear down everything you touch!"

There were the ingredients of a quarrel here, but my father was anxious to avoid trouble, and he quite conspicuously disregarded the incident by holding out the will and beginning to read in a loud voice:

In the Name of God, Amen.

I, Jacobus Westfall, being of sound and disposing mind and memory, and realizing the uncertainties of this transitory life, do hereby make, ordain, publish, and declare, this my last will and testament in way and manner following, that is to say: First—

Sometimes when he finished reading a will there would be questions; but this time there were no questions at all. He had hardly spoken the last words when Stanley stood up, every one of his two hundred pounds tense with anger. "So he thought I needed a guardian over me! Well, I'll tend to *that!*" He picked up his hat and stalked out of the house, the floor trembling beneath the impact of his steps.

"Expects me to live in that dower house, does he?" shrilled Granny. "I'll never do it—so there—!"

Cordell, who had been named with a neighbor, Calvin Porter, as executor, turned to my father. "File it for probate," he said. "I'll be in and sign the papers tomorrow."

And the fight was on. Part of the time it was a five-way fight, with no two of the interested parties able to agree on a single point of the controversy. Each had a separate attorney. My father represented the executors. His position was that the will had been drawn exactly as the testator desired, and he meant to see it through so far as he was able. He filed the will for probate without delay, and when objections to its admission were filed he had the cause transferred to the Supreme Court, where the issues could be submitted to a jury. More than three weeks were spent in taking the evidence, and there were two full days of oratory before the case went to the jury. The jury did much better than that and were back in half a day with a verdict sustaining the will.

My father thought that with this verdict the troubles of the Westfall estate were practically over; but actually they were only beginning. Three of the heirs filed separate appeals. Two of these appeals ran into unanimous affirmance in the General Term and died there, but the other went on to the Court of Appeals. When the high court sustained the verdict my father felt pretty sure that matters *were* settled. But they weren't. For nearly twenty years they weren't settled.

The temporary administrators who had been appointed to conserve the estate during the will contest had just finished turning the assets over to the executors when the executors found themselves involved in a proceeding for the construction of one of the provisions of the will. From that time on every step they took was challenged and contested. If the Surrogate granted an order, a motion was immediately made for a reargument. If the motion was denied, an appeal was taken, and usually some other party had already appealed from the original order. Whenever estate matters became dull somebody would ask for the construction of another clause of the will. But it was not until the executors came into court for their first accounting that the case really began to blossom. Motions and objections and exceptions filled the usually calm judicial atmosphere of the Surrogate's Court in Canandaigua. Appeals flew in all directions. At one time the Westfall estate had appeals pending in both the General Term and the Court of Appeals and motions or orders to show cause on the Special Term calendar of every Supreme Court Justice in the district. There was probably not an attorney in the county who did not appear at one time or another in some phase of the settlement of this embattled estate, and most of the leading attorneys in the surrounding counties had their fling at it, too. Before he was through with the matter my father felt almost as much at home in the General Term and the Court of Appeals as he did in the Surrogate's Court of his own county.

By the time the case was six months old my father was acutely aware of the filing problem; all the facilities he had were strained to the utmost. Before the first year was out he had Elder Woodruff build him a special pigeonhole cabinet for the Westfall papers alone. Then he had drawers built for the appeal books and the larger records and exhibits that would not go readily into pigeonholes. The time came when one entire side of the office was devoted to the papers of the

Westfall estate. But even this was not enough, for periodically large wooden boxes marked "Westfall Papers" and bearing mysterious dates and numbers found their way into our attic. There must have been a dozen of these in all, and on rainy days when we went to the attic to play we used to build forts out of them to keep off the Apaches or Cherokees.

It had been the desire of old Jacobus to continue the distillery, and for a few years Cordell did continue it with some success. He was so hampered by the family hostilities, however, that he finally closed it out. This was exactly what Stanley wanted, and he set up a distillery of his own, using the Westfall name for his product. But Stanley was too good a customer of his own wares to make any considerable success of the distillery business.

For all their contentiousness, however, the Westfalls were not a long-lived tribe. Old Granny died before the battle was five years old. The next to go was a daughter who, after bringing numerous progeny into the world, expired in childbirth. The other daughter moved to Iowa, which proved to be too far away for very effective hostility, and from that time on it was the two brothers who kept the fight going with stubborn endurance until the sudden death of Cordell. This left nobody but Stanley and Calvin Porter to go on with the contest. Porter had been in the thick of it from the first and was well qualified to carry on; but with the death of Cordell something seemed to go out of Stanley. He lost all zest for the fight and withdrew to his distillery business, leaving the field to Porter and the next generation of Westfalls who turned out to be a lot of weaklings—that is, they preferred money to a good fight, and in this case the money lasted all the way through. The large stock of liquor in bond kept appreciating. As long as Cordell had run his father's distillery he had made enough to take care of all the costs of the litigation justly chargeable on the estate.

108

But even after the cessation of hostilities there were many tag ends to be cleared up, and it was fully five years after the death of Cordell when my father thrust the last paper into a pigeonhole and wrote with a large blue pencil, "Case Closed."

Warring families are not so numerous as they used to be. Perhaps size may have had something to do with the case; for surely the number of children per family has decreased since the nineteenth century, and the proportion of those who remain under the parental roof or the parental influence is greatly diminished. It is hard to tell why some families are filled with clashing personalities, whereas other families never clash at all. Lawyers can hardly be blamed for litigating cases where the members of a family are spoiling for a fight, even though the differences might have been compromised or settled at half the cost. There are still people in the world who enjoy a good fight, as any lawyer knows, though the machine age, with the radio, the automobile, and the motion picture house within easy reach of anybody with a car, has furnished distracting interests. It might even be said in this case that science has furnished mankind with a more civilized outlook.

In the country town no man's private business is allowed to take his mind entirely away from civic affairs. Almost without exception local offices are honorary—that is, they carry no emoluments—and everybody is expected to do his share of the work. No matter how immersed a man may be in his own business he is supposed to lay it aside when some interest of the community is in need of him. This is especially so in the case of the country lawyer, who does a vast amount of unrewarded worrying over the well-meant though bungling efforts of public servants as well as the failure of the community to grasp the importance of some public need.

For example, my father, with one or two others, regarded the town as almost criminally backward in the matter of water supply. They were gratified, of course, to see that the buildings destroyed by the big fire were being rebuilt with brick and fortified with substantial fire walls; but they were still of the opinion that the town would never have any real security from fire without an adequate water supply.

The fire had furnished them with an unanswerable argument, and they had gone quietly to work almost before the embers were cool. But this time they wanted proceedings to seem to originate with the Village Board, and they wanted first of all to be assured as to the adequacy of their proposed water site. So my father went to Rochester and consulted an engineer as to the best way to proceed. The engineer came back with a volley of questions. How much water was in sight? Would it flow, or must it be pumped? What were the natural storage facilities? Would a dam be necessary?

This had my father groping. He had his eye on some springs, he said, but he hardly dared to explore them for fear of arousing the avarice of the owner. The engineer suggested that since he was fond of hunting he might come down with his shotgun and tramp over the territory. He came the following week, and, though he bagged few birds, he was able to report a plentiful supply of water with a gravity flow into town. My father's next move was to get an option on the water site under a fictitious name—to be assured of keeping the price within reason—and then to spread the rumor that a neighboring village was negotiating for the property.

The rumor brought the Village Fathers on the run. They did not want anybody else to get that water site, and would my father see what he could do about getting possession of the option? My father was only too happy to accommodate them, and the town was soon in the throes of another water fight, brought on at the instance of the Village Board. This time the side of progress won, and before the year was out a contractor from Rochester with a large gang of laborers began digging up the streets. They were the first Italian workmen ever seen in town, and although the natives were amused by the dark-skinned outlanders with their great handle-bar mustaches and their wooden-soled shoes, they were a little afraid of the foreigners and kept out of their way after nightfall. However, the Italians proved to be good workers, and by fall our family were taking their Saturday night baths in "the bathroom" instead of in the big round tub before the kitchen stove.

At first our Saturday nights were as busy as ever. We could not seem to get over the idea that the whole family must be clean at the same time. Ablutions usually started with the youngest children immediately after supper and went on progressively according to age far into the night. Occasionally there would have to be an intermission while the water in the tank was heated, and this eventually led to a system by which each member of the family was assigned a regular weekly period for bathing. A written schedule was made out and tacked on the back of the bathroom door to prevent misunderstandings. Of course, there was nothing to prevent any member of the family from taking a bath at any unscheduled time, though it was quite a while before any of us thought of it. In all cases of argument—and with so many children around there were bound to be arguments —the schedule was to prevail. And there was nothing that I enjoyed so much as ordering my brothers and sisters— especially the older ones—out of the bathroom when I heard one of them running water in the tub on my time.

This written schedule on the bathroom door was not at all exceptional in our household. My father believed in schedules. He had them for nearly everything. Our garden was no haphazard affair to be hoed merely when hoeing was needed; it was divided into sections, and each section was hoed or thinned or weeded strictly according to a schedule tacked on the inside of the barn door. The lawn was not cut because the grass was too long, but because a certain day had arrived on the schedule. The room stoves—before we got a furnace and, afterwards, the furnace itself—were filled and shaken down by schedule. My father even changed his underwear by schedule.

I distinctly remember finding a calendar in his desk on which the letters *S* and *D* appeared at regular intervals all through the winter months. When I asked my mother what the letters meant she said that the calender was my father's underwear record and quickly took it away from me. The explanation was that in those days of heavy flannels he disliked the intense itching that came from changing both shirt and drawers at the same time and had arranged the schedule to keep from cheating himself unintentionally.

While not technically a schedule, the bulletin board on our library wall performed a similar function. A family the size of ours was sure of being together only at mealtimes. When we were not in school we had plenty of other projects on hand and were in and out of the house at will. The boys who had swimming and fishing to attend to in summer and skating and hunting in winter were often away for hours at a time and not infrequently were gone all day. There had to be some way of knowing where the various ones were, what they were doing, and when they would be available again. The bulletin board acted as a clearing house. We were presumed to take judicial notice of anything posted there, and if I went off for a day's jaunt in the woods without attending to a previously posted errand—it was just too bad. But good news as well as bad used to be posted there, and my brothers and I had code words to indicate such things as that there were fresh cookies in the pantry or that the gang were skating on Frisbie's pond.

10. Country Squire Supreme

I T WAS true in my father's day, and is undoubtedly true
to some extent today, that a large part of the practice of
a country lawyer is derived from correcting the errors
made by justices of the peace, notaries, and other ill-
equipped purveyors of legal advice. The lawyer is strictly
forbidden to practice until he has passed the bar examina-
tions, which, of late years at least, have been extremely
rigid, and until he has satisfied the requirements of the
Appellate Division as to his moral character. On the other
hand, the country squire needs no such qualification. All
he requires is one more vote than his competitor, and then
he can hang out his shingle and compete for business with
lawyers who have spent some eight years in study.

Of course, the country squire is unable to practice in a
court of record, but there is nothing to prevent him from
drawing wills and deeds and mortgages affecting the life
accumulations of his neighbors and furnishing legal advice
to all and sundry. Usually the position of justice of the peace
is a spare-time job, a side line. The most capable justice I
ever knew was a harness maker. While he was handling
some of his minor cases he used to keep right on working at
his bench; he said it sharpened his wits. Not only was he
honest and fair-minded but he possessed judicial tempera-

113

ment. Educated in the law, he would have made an able jurist. He was a shrewd student of human nature and was rarely misled by the blather of a witness—or an attorney either. Naturally a careful man, he was seldom tempted beyond his depth. He would draw a simple will, but the moment the testator proposed any complications with which he was not familiar Squire Cornford would tear up what he had written and send him to a lawyer.

On the other hand, old Justice Redman would tackle anything. He had retired as a merchant, and, having endeared himself to the people of the town by his benefactions, he was re-elected justice term after term as long as he lived and devoted his entire time to his practice as squire. Nothing in the way of a legal problem ever daunted him. His library consisted of a battered copy of a book containing the penal and criminal laws of the state and a form book that must have been more than twenty years old when he acquired it. But with nothing more than these for working tools, he never hesitated about drawing contracts, leases, and agreements affecting the most intricate and complicated situations. His wills were fabulous and fantastic, drawn with no regard whatever for the existing laws. The descriptions in some of the deeds he drew were more picturesque than informative. One of my father's clients spent several hundred dollars and weeks of investigation trying to locate a row of currant bushes which Squire Redman had given as the boundary line of a parcel of land in one of his off-hand deeds of many years before.

The old Squire never could grasp the meaning of surveyor's measurements. He copied them off as best he could, but he never was an accurate copyist, and, since the phrases that he was copying made no sense to him, he could drop a word occasionally without ever missing it. He could also say "east" where he meant to say "west"—he explained to my father once that the words meant practically the same thing and merely depended on the point of view. As a matter of fact, surveyor's measurements are quite simple. The dimensions are given in chains and links. A link is 7.92 inches in length. A chain contains 100 links. The reason for adopting these measurements for agricultural lands is plain when one stops to recall that 10 square chains make an acre. It must have been the courses that baffled him, as they often baffle the layman.

A surveyor's description always begins at a fixed point. His last course returns to this point. The parcel described is the land included within the courses. Chains and links give measurements, and courses indicate direction. Beginning at a certain point, a line runs, let us say, "north, six degrees east, one hundred chains and two links." This means that the line does not run due north but slightly east of north. Thus far it is easy. It is the second course, however, which usually misleads the layman. Here the course reads, "thence north, ninety-six degrees east."

"What!" says the layman. "North again? Is there a jog in this west line?"

There is no jog. Ninety-six degrees east of true north will make a right angle to our first course. Ordinarily a piece of land will be described by four boundaries, unless it happens to be irregular in shape. In that case there may be five, six, or any number of courses, though the final course will always run "to the point of beginning."

In following a surveyor's description of a valuable farm, Squire Redman made a mistake in his bearings and wrote "east" where the surveyor had said "west," with the result that the parcel he described covered only three sides of a square and left the property with no southerly boundary at all. In another of his deeds the old Squire went *north* on his third course when he should have gone *south*. The result was a zigzag line roughly the shape of the letter Z, and his final course to the place of beginning, instead of describing a square, made two triangles standing point to point like an hourglass. It unfortunately included a large corner of the property to the north and constituted a cloud on the title which a future buyer insisted on having removed by suit to quiet title. A second suit for reformation of the description of the lands attempted to be conveyed also became necessary before the title could be cleared to the original premises.

Had these errors been discovered soon enough they might have been rectified by the signing of new deeds containing a correct description, with a quitclaim as to the parcel inadvertently included. But, alas, by the time that my father detected the errors some of the parties were dead, some had moved to an unknown destination, and one was an inmate of a state institution for the insane. Thus recourse to the courts was the only solution, and the innocent land owner was left to foot the expense.

The old Squire's wills were full of unbelievable provisions, many of which violated a clearly expressed statute. Often these provisions were of such a nature that they could be nullified by the Surrogate without the necessity of a special suit. One of his most frequent errors was a clause which tied up the ownership of real property for more than the duration of two lives in being. He would have his testator attempt to leave his farm to his wife for her lifetime, after her death, to his two daughters for as long as they should live or to the survivor of them. Upon their death the title would become vested in the child of his deceased son.

This was one life too many. Our law, which was definitely opposed to the entailment of estates, in an endeavor to prevent an unreasonably long suspension of the power of alienation (the right to convey) of real property, had put a limit of two lives in being. But the Squire never suspected this, and in some of his wills he attempted to suspend the power of alienation for four and even six lives in being. His legal vagaries were good for the lawyers but expensive for the clients—even though they may have paid only half a dollar for the drawing of the will. The Squire, however, outdid even himself when he drew the will of old John Gilson.

John Gilson had made a fortune in the malting business. He had built and managed several successful malt houses when the business was in its prime and had invested most of his savings in local loans and enterprises. He had built the largest business block in town, which, with the exception of the Inn, was the first building to go up three full stories. His Gilson Block fronted on Main Street at the head of Church and had a fine view down Church Street all the way to the railroad, so that by standing in the doorway one could see who came and went on the trains. Four large stores were built on the street level, with roomy offices above them on the second floor front. On the second floor rear was the Gilson Opera House, the only theater in town, which had a seating capacity of about four hundred, with removable benches which could be taken out for a dance or a banquet. It was a complete little theater with two fair-sized dressing rooms and scenery which rolled up to the ceiling by means of ropes and squeaky pulleys.

A third floor was reached by means of a winding stair-way from the second floor hallway. The third floor front was occupied as a lodge room by the Masons. Space had been left for another large auditorium in the rear, but this had never been finished inside. It had not even been floored.

The approach to the Opera House from the street was by a stairway which came up at about the center of the build-ing. At the top of this stairway was a long hallway extending the full length of the building. My reason for giving all these details is merely to show what can be done by a determined scrivener.

It was undoubtedly John Gilson's intention to have his six children share equally in his estate. If the will had been drawn in such a way as to say just that, little difficulty would have arisen in the settlement of his estate. The children could have divided it by agreement, or, if they were unable to agree, the property could have been sold under court supervision and the proceeds divided. It was as simple as that. When, however, the matter was presented to Squire Redman, it at once began to take on a very complex flavor. He was for having old John carve the block into imaginary pieces and tell each child exactly what part he or she should have.

As the will was drawn, he devised one of the four stores on the street level, together with the land underneath, to each of his daughters. To his son, Jacob, he gave the Opera House and all its contents as well as two of the office rooms on the second floor. The remaining two offices and the Masonic Hall went to his other son, Peter. And since the testator thought the Opera House was worth more than the Masonic Hall, he also gave Peter the loft above the Opera House. This will had some other original Redman features, but those I have given will suffice to illustrate the point.

My father gasped when, after old John's demise, the will was brought to him for probate. He could see trouble coming before he had finished reading the first page. If there had been no will at all, matters would have been much simpler and fully as equitable. But when there is a will, no other course remains but to offer it for probate.

Curiously enough, the first dissension arose over the stairs and the second-floor hallway. These had not been mentioned in the will, and the Surrogate ruled that as to them the decedent had died intestate. The same question was raised as to the box office and dressing rooms. These were not within the theater proper. The box office was across the hall and the dressing rooms at one end. The Surrogate also ruled that the box office and dressing rooms had not been mentioned in the will and were therefore owned by all the heirs jointly; but he was forced to modify this ruling when the Supreme Court held on appeal by Jacob that the box office and dressing rooms were a necessary part of the theater and were thus included in his legacy.

Jacob's victory was not without its Pyrrhic qualities, however, for it enraged his four sisters to the point of demanding compensation from him for the use of their undivided four-sixths of the stairway and the second-story hall. Peter tried to refrain from taking part in this argument, but he was eventually drawn in. Although his sisters had been receiving nothing from him for the use of their share of the stairs and hallway by his tenants, they were not angry with Peter.

When Jacob flatly refused to pay for the use of a stairway that was partly his, the sisters obtained an injunction against him and had the stairway padlocked by the sheriff. My father, who was representing Jacob, quickly had the injunction vacated and started a suit in partition, by means of which the right to use the hall and the stairway could be sold by the court and the proceeds divided.

This suit was resisted by the attorney for the daughters on the ground that an easement was not subject to partition apart from the land to which it attached, but the court ruled that the stairway and hall amounted to a tangible asset subject to partition. And in the meantime, just to keep up a vigorous offensive, Jacob started another suit to recover from the sisters four-sixths of the money he had spent for repairs and upkeep of the stairway and hall.

On the sale under the partition action Jacob and Peter bid in the stairway and hall and signed a written contract which provided for joint use and upkeep.

Now for a time quiet reigned among the Gilson heirs, though it was not in the cards that permanent peace should come in this way, and soon Jacob was quarreling with Peter

119

over the damage from a leak in Peter's roof which let the rain water come in and soak through into the theater, where it ruined some of Jacob's best pieces of scenery. Peter retaliated by demanding reimbursement for repairs to a chimney which he claimed was of no use to him, since the only flue was used for the heating appliance of the theater. These difficulties were rapidly approaching the point of litigation when the big fire came along and burned the entire building to the ground.

My father's first thought was that an end had come to contention among the Gilson heirs, but it was not long before Jacob came around to inquire about his rights to that portion of the atmosphere formerly occupied by the Opera House. He was well aware that he did not own the land, though he was very positive that he owned the space above it where that theater had been. He said he wanted to rebuild and asked my father how he was to proceed. Peter, too, wanted to rebuild, and he had many questions to ask about how they were going to tell just exactly where the hall and the stairway used to be. The sisters also wanted to rebuild and were inquiring where their "upper boundaries" ended.

Here was a legal puzzle to challenge the ingenuity of the most resourceful man of law. No doubt my father blessed and damned old Squire Redman in the same breath for drawing so magnificently asinine a will, and then he proceeded to circumvent it in such a manner as to avoid all future trouble by an agreement making them all tenants in common of the new building together with the lands on which it was to stand.

He was too wise to call them all together to consider his plan. By this time he had treated with enough litigious families to realize that the one thing *not* to do was call them together if they were to be brought into agreement; he had learned that if there was to be any hope of an agreement they must be handled separately. So one by one he sold them his idea and got their names on the dotted line. When the Gilson Block was rebuilt, it was a joint venture in which each heir owned an undivided one-sixth part. All were agreed from the first that it should be constructed of brick with substantial fire walls on either side. And soon the doves were nesting in the cornices, and peace had settled upon the Gilson family for the first time since old Squire Redman's will had come to light.

My father must have looked upon his handiwork and found it good, though there was no telling when another posthumous will by the unpredictable old scrivener would upset the peace and placidity of some other family with testamentary provisions equally stupid and equally daring.

It was not Squire Redman but another justice of the peace whom I need not name who drew a bill of sale by which one thrifty citizen of a benighted corner of the township deep in the pines, for and in consideration of six dollars and one yearling heifer, sold, assigned, transferred, conveyed, and delivered to a neighbor the following property to wit:

> my wife, named Mary, white with brown mole on left cheek, 38 years old, and weighing about 160 pounds.

The buyer came to my father one day and said that his "woman" had run away and was working as a scrub woman in a building in Geneva. He wanted to know his rights. The word "woman" may mean wife, and it may mean something else; and when my father asked him what the woman was to him he replied that he had bought her from Ern Skinner, and he produced the bill of sale. He seemed greatly surprised when my father explained to him that human bondage had been abolished throughout the nation since the Emancipation Proclamation of January 1, 1863.

"But how's a feller gonna get him a wife?" he asked dejectedly.

"The only way I know of now," replied my father, "is by marriage."

Deeply disappointed, the native went away, shaking his head, presumably to consult the justice of the peace who had "drawed the writings." What relief, if any, the author of the bill of sale may have been able to render my father never heard.

Just how it had happened that Squire Redman had never attempted a divorce in his justice court my father could never understand, though he was asked to pass upon several very elaborate contracts for the separation of warring couples, all of which he found illegal for one reason or another and entirely unenforceable.

Another justice of the peace, a raw-boned old fellow called Doc Green, who used to sit with his feet on the desk while cases were being tried before him, once undertook to dispose of a bastardy proceeding pending before him by marrying the erring couple. When he proposed marriage to them and found them only lukewarm to the proposal, he gave them an extended argument on the importance of legitimacy to the coming child. They listened, but they were unimpressed. They said they could not think of such a thing. The justice was not a man who gave up easily, and after he had spent a reasonable time insisting that legal marriage was their duty to posterity, he suddenly turned on the putative father and threatened to send him to jail if he persisted in refusing.

This apparently went against the grain, but the putative father was game, and rather than go to jail he took the hand of his accomplice in sin and stood up before the court for the tying of the nuptial knot. The justice had completed the ceremony and was giving them a rather flowery blessing when my father happened to come in.

"Greet the happy couple, Counselor," said the Squire jovially. "I have joined them in the sacred bonds of holy matrimony. Just pronounced them man and wife."

122

My father looked dubiously at the groom. "Impossible," he said. "This man already has one legal wife that I know of. Do you want him sent up for bigamy?"

"Is this so?" thundered the justice.

The groom nodded guiltily. "I tried to tell you, but you wouldn't give me a chance."

"In that case," said the justice pompously, "I unpronounce you man and wife—and restore you to your former status of seducer and victim. We will now proceed with the bastardy charge."

11. The Coming of the Typewriter

W E WERE all thrilled when my father came home with his first typewriter. It was not so much the fact that it could print the words on paper without setting type that impressed us as the knowledge that it could perform the miracle of making three copies at once, two of which were plainly readable. To us it was the first faint glimpse of the approaching end of the drudgery of copying. The light of a new day was, indeed, showing in the eastern sky, though it did not actually dawn to any great extent with this early Hall typewriter.

In size, the Hall would compare with the portable machine of today, but otherwise they would have little in common. The keyboard was a plate of metal about three inches by four. It was as full of holes as a punchboard. These holes, about the diameter of a straw, were an eighth of an inch deep, with a letter of the alphabet neatly hidden at the bottom of each. A metal pointer, hung on a little wooden crane, was suspended over the keyboard. The *modus operandi* was to take the wooden arm between the thumb and forefinger and push the pointer down into the hole in which the desired letter could be seen—whereupon the machine would give a thump and a shudder, and the letter would appear as if by magic on the sheet of paper which had been previously placed beneath the keyboard, though the hinged keyboard would have to be raised before it could be seen.

Not very fast, as may be imagined, but to us it was the marvel of the age.

It was always my father's boast that this was the first typewriter in the county. I would not know about that, though I do remember that two lawyer friends of my father's, Tom Bennett and Frank Rice, drove down from Canandaigua especially to see it work. Another friend of my father's, a Geneva banker named S. H. Verplanck, drove over one day to see if it would be practical for use in his bank. His decision was unfavorable. He felt that bank letters and papers might be too easily tampered with if reduced to print.

Of course, we were all anxious to learn to write on the new machine. One of my sisters did learn, and she soon became so proficient that she could copy a page on the Hall almost as fast as the rest of us could write with a pen. We thought such speed was really quite remarkable if one stopped to consider that she was making three copies at once.

For a time the papers emanating from my father's office were a heterogeneous lot, some typed and some written. Ordinary copies, those which were to be served on people, might be written out in longhand, but the court copies for filing were from this time neatly typed—at least they were typed.

The Hall typewriter speedily wore out and was replaced by a Hammond. This early Hammond bore no resemblance to the portable. If it were to be compared with any machine, it would be with the Mergenthaler Linotype; for it was nearly as large and surely as noisy. The keyboard of the Hammond was built around a court, with some of the letters almost at arm's length distance. The type, which was on a central sleeve, spun around dizzily while in operation, but the machine was capable of real speed and could make five perfect copies. It was not until the arrival of the Smith Premier, however, that the typewriter took on the appearance of the machine of today. The Smith had a universal keyboard. Indeed, it had *two* universal keyboards, one for capitals and one for lower case letters. And the Smith was the first machine in my father's collection to be inked by a ribbon.

My father had a great deal to say about that ribbon, which makes me think that high-pressure salesmanship must have been getting in its work even in those old days. After he had occasion to change a ribbon, however, we heard less about that particular improvement. It was on a very hot day in midsummer that he undertook the job. The ribbon had been sent on from Rochester and was inked for making wet tissue copies in the letter press; "black-copy-black," it was called. He had taken off the coat of his white linen suit before starting the task, though he had not rolled up his sleeves or even removed his cuffs, which were removable in those days.

A glance at the machine told him that in order to take off the old ribbon he would have to unwind it from the spool. So he detached one end and began to unwind it. He found the ribbon much longer than he had thought, for he had one hand quite full of small loops of the smudgy tape before the spool had really started to unroll. He made the loops larger as he began to fill his other hand, but he evidently did not make them large enough, for soon both hands were full, and still the ribbon was showing no signs of unwinding. Never a patient man with any sort of mechanical difficulty, my father now began to lose his temper and undertook to empty the spool by giving angry yanks at it, first with one hand and then with the other—and before he realized what he was getting into he had himself completely draped with Smith Premier No. 2 black-copy-black ribbon. It not only hung from his hands and arms but was festooned from the pencils sticking out of his vest pocket and dangled from his watch chain. Even his feet had become enmeshed by the time that I chanced to enter the office door.

I realized at a glance that this was a situation with no immediate aspects for humorous treatment, in spite of the fact that my father looked very funny with his hands and face and shirt and white linen pants smeared and mottled with black-copy-black ink. I managed to keep down my mirth and went to his assistance—and soon there were two of us enmeshed in the inky tentacles.

My father's temper was not noticeably improved by my efforts to help him. In fact, it had begun to look as if he did not appreciate what I was trying to do for him when the spare form of Libby Weston was outlined in the doorway.

Libby may have been prim, but she was practical, and after a few disapproving clucks she took the office shears and released us. Then, with a grim but unflinching air, she put on my father's stove-tending gloves, emptied the spool by unwinding it into the wastebasket, and rewound it with the new ribbon. This done, she seated herself at her desk and went on with her copying—in longhand of course.

For Libby the age of science had arrived. She was, without doubt, the first person in town to feel the jolt of the oncoming machine. The typewriter had come to take away her job, and she surrendered without a struggle. She never even attempted to master the little black and white keys. Her explanation was that she was too old to change the writing habits of a lifetime. My father never quite believed this; it was always his firm conviction that Libby regarded typing as something not quite ladylike.

If anything went wrong with the typewriter my father was completely at sea. At first he used to take the heavy machine to Rochester to a repairman, but after a little he found that Austin Lamb, the jeweler, could fix it just as well at only a fraction of the cost and with no bother at all. It seemed strange to my father that one man should know instinctively about the workings of another's machine. It never occurred to him that all machinery was based on mechanical principles, just as jurisprudence was based on legal principles. Anything of a mechanical nature was simply beyond his comprehension. Even so simple a matter as the hanging of our front gate baffled him for days.

My father was extremely fussy about his lawn and flower beds and had built a substantial fence around the yard to keep out wandering stock which was inclined to pasture wherever the grass grew greenest. Directly in front of the house was a large gate which closed with a spring. A heavy latch usually gave notice to the household when someone was entering. Of course, this handsome gate was a great temptation to the boys, and every year after Halloween my father had to rescue it from the porch of a near-by neighbor or even from the roof of a barn.

One year, however, as he emerged from his front door the morning after Halloween, he noted with satisfaction that instead of having being carried off the gate had merely been lifted from its hinges and set to one side. He thought that the prankster had been unusually considerate and walked over to restore the gate to its proper place. This he found to be not so easy as he had anticipated, and after struggling with it for a while he gave up the job temporarily, since he had appointments that must be kept. He struggled with it again when he came home that night, but the gate resisted all his efforts. He was finally driven indoors by darkness, but he went into the house more annoyed than discouraged. "That gate came off those hinges," he muttered stubbornly to my mother, "and it will go back on again."

As he was starting for the office the next morning, he thought of a different method of approach; so he set down his walking stick and had another go at the gate. A trio of passing boys stopped to watch him and offer advice. For some reason their presence as well as their counsel annoyed him, and after enduring them for only a short time he angrily picked up his stick and stalked into the house. At intervals during the next few days he would attack the problem again—but the solution always evaded him.

"Did you get it on, dear?" my mother asked one day as he came sputtering into the house, his coat in one hand and his hat and stick in the other.

"Not yet—probably would have if I hadn't had so damn much help."

My mother glanced up to see if any of the children were within hearing. "I wouldn't add bad language to ill temper if I were you."

"You would if you'd been in my place. The little devils—they stand around there and ask me sweetly why I don't try this or that or some other thing."

"Wouldn't you rather have them sweet than otherwise?"

"That's just the trouble," my father growled. "They're too *damn* sweet. They stand around in such open-eyed innocence that I'm perfectly certain they're the little swine who took that gate off in the first place."

"Is that any way to speak of your own sons?"

"Well, I don't doubt that they had a finger in the pie. They're as bad as the rest, only they don't dare to laugh at me quite as openly as the others. But they've had their last laugh at my expense. I'm through!"

"But what are you going to do? You can't leave the gate off indefinitely—dogs and other animals will come in and dig up the bulbs and trample the shrubbery."

"I have no idea of leaving the gate off. I'm going to Mr. Beach, who built it—and who hung it. He ought to know how to put it back on—if anybody does."

When my father came home that night he found the gate in its accustomed place. He stood and looked at it in wonder. He swung it open and shut a few times. It worked perfectly. He was still shaking his head in a puzzled way when he went in the door. "How long was Mr. Beach here?" he asked.

My mother smiled. "Only a minute or two. I saw him drive up with his wagon—and when I looked out again he was gone. But the gate was on!"

"So I see," said my father, and the matter was dropped.

He met Mr. Beach on the street a few days later. "Have any trouble with that gate of mine?" he asked.

"Not a bit."

"How much do I owe you?"

"About half a dollar."

My father paid it. "Sure you didn't have any trouble with it?" he asked.

Mr. Beach shook his head. "They weren't no pertic'lar trouble with that job. One look was all I needed to tell me that it was a right-handed gate. And let me tell you, Judge, no right-handed gate won't never go onto a left-handed set of hinges." Mr. Beach cackled with squeaky laughter.

My father looked puzzled. "You mean to tell me my hinges are left-handed?"

"Sure they be."

"And the gate was right-handed?"

"That's correct."

"But what did you do about it?"

"I recollected buildin' a fence like yours fer Abner Pardee a coupla years ago. They was both painted white there at the same time. On account of that big tree in front of Abner's I had to swing his gate right-handed. And the minute I seen the gate you had I knowed it was Abner's. So I chucked it into my wagon and took it up to his house. I could see your gate standin' there side of his gateway, and without sayin' nuthin' to him I changed the two gates and put the one that belonged to you into the wagon. Then I went out back and hollered to him. He was diggin' taters in the garden. 'What's the matter o' yer gate?' I says. He shook his head. 'That's what I'm a-wonderin',' he says. 'The dern kids took it off Halloween, and I can't get the danged thing back on again.' I kinda smiled. 'Let's have a look at it,' I says. 'I ain't never seen a gate I couldn't handle yet,' I says. Well, we walked around and took a look at it. 'Looks all right to me,' I says. 'Then why don't you put it on?' he says. So I did." Again Mr. Beach cackled with his squeaky laughter.

"What did Abner say to that?" asked my father.

"Not a dern thing! His mouth fell open so wide he couldn't say a word. Just stood there a-gappin' when I drove away."

"It's all very simple—except one thing," said my father. "How did the boys know the difference?"

131

Mr. Beach shook his head. "Now you're gettin' outa my line," he said. "Ask me all you want to about gates and fence buildin'—but don't ask me nuthin' about boys. You oughta know somep'm about 'em yourself—you got enough of 'em."

Mr. Beach was right. My father couldn't hang a gate, but he did know about boys. He understood, for one thing, that there are times when boys must fight. He used to shock my mother by saying that fighting was good for boys. As soon as we were old enough he gave us boxing gloves with which he insisted that we must settle our disputes. His only question when one of the boys came in with a black eye was, "How did you happen to let your guard down?" He took no apparent interest in our troubles with other boys, though he never failed to take our part when my mother scolded about clothes torn in a fight at school. Necessary wear and tear, he used to call it, and he would explain that no fight could wait while a boy went home to change his clothes. One thing that he was positively telepathic about was our running away from school; he could sense the day when a boy would fall for the call of forest or stream—and he was the hardest man to lie to that I ever saw. Trying to tell him a lie was seldom worth the effort.

He could not mend a doorbell or regulate a clock. A can opener was a mystery to him, a fountain pen an enigma. The only machinery of which he had any grasp was the machinery of the human mind.

It was to my mother that we always went when anything was broken. She was the mechanical genius of the family. No fractured doll, no disabled toy was too much for her capable fingers. With her glue pot, a pair of scissors, and a bit of wire she could mend practically anything. If the children of the neighborhood came in with some novelty she would copy it for us. But it was in the mending and repair of clothes that her touch was most magic. She could

132

reweave a stocking so that you could hardly tell where the darn was, and she could mend a tear in your clothes so that you could not find it afterwards.

My mother was a small woman with brown hair and dark, lustrous eyes. She had been quite a beauty in her youth. In spite of the fact that she had married in her 'teens and at once embarked on the serious business of raising a large brood, she was always a lively spirit and believed in having a gay time. She was one of a family of nine and was quite familiar with all the economizing, quantity buying, corner cutting, and making over that went with mass production. I am appalled when I think of the numbers of pairs of shoes, overshoes, and rubber boots that she would buy on a single visit to the shoe store in the fall before school began. Just our family alone would keep the shoe man busy for an entire afternoon.

Another of the collective family projects that I remember most vividly was our annual pilgrimage to have our teeth put in order. The town was, at that time, without a trustworthy dentist. White-bearded old Dr. Snow had an office, but he was getting along in years and could no longer see through his octagonal iron-rimmed spectacles a cavity much smaller than a thimble. He was still making extractions with a turnkey. Once in an emergency he twisted out a wisdom tooth for my father—but he accidentally twisted out at the same time a perfectly good molar which happened to be alongside. So we were never taken to Dr. Snow. Instead, we used to reserve an entire day with a dentist in Geneva and get the family teeth all overhauled at once.

The journey to Geneva, eight miles away, was always a welcome diversion for the younger children, who did not get around much, but as I look back on that annual dental appointment the scene reminds me of an old Hogarth print. We usually went on Saturday so as not to interfere with school. Since my father was nearly always in Special Term

133

on that day, my mother had to mobilize and transport her army single-handed or with such help as she could get from the older children. We were usually rather well behaved on the train and up to the time when we were inside the dentist's office; but after he had begun his poking and boring and scraping and filling—and especially after he had broken the news that extractions were to be made—the place became a bedlam.

I remember quite distinctly screaming and resisting and fighting that harried dentist when he tried to extract a loose tooth of mine and putting up such a lusty opposition that during the argument the tooth fell or was pushed out.

Fortunately there were no other patients around to hear our goings-on. We had the office all to ourselves—and we needed it. If my father had been there I am sure discipline would have been better. Perhaps he would have set us an example, as he did when we were having family vaccination; he always led off and was vaccinated first, just to show us that it did not hurt. In all, he must have been vaccinated half a dozen times—but with him it never worked. He was immune.

Had my father been present, I am sure that I never should have shown the white feather over that loose tooth. There was nothing in the world that he so detested as a coward, and I was too anxious for his good opinion ever to have thrown such a fit. My father's great dread was that one of his boys might grow up to be a weakling or a coward. He would have preferred to see all of us bandits—if we were courageous ones. As for himself, he simply was not afraid of anything. Even as a little lad he stood up to his austere father in a way that was indicative of his courage in years to come.

According to family tradition, his most famous stand was in 1848 when he was nine years old. The family were living in New York City on West Twenty-third Street, then a tree-

134

grown thoroughfare lined with detached residences having fenced yards with lawns and gardens and even fruit trees. My grandparents' house was near the river, and when my father played in the yard he was always in sight of a forest of masts and spars of the innumerable sailing ships moored to the docks or anchored just off shore.

His mother, who was one of the Rochester Seldens, had died soon after he was born, and his father had remarried. The young man did not find the new stepmother, who had children of her own, any too cordial, and by the time he was nine years old he had decided to get away from it all by running off to sea. So he watched for his chance, and one day he slipped out the gate and made his way to the waterfront. He wandered along from one windjammer to another, seeking a place as cabin boy. But he was so small for his age that even if a vacancy existed he was gruffly dismissed and advised to go back to his cradle. He was persistent, however, and finally found a berth on a ship that was about ready to cast off. The captain, taking the lad's word that he was twelve years old and an orphan, put the little fellow at some task below decks, where he would not be seen.

If the vessel had sailed as planned there might be a different tale to tell. But the wind failed, and the ship was still tied to her moorings when, deeply perturbed, the boy's father came along, searching for the fugitive. He was an imposing man in a broadcloth suit and a beaver hat, domineering, without the slightest trace of a sense of humor. He was the one man who, starting out from a Vermont farm at the age of fourteen with a ten-dollar gold piece sewed into his underwear, to make his way in the world, never took pride in producing the identical gold piece in after years. Perhaps what he lacked was imagination, though he did have enough to suspect that the youth might be contemplating a future on the bounding deep.

When he enquired of the captain if he had seen anything of a nine-year-old lad, the captain stroked his whiskers for a moment and then asked him to come aboard. Word was sent down that the new cabin boy was wanted on deck, and the little fellow promptly reported to the captain. For a few moments the captain watched him closely, and when he saw that the lad took no apparent notice of the man in the tall beaver, he asked:

"Ever see this gentleman before?"

The lad looked his father up and down, "I never saw the old cuss before," he answered.

It was a noble attempt, and though it failed to work it showed no lack of nerve on the part of the boy. That same nerve was with him all through life. He was living with his mother's family in Rochester when Fort Sumter was fired on and was among the first to enlist upon Lincoln's call for volunteers. He fought in the Thirteenth New York Volunteer Infantry until the regiment was mustered out of service. It was when the remnants of the regiment returned to Rochester and were being received with a great ovation that my mother first saw her future husband. He was on a white horse out in front of the regiment, a sunburned stripling with long wavy hair showing beneath his campaign cap.

"Doesn't that one on the white horse think he's smart!" she said.

And only a year or so afterward the minister was asking her, "Do you take this man?" and she was answering with a tremulous, "I do."

No alarums by night ever fazed my father in the least. Piercing screams of animals from the backyard, angry shouts and bellowings from the street, ominous pounding on the door after midnight, squeaks from the floor boards which sounded like marauders sneaking up the stairs, eerie lights, mysterious knockings—all were taken in his stride.

He never failed to investigate when my mother thought she heard a burglar in the night, which was not seldom. How much was utter fearlessness and how much was bluff to make us brave only my father knew. But I can truthfully say that I never saw him show any fear of God, man, or the devil.

12. Bailiff: Handy Man of the Law

THE country lawyer, who rarely had a clerk in his office, was largely dependent on the constables for many things. It was the constable who ran his errands, who served his papers, rounded up his witnesses, and acted as messenger during a trial. And it was often the constable who rode herd on the witnesses when the trial lasted for several days; for witnesses will stray, and someone must be on hand to keep them sober and see that they are in the courtroom when needed. In my father's half century of practice he worked with hundreds of constables. His stories about them ran all the way from farce to tragedy, though they were on the whole an amusing lot.

Payment of the constable was by the fee system. No work, no pay. The term of office was two years. Many a constable did not earn from his official duties as much as twenty-five dollars a year; and still the position was one of the most stubbornly contested in every election. No matter how hard it might be to find a suitable candidate for village president or path master, for assessor or school trustee, whenever there were constables to be elected a host of aspirants would appear.

Quite obviously the candidates did not go in for the money. Nor could they possibly have hoped for the glory of detecting sensational crimes and bringing the perpetrators to justice; few serious or sensational crimes were committed in country towns, and when they were, the sheriff's office immediately took charge. The post of constable was, however, the underdog's one chance to achieve preferment, to become important in the eyes of his equals. It was possible for anybody without a criminal record to become a constable if he could get enough people to vote for him. There was no physical or educational requirement to be met. The candidate did not even have to be literate. Indeed, the constable who held the brightest spot in my father's memory was unable to read or write. He always signed by making an *X* for his mark, and in time he came to be known as Abram X. Van Tyle, to distinguish him from an uncle whose name was merely Abram Van Tyle. He even ran for office as Abram X. Van Tyle and was handsomely elected time after time. Abram X. was quick at mental arithmetic and could compute interest in his mind faster than my father could look it up in the tables.

Another of my father's favorite constables was a gigantic redhead, nearly seven feet tall, called the Red Cloud. My father was a little inclined toward the Paul Bunyan tradition whenever he began to tell about the Red Cloud. Red's hands were like "hams from which the bristles had not been removed," his feet were "pigeon-toed flatboats," and the freckles on his face varied in size from the diameter of a three-cent piece to that of a quarter. For all his size the Red Cloud was not noted for his courage, though he held the record of having arrested twenty men at once and taken them all to the lockup. It happened one night in the coldest part of the winter when he was sent to quell a disturbance in a saloon just before closing time. He was told to arrest the culprits and put them in the lockup to sober up; the justice would attend to them in the morning.

By the time the constable reached the scene the actual fighting was over, and he had some difficulty in finding out who the culprits were. But as closing time approached and the proprietor was about to turn all his customers out into the cold, two tough young fellows went to the constable and admitted their participation in the fight.

"All right," said the Red Cloud firmly. "You come along quietly now and there won't be any trouble."

At that point four more of the rowdies interrupted to confess that they also were in the melee.

The constable was a little surprised, but he was equal to the occasion. "You admit it, hey? All right, fall right in behind these other two, and if you behave yourselves I won't make you any trouble."

"Oh, hell," said the spokesman for another group, "if the rest of the fellers are goin' to tell the truth and confess, we might as well confess and go along with 'em. That wouldn't be no more'n fair."

By this time the constable was scratching his red head. "This musta been some ruckus!" he muttered.

"It was," said Jimmie Dooley, the proprietor, who had quickly caught the drift of affairs. "I thought they were going to wreck the place."

"All right," growled the Red Cloud. "Get in line there. Anybody else?"

There were twenty culprits in all and only two cells in the lockup. The entrance to the lockup was through a dark alley which led behind the stores, with one branch extending through to Church Street and the other ending in the yard of the livery stable. The constable had an idea that he might lose some of his prisoners in going through this alley; but he did not, and when he had unlocked the door and turned on the light they all filed into the warm corridor of the lockup.

It was at this point, as the Red Cloud told my father, that he began to be disturbed. He realized that twenty men

140

could not be left in that small space all night without danger of suffocation. It never occurred to him that he might make a "token" arrest by holding two or even four of the culprits and releasing the others on their own recognizance. Nor did it occur to him that since they were all local boys he might let them all go and rearrest them from time to time whenever he happened to see them. The mind of a constable does not work that way. On the contrary, it worked like this: he was ordered to arrest the trouble makers—he had arrested them—and it was up to him to hold them until he was ordered to release them. And it is very likely that he did not entirely forget that he was entitled to a fee for every man arrested.

The town lockup was located immediately in the rear of the town clerk's office, a large airy room containing several tables and a number of chairs. A door led from the lockup corridor directly into the clerk's office, and the constable had in his pocket a key to this door. After considering the problem for a few moments, the constable informed his prisoners that they could have the run of the clerk's office during the night if they would promise not to molest any of the papers on the desk and would agree to leave the place in as good order as they found it. They readily agreed, and after the constable had reassured himself that all outside doors of the clerk's office were securely locked, he went out by the alley door and locked it behind him. He had left the doors of both cells open so that the bunks in them could be occupied, for it did not seem fair to him to lock up part of the men and leave the others loose.

When the town clerk opened the door of his office the next morning his first thought was that the place had been sacked by thieves, so great was the state of confusion. On looking a little farther he concluded that all the tables and desks had been slept on by persons unknown who had used for pillows boxes of town stationery as well as bundles of

141

newly printed tax blanks and other similar sleep-promoting objects. He found sixteen empty whiskey bottles of various brands and sizes. The door into the lockup was wide open—as well as a window of the clerk's office which looked out on the alley.

The justice who had ordered the arrests was very much upset when he learned what had occurred. No legal charge had been made against the persons arrested. Indeed, there was no evidence that any one of them had committed a crime. Trembling with indignation as well as nervousness over the prospects of twenty possible damage suits for false arrest, the justice came to my father for advice.

After a brief investigation of the circumstances under which the arrests had been made, my father advised the justice to note in his docket that the prisoners were detained after a voluntary surrender. He also advised that a charge be entered against each malefactor for malicious mischief in littering and defacing town property, conspiring to escape, and being a fugitive from justice. Having made the entries, the justice was advised to let the matter rest.

There was only one trouble with this advice—the Red Cloud could recall the names of only eighteen of his prisoners; so the ubiquitous John Doe and Richard Roe were brought into the case—but there were no suits for false arrest.

A more courageous constable of this period was Philo B. Navis. Philo took his office with great seriousness. If he came to grips with a malefactor he never failed to bring in his man, and he always brought him back alive. Philo was a thickset fellow with a short neck and an undershot jaw, and he did not know what fear was. When, early one summer morning, the town was aroused by a dull explosion and leaped out of bed to find that the post office had been robbed, Philo was one of the first to reach the spot.

"Anybody see 'em?" he asked. "Which way did they go?"

142

The country lawyer at forty-five.

Somebody had heard a horse being driven rapidly out West Main Street soon after the explosion, and it was not long before it was discovered that a fast horse had been stolen from a near-by stable. With this as a starting point, Philo ran home and harnessed his undersized black mare to his topless side-bar buggy and started in pursuit. Somehow he picked up the trail and followed the safe crackers out of town. They had turned north and headed toward Newark, but when their horse had begun to tire they had turned off the main road and made for a thickly wooded tract known as Cedar Swamp. Philo traced them to the edge of the swamp, and there among the trees he found their abandoned horse and buggy.

Cedar Swamp was a dark and tangled morass into which few human beings had ever ventured save in the dead of winter when the treacherous bog was frozen over. Any other constable would have turned back at this point; but not Philo. He inquired at a near-by farm concerning the size of the swamp and the possibility of driving around it. The farmer did not know much about the size, but he did happen to mention the fact that the main line of the New York Central crossed it on an embankment only a mile or so away.

Philo drove around the west end of the swamp and made for the embankment. Far down in the swamp he could see three men walking along the track. They were so far away that he could not tell whether they were coming or going, but after watching them for a time he concluded that they were coming toward him. He crept down the embankment and hid in the grass. When the three men were within fifty feet of him he suddenly scrambled to the top and demanded their surrender. In his haste to get away from home Philo had forgotten his gun, and he had no other weapon on him. All he had in the way of man-chasing implements was a pair of handcuffs, and he brandished these to good effect.

Two of the safe crackers immediately threw up their hands, but the third dropped a bundle he was carrying and whipped out a pistol. He drew a bead on Philo, and as the constable started for him on a run the fugitive pulled the trigger. A wreath of autumn leaves or a cross of lilies of the valley might have come into our story at this point except for the fact that the gun did not go off. Philo kept right on going while his would-be asssilant recocked the pistol—but again the weapon failed to go off. Twice more the pistol snapped harmlessly before Philo could get close enough to deliver a blow with his handcuffs. The fifth attempt, however, did not fail. The pistol went off with a loud report—but not until the moment just after the handcuffs had crashed down on the gunman's head with force enough not only to spoil his aim but to put a very painful dent in his skull.

The constable brought the three back to town with him in his side-bar buggy, together with the package which contained their loot. This package was so heavy that Philo felt sure it must be very valuable. It did contain the total loot; but this, alas, consisted of ten dollars in pennies, or one dollar for every year that the trio ultimately spent in prison. The safe crackers were greatly relieved when the sheriff came and took them out of the custody of the constable. They said he was the roughest man they had ever met. Philo was equally relieved to get rid of the prisoners. He said he was in a hurry to get home to hoe an acre of onions that he was raising.

Physically, Constable Mark Reedy was no match for Philo. Mark was so very much under-sized that a good many people refused to vote for him, though he was otherwise well qualified for the position. But like many under-sized men I have known, Mark used his brain to accomplish the things to which larger men devote nothing but brawn. With his five feet of height and his hundredweight of avoirdupois,

144

Mark was no rough-and-tumble fighter like Philo Navis, and he was bright enough to know it.

In making an arrest Mark usually *invited* the victim to come along with him—and the man usually came. If he did not come Mark would give him an argument about the serious consequences of resisting arrest. Should that fail to produce results there was no telling what Mark would do next; he seldom tried the same tactics twice. He was as quick as a cat. Once he started fisticuffs with a rough customer who must have outweighed him two to one. When the astonished prisoner came back at him Mark leaped behind a maple tree not much larger than his arm and began to dodge back and forth. The felon reached around the tree to grab him and succeeded in getting hold—and then suddenly he found himself manacled, with his arms circling the tree trunk.

"Just wait here, will you?" asked Mark with a laugh, "while I go and get some help?"

Mark had no taste for heroics, however, and left the criminal work to others if he could. What he really liked was serving papers, and after he had been stopped a few times by doors slammed in his face or a bucket of water thrown on him he developed a technique of his own. His method consisted almost entirely of sleight-of-hand. He would appear to be handing the victim one thing—and would hand him quite another.

There was a case of my father's in which a woman had evaded service in an action of partition. She did not want the property divided, and she did not want it sold and the proceeds divided. She shut herself up in her house and defied process servers to get her. The one or two who tried it found themselves compelled to dodge boiling water thrown at them through the crack of the door or from an open window. Mark heard of the situation and asked to be given a chance to show what he could do. My father acquiesced and furnished him with a set of papers to serve. That evening at dusk, when it was still light enough to see a person's size without distinguishing his features, Mark appeared in front of the house with several bundles. He set them all down on the sidewalk, and, after sorting them over, picked up one of them and started for the door of the house. His knock on the door was answered by a woman's voice from inside.

"Who is it, and what do you want?"

"Express package for Mrs. Swan!" he called in a piping voice that sounded like a boy's.

"Where's it from?"

"Looks like Buffalo." He knew Mrs. Swan had a son in Buffalo.

"Well, all right—set it down and I'll come and get it. I ain't dressed."

"All right. I'll leave it here by the door—but you'll have to sign the book. Guess I can shove it through the crack of the door if you'll just open it a little."

He heard the key turn in the lock and the rattle of a chain. She was not going to have him shove the door open unexpectedly. Then the door opened a crack and Mark held out what appeared to be an express receipt book. It looked harmless enough, but when she reached for it she suddenly found in her hand a copy of the papers that she had been evading for weeks.

Mark once seized an armful of auction bills from a boy and walked down the street shouting "Auction! Auction!" He went along in a very businesslike way, thrusting the bills into the hands of passers-by. He apparently did not look up at the faces at all but thrust a bill at every hand that came along. Then suddenly one of the outstretched hands received an auction bill that seemed to have something underneath—and when the recipient looked to see what it was he found a copy of a summons and complaint that process servers had taken out to his farm no less than twenty times, only to be informed that he was not at home.

It was my father's observation that political careers which started with the office of constable usually ended there. Only one of my father's galaxy of constables used the office as a stepping stone. And he leaped in a single bound from the lowly post of constable to that of lord high sheriff of the county. His name was Si Peckham, and before his preferment he had been a small but successful market gardener. Si was a natural-born agriculturalist. He loved the earth, and the earth loved Si. When Si planted seeds the seeds grew. The earth turned its fertile belly up to the sun when Si scratched it with a hoe, and after that things began to happen.

Personality had nothing to do with Si's political success; it was a matter of simple geography. To keep the voters in line some job had to come to the town from time to time.

"Who we gonna give sheriff to?" the county chairman asked my father.

"Peckham wants it."

"Which one is Peckham?"

"The old square-rigged fellow there."

"The one with the hickory walking stick?"

"That's the man."

"Does he always talk like that—with only half of his mouth?"

"Always has."

"Can he make a speech?"

"No—but he can knock down an ox with his bare fist."

"Is he honest?"

"Honest enough to get bondsmen."

"Will you nominate him when the time comes?"

My father nodded.

As a sheriff, Si, though a nonentity to others, became very important to himself. He began to feel that so great a man should wear some distinctive form of regalia and had hit upon double-breasted navy blue with brass buttons as suitable for his rank. He subsequently adopted a yachting cap with a stiff visor as a suitable form of headgear, and the outfit really set off Si's chunky frame to good effect. Si himself was so well pleased with his new uniform that he made it his regular wearing apparel for the rest of his life, even after his retirement from public duty.

Si was a strong-headed old fellow, stubborn and profane. He could be and occasionally was a good friend, but he could always be counted on as a good enemy. He had a neighbor named Tully, a small man of violent temper who was equally stubborn and equally profane. Their properties adjoined, and of course they had trouble over the line fence. If it had not been the fence it would have been something else, for the two were natural enemies.

Both men were accustomed to drive to the post office every day for the mail, and it so happened that this daily jaunt would occasionally bring them together on the road. Though neither would condescend to speak to the other except for purposes of insult, a number of hair-raising horse races resulted. Any attempt on the part of either to pass the other from behind would be the signal for a quick whipping up, loud profanity, the sharp cracking of whips, and the wild pounding of horses' hoofs along the usually quiet street.

The two horses seemed to share the enmity of their owners, whom they sometimes plunged into races that might otherwise have been avoided. None of the contests was run with any idea of sportsmanship. It was only now and then that there was a real test of speed, for the encounters usually ended with one or the other of the contenders in the ditch or so far off the road as to be out of the running. This feud lent no great dignity to the advancing years of either of the participants, but it did add somewhat to the excitement of the life in town. In time the sheriff's horse suffered an attack

148

of colic from which it died, and, since he did not replace it, the horse racing came to an end. But the two neighbors continued to hate each other as cordially as ever.

It was only a few days after the demise of the sheriff's horse that Peckham and Tully met face to face in the post office one morning. At the sight of his enemy a sour smile appeared on the wizened visage of old Tully, and a wicked gleam shone in his faded blue eyes, which were ordinarily about as lifeless-looking as a washed-out pair of overalls.

"Hear y'lost yer horse!" he said jubilantly.

The sheriff nodded. "Yes, sir, he's gone all right. Quite a loss—fastest horse in town. Sorry to lose him, but I'm much obliged for your sympathy." Unexpectedly he extended his hand to Tully.

Tully, taken by surprise, did not withdraw his hand in time to keep the sheriff from gripping it. He instantly wished that he had, for Peckham shut down on it like a vise with his enormous hand and squeezed so hard that Tully could hear the bones crunching, as he afterwards said, with a sound like that of a horse eating oats. The terrific pain caused Tully to buckle slightly in the middle and drew from him an agonized oath of remonstrance.

The sheriff grinned with half his mouth, and instead of loosening his hold he tightened it. "What's the matter?" he gloated. "Too much fer ye?"

The taunt brought Tully up standing. "No, it ain't any too much—" he snarled through his blackened teeth, and he caught the sheriff by his snow-white side whiskers and began wrenching and twisting with all his strength. "How do you like that, you red-faced old buzzard?"

For once in his life the sheriff used all his mouth when he spoke. "Leggo them whiskers!" he bawled in a voice like the roar of a lion, with an appended string of profanity. "Leggo or I'll take home what's left of that hand of yourn and feed it to the hogs!"

149

Tully took another turn on the whiskers. "Yer hogs won't know you," he bleated, "when I get through pullin' this ornament out by the roots!"

"Leggo them whiskers!"

These were only a few of the comprehensible phrases that arose above the steady stream of profanity that each contestant was pouring into the face of the other. It was my father who finally parted them. He shoved his way through the crowd that had gathered and forced himself between the panting gladiators.

"You'll have to settle this somewhere else," he shouted curtly. "You are obstructing the United States mails!"

The postmaster caught the cue and shouted lustily, "Gangway for the U. S. mail!"

The two fell apart, and while my father hauled Peckham into the postmaster's private office bystanders shoved Tully into the street. Tully's hand, though painfully bruised, was, after all, made of pretty tough material and within a day or two showed no signs of the ordeal it had been through; but the sheriff's whiskers had been so badly mangled that he had to cut them to give the bare spots time to grow in again.

13. Words—Words—Words

WHEN Hamlet was asked by Polonius what he read he made the oft-quoted response, "Words, words, words." The reply would have been equally apt if the old man had asked him for a definition of the law. The painter works with a great palette of colors, the etcher, with lines and lights and shadows, the musician, with majestic chords or lilting melodies, but the lawgiver must confine himself to words, words, words.

Words, words, words. The legislator puts his law into words. To know the law, the populace must know the meaning of those words. If words had an exact meaning legal troubles would end instead of beginning at this point. But since few if any words have exact meanings, being among the most slippery and evasive inventions of man, courts must be set up to interpret the words of the lawgivers and tell the puzzled populace—by means of more words—what the lawgivers mean by the words their laws make use of. And then, with many more words, the lawyers try to help the courts in their quest of truth by calling attention to previous words used by that and other courts in the interpretation of words of a like nature promulgated by lawgivers at some earlier time in even more words, words, words.

Already the situation begins to sound hopeless, though it is not really so bad as it appears. Although it is impossible by its nature for the law to be exact, it is not at all impossible for it to be precise about the words it uses. And for a lawyer to attempt anything less than precision is to go the way of chaos.

The drawing of legal papers was to my father one of the fine arts. His attitude was that a carelessly drawn paper was as dangerous as a carelessly loaded cannon; it was as likely to shoot through the breech as through the barrel. In drawing a paper, his idea was to make it say precisely what it was meant to say so far as was verbally possible. He tried to put into his legal papers words and phrases that could mean only one thing. When I first began to copy his papers I was attracted by the resounding phrases, though they meant little to me. I must have copied the words "Know All Men by These Presents" hundreds of times before it ever occurred to me that what was meant was, "*Take Notice.*" Another phrase that caught my eye was, "In Witness Whereof I have hereunto set my hand." I remember shouting that at one of my brothers one day as I socked him for some fancied grievance. I little thought at the time that the business brevity of the future would boil this lovely phrase down to the single word "Signed."

For a long time I copied these old legal forms with little or no curiosity as to what they might mean. Then one day I came across a clause in a will which left certain property to Cordell Westfall, "his heirs or assigns forever."

"When it's left like that," I asked, "which one of them gets it?"

"Oh, that's just intended for Cordell."

"Then why not say so?"

My father smiled. "The court took some three hundred pages to say just that in a famous old decision called *The Rule in Shelley's Case.*"

The words used in these legal phrases are not all hocus-pocus to impress the layman. Most of them derive from old cases under the English Common Law, and many of them are to be found in the Magna Charta itself. For centuries the courts have been ruling on these phrases, which have been challenged and interpreted from so many angles that they are now practically impregnable. The courts have firmly established that they do mean this and do not mean that. A new phrase, as my father explained, was subject to no such protection. It might mean one thing to you and another to me, but we could not be sure of the legal meaning until it had been passed upon by the court.

These well-rounded phrases, properly used, give to a document not only the quality of legal precision but a positive characteristic of authority. Some of these ancient forms of expression fairly rumble and thunder with importance. All my father's contracts and conveyances were built upon a framework of this old phraseology. Thus the fundamental structure was sound beyond peradventure, and only in putting in the specifications was there a chance for misunderstanding or misinterpretation.

Nothing so irritated my father as a carelessly drawn contract or other instrument containing loose statements or terms and conditions that were expressed in obscure or sloppy language. It was his firm belief that a concise, well-drawn contract, even though pompous in phraseology, was much more likely to be faithfully performed than a loosely drawn agreement more liberal in terms but less authoritative in expression.

People who live in the country cannot drop into a lawyer's office every time they want a paper drawn. This was even more true in my father's time than it is today. Country people used to draw their own notes and bills of sale. Nor did they balk at leases and agreements; and all too often they would attempt their own wills and deeds as well as satisfactions of mortgage. My father was not long in discovering this practice, and during the next fifty years further evidences of it kept drifting in, usually in the form of an instrument that was deficient in some vital particular.

One of the mistakes most frequently made by the home conveyancer was the assumption that a mortgage was automatically satisfied by being paid. Nothing could be further from the truth. A bond is a promise to pay—the mortgage is security for that payment. A mortgage is an encumbrance against the land. Only if it is recorded does it take precedence over subsequent encumbrances. And once it has been placed on record it can be extinguished only by recording an instrument of discharge signed by the holder. Payment of the money merely extinguishes the debt; it does not discharge the mortgage from the record.

At not infrequent intervals during my father's practice an old mortgage would show up on the title search. Some of these were no more than fifteen years old, though occasionally there would be a well-seasoned encumbrance thirty or forty years old, and in one case that I recall the mortgage, though paid, had been undischarged of record for over sixty years. One aged tiller of the soil whose title was thus clouded triumphantly produced the mortgage from which the signatures had been torn off, and my father had a hard time to make him understand why that did not clear the record.

If the person who held the mortgage was still alive and could be found, the matter could usually be straightened out by a properly acknowledged release. But if the holder happened to be dead or unknown or otherwise unavailable, a suit in court to quiet title was the only alternative.

Another form of home scrivening which cost innocent people thousands of dollars was the promissory note. Simple as the promissory note seems, it has probably been the basis of more lawsuits than have wills. Even with the printed forms everywhere available today the number of promissory notes which get into court is almost unbelievable. The layman has a way of forgetting to put down the date, so that a note that promises to pay "thirty days after date" never becomes payable. The printed forms always contain the words, "For value received." But in the old days neglect to specify "consideration" was one of the most frequent causes of failure in a homemade note. In an old bundle of my father's papers is a note in which the personal pronouns were so confused as to invalidate the instrument. It reads as follows:

April 15, 1881

He promises to pay me Three Thousand Dollars ($3,000) on demand in case we get along good.

John Garson

This alleged note was presented to the estate for payment by the widow of John Garson soon after his death. She was a second wife and a very grasping one. This note had been exacted while she was still a bride. There were children by the first wife, and the second wanted to be sure that her own nest was properly feathered. The family gossip was that Number Two was very sparing with her favors unless old John paid handsomely for her smiles. Some of the large notes she produced after his death were incontestably valid. This one, however, the executors rejected, and the widow promptly sued the estate. The trial court held that "getting along good," properly proved, was a sufficient consideration. But it also decided that the note contained no promise to pay by the maker and no payee definite and certain enough to be recognizable in the eyes of the law.

The widow was so stung by this decision that she sat down and wrote to my father an eight-page letter of vindication telling what a difficult husband old John had been. Louella Garson has long been in her grave, and still the yellowed scrap of paper she wrote remains as a warning of how not to draw a promissory note.

My father tried in every way to get people to come to him to have their papers drawn. He charged practically nothing for counsel and would for a dollar draw with skill and accuracy almost any instrument they had need of. But for a time they were slow about coming. People are always slow about learning to pay for anything that has formerly been free. Gradually, however, he won them over, and in time he had a conveyancing business that was often more than he could attend to.

In only one instance did I ever know him to encourage a layman to draw a legal paper for himself. A slippery codger named George Mason who used to run a sales stable had succeeded in getting himself deeply enough in debt to make bankruptcy look attractive to him. Only a day or two before filing his petition he had borrowed $300 from a slow-witted old farmer named Albert Westgard. Al had fallen readily for the glib talk of the horse dealer, but when he met Mason on the street the day after the petition in bankruptcy had been filed there was blood in the old fellow's eye.

Mason was a little perturbed; he had not expected the old farmer to show fight. He took Al aside and assured him privately that the loan would be taken care of. "Just keep your mouth shut," he said, "and after I get this bankruptcy business out of the way I'll clean it up."

The farmer did keep his mouth shut until after the discharge in bankruptcy, he said, but all he was ever able to get was promises. My father had long known that Mason was a scamp. He had haled the fellow into court any number of times and had come very close to sending him to jail over one of his crooked horse deals.

"Do you mean to say that he is still promising to make good—even since his discharge in bankruptcy?" my father demanded of Westgard.

"He certainly is," said Al. "Told me again only yesterday."

"Of course, you know that such a promise is worthless, don't you?"

"That's what I wanted to find out."

"A promise to revive a debt discharged in bankruptcy must be made in writing," my father said.

"Well—mebbe I can get him to put it in writin'," said Al imperturbably.

"You haven't got a chance. He's too slick."

"You write me out a little some'pm and I'll see."

My father shook his head. "He'd never sign such a thing as that. You'd be wasting your time to ask him." He stopped and looked out the window, smiling thoughtfully. "Tell you what he might do, though—he might sign a paper if he thought it was something you cooked up yourself—something he saw you write."

He picked up a pencil and wrote out a rambling, bungling statement about Westgard's claim in bankruptcy, with vague references to "wanting to reach a friendly understanding." The nonessential parts were extremely vague and meaningless; but hidden underneath were all the legal requirements to make it a binding promise. He gave the paper to Westgard and told him to study it until he could write out a perfect copy from memory.

A day or two later Westgard came upon Mason in the lobby of the Inn and led him over into a deserted corner near the writing desk for a private talk. He told Mason that he was tired of promises and wanted to know when he was going to get a little money. Mason tried to soothe him, but Westgard was obdurate; he wanted more than promises.

"But what more can I give you?" Mason demanded. "I got no money."

"Well, at least you might give me more'n a bare promise," Westgard grumbled sullenly.

"Such as what?"

"Well—" Westgard acted as if he did not know quite what he wanted himself. "You could give me a little—

well, a little writin' or some'pm to the effect that you'll fix this thing up sometime—say in six months or a year."

"Sure I'll fix it up in six months or a year." The bait was beginning to work. "Sure I'll fix it up—but what kind of a writin' do you mean?"

"Oh, a little writin' so I'll have confidence I'm gonna get my money back sometime." Westgard sat down at the desk and picked up a pen. "Ain't afraid to give me that much comfort be you?"

"You gonna write some'pm out?"

Westgard scratched his head. "Yes, I'll write out a little some'pm." And he wrote out the rambling form he had learned from my father.

Mason had a hard time keeping his face straight when he read it over. "Looks all right to me."

"Shall we make it six months or a year?" asked Westgard.

"Oh, I guess we better make it a year."

Westgard made it a year, and Mason signed it. When Westgard brought suit on it after the expiration of the year the court sustained it as a valid promise to revive a debt discharged in bankruptcy and granted a judgment. Meanwhile Mason had brought an action against the railroad company for personal injuries. He succeeded in recovering a sizable amount, of which my father was able to attach enough to pay Westgard's judgment in full.

"Funniest lookin' paper you ever see in your life," Westgard said to me long afterwards, "and still the damn thing held water."

There was nothing funny about that to me. My father's papers usually did hold water.

The country doctor was not the only one who was routed out of his warm bed at night to minister unto some unlucky mortal who was *in extremis*. On a number of occasions my father was called to draw a deathbed will for somebody not

158

expected to live until morning. I made two such midnight excursions myself, and I realize to the full the dreariness of those drives through the rain and darkness, with the horse never able to go faster than a walk, the wheels sunk in mud halfway to the hubs, and the gnawing uncertainty about getting there on time.

On one of these expeditions I found a woman in bed with quinsy and the house filled with sympathetic neighbors who were keeping themselves awake by drinking quantities of her hard cider. The patient was unable to speak above a whisper, but she was so alert and showed such vitality that I was somewhat annoyed to have been summoned in the night when the morrow would have done just as well. I felt a little sheepish the next day when I found that she had breathed her last within an hour after I had left her bedside at about three o'clock in the morning.

I had no difficulty in finding witnesses right in the house. But on the first occasion that my father was called out in the

night to draw a bedside will he found no visiting neighbors present, and when he asked about witnesses he was informed that the brother and sister of the patient were the only ones available. This would have been all right if the patient had not desired to mention them in the will, for beneficiaries under a will are not acceptable witnesses.

Finding witnesses in the country between two and three o'clock in the morning, with the nearest neighbor half a mile away, took some time, during which my father finished his writing and read the will to the prospective testatrix, who approved it and said she was ready to sign. When my father explained that the law required her to sign in the presence of the witnesses, the sick woman at once began to pant and said she was afraid she would not be able to last until they came. My father picked up a palm-leaf fan and began to fan her while her sister ran for a basin of cold water. Between them they managed to revive her, and for an hour they continued the fanning and the cold applications, but still the brother did not return.

As the patient recovered her strength, she began to show some agitation because of the brother's long-drawn-out absence. She kept calling for him and asking what could have happened to him. By the time his footsteps were heard on the veranda she had worked herself into a state of extreme agitation. She was so flurried that my father was afraid she would not be able to write. However, she was propped up on the pillows, and the atlas that was to serve as a writing board was placed before her. My father noticed that she was breathing lightly, but she was equal to the amenities, and as the two witnesses came in the door of the sick room she smiled at them and moved her lips in greeting —and then she passed out.

At first my father thought that she was dead, but this proved to be an error, and with the aid of smelling salts, fanning, and cold applications she was brought back. When she thought she was strong enough to sign, my father spread the will in front of her and put a dipped pen in her hand. For a time her hand hung over the paper trembling feebly but making no mark. Then slowly the pen went down to the paper—it touched—it made a mark—and gradually, almost painfully, the letters of her name began to form.

Standing with their wraps still on, the witnesses were watching her with tense fascination. The man was working his mouth with each labored movement of the pen as if by twisting his lips he could help the pen along; his wife, equally rapt, was bending over, almost breathless as she watched the faint line of ink bend itself into letters.

At last the first name was finished. *Emily*—there it stood for all to see. The witnesses straightened up and drew a long breath. The sister administered the smelling salts. My father plied the fan. After a little the patient indicated that she was ready to go on. As my father dipped the pen he thought with apprehension of the length of the last name, which was Stoutenburg. If it had been a short name like Dix or Bird she might have made it; but Stoutenburg was simply too much of an effort for the woman's fast-ebbing strength. She took the pen in her hand and for a moment held it over the paper. Then suddenly it dropped and rolled down on to the bedclothes, where it made a dark spot. This time she did not come back. Emily Stoutenburg was dead.

Of course the will was invalid, and the estate which might have been administered quite simply under the will was compelled to go through a complicated intestacy which vested a goodly share of the property exactly where Emily Stoutenburg did not wish it to go.

My father's memory was brought back vividly to the scene of Emily Stoutenburg's deathbed some years later when he again saw the pen faltering on the dotted line of an important instrument. This, however, was not a will but a deed. Philip Tarbot, an old friend, had called at the office and asked my father to prepare a deed of the house and lot in which he lived with his daughter, Annie, a school teacher and a very superior person.

He explained that although the deed stood in his name all the payments had been made by Annie, and he wanted the property made over to her.

There were a number of grown sons, mostly worthless, some of them rather accomplished dead beats, and Philip realized only too well that if he should die with the property in his name Annie would lose everything she had put into it. The deed was ready the following day, but Philip did not come in to sign it. My father heard nothing from him for two or three days, and then he received a message asking him to bring the deed to the house. The messenger said that Philip had suffered a heart attack and was confined to his bed and that Annie had given him the idea the matter was rather urgent. It so happened that my father was not occupied at the moment and he at once put the deed in his pocket and started for the house.

He found old Philip propped up in bed, looking very pasty. The sick man did not even take the time to return my father's greeting but began fidgeting with his fingers. "Got the papers ready?" he asked as my father entered the room.

"Yes, they're right here." My father drew the deed from his pocket and opened the portable bottle of ink that he carried whenever papers were to be signed outside the office. He had caught the need of haste and was wasting no time. "We won't need to read this over, Philip," he said. "It's a deed of this place and conveys the title from you to Annie, just as you told me. Is that right?"

"Yes—yes—that's right." His breath was coming in short gasps. "Annie—the book—"

Annie had already picked up a geography from the table and was handing it to my father. He placed it in front of

Philip, spread the deed upon it, and put the pen in the sick man's hand. It was when Philip's hand hung trembling over the paper but did not write that the thought of Emily Stoutenburg flashed into my father's mind. Then suddenly Philip's hand began to move. It did not form any letters but slid gradually down the page, making a vertical line which was already some two inches long before my father caught hold of his hand. "Guess you need a little steadying," he said. "Let me help you."

He guided the pen into a semblance of Philip's signature and withdrew it from the inert fingers, which collapsed as he released them. "You acknowledge the execution of this instrument for the uses and purposes therein set forth?"

Philip's head nodded to his breast, and my father did not wait for any further answer. He picked up the deed and busied himself with folding it and capping his ink bottle. "I'll sign as a notary after I get back to my office, and I presume you'll want me to attend to the recording."

Annie was bending over the bed. "If you will."

"I hope you'll be feeling better, Philip," my father said as he started for the door.

There was no answer. And as my father was going into the post office an hour later to mail some letters he heard that Philip Turbot was dead.

When he told me the story I asked him if he ever found out the exact time when Philip's death occurred.

He shook his head. "I never pried into the matter. I could see no reason for stirring up such a question. Philip was doing his best to make a deed of the place to Annie. As his attorney—I helped him see it through."

"But what about the deed—was it ever questioned?"

"Never. It was placed on record that same day—and there it stands today unless Annie has disposed of it without telling me."

"But didn't Annie ever mention it to you?"

163

He shrugged his shoulders. "Why should she?"

Some years had passed, and I had been admitted to the bar and was practicing with my father when one day Annie Turbot Wilson, then a widow in the sixties, came into the office. She said that since her daughter's marriage she had found the place too large for her and was selling it. She wanted to know if I could have the deed ready that afternoon.

"Have you the old deed?" I asked.

She opened her bag and handed me a deed in my father's handwriting. It was not until I had looked at the signature that the story came back to me. This was the identical deed my father had told me about. I knew it at once by the long vertical line running down toward the bottom of the page, and the signature bore abundant evidence of my father's assistance. It might almost have passed for his handwriting.

"This was drawn by my father," I said.

"Yes, it was a long time ago," she said slowly. "But I remember it very distinctly. He brought it up to the house for my father to sign."

"The signature looks pretty shaky. Was he—very ill?"

"He was on his deathbed."

"You mean—he died soon after—signing it?" I could not help asking.

She nodded. "Yes."

"Was it—very soon?"

"It was—the same day." She did not amplify the statement, and I did not feel that I could press the matter any further. But I would have liked to know.

164

14. Country Lawyer in Politics

IT IS practically impossible for the country lawyer to keep out of politics. Whether he has a real interest or not he is likely to be dragged into every campaign. Practiced speakers are needed, either to discuss the issues for the voters or to preside at the rallies and introduce other speakers, and in the country town there are few men who can talk on their feet except the lawyers and the clergy. As a rule, men of the cloth consider politics a little beneath their dignity, and in the small town this leaves the lawyer holding the gavel.

All his life my father was interested in politics. By this I do not mean that he always wanted to run for office. With the exception of the position of school trustee, he never actually ran for office in his life—though on one occasion he moved all that part of heaven and earth that he could get his fingers under to win the nomination for surrogate; but owing to a slight error in judgment made during the earlier years of his practice, he was, to his great chagrin, ignominiously unhorsed.

The error in judgment occurred back in the days when he had a very small practice and a very large family. The ratio of increase between the two had somehow been miscalculated so that the family was running far ahead of the income.

My father was lying awake nights trying to figure out some way to enlarge his income when the term of Rutherford B. Hayes expired as President, and the term of the village postmaster likewise expired; and my father had the novel idea that he could serve as postmaster without seriously interfering with his practice.

He mentioned the matter to some of the local political strategists, but they received the suggestion with coolness, having, it seems, a tacit understanding among themselves about the succession. So my father went higher up; he mentioned his ambitions to the county leader, without whose approval no political plum was supposed to be passed out, no matter how puny. He received my father's application with every courtesy, but he insisted that the candidate for postmaster must have the approval of the county committeeman from his own town. My father realized that this was quite impossible, since it was the committeeman himself who wanted the appointment.

So he said no more to the local authorities but sat down and quietly wrote to a relative in Washington who knew her way around. She replied cryptically that she would speak to the judge about it. That was all. He heard nothing more about the matter until the list of postmasters for Ontario County was released—and behold! his name led all the rest.

He got the job. He put the local politicians in their places, but he had violated the code. He had aroused an enmity that had to be avenged though it took years to get the knife into his back. The stroke would not have been delayed so long if my father had evinced the slightest desire to run for office again. But a number of years passed before he felt the urge. Meanwhile, he had built up a large practice. He was one of the substantial citizens of the county and a wheelhorse of the Republican Party. He had long since forgotten about his youthful indiscretion of putting the town and county politicians in their place. But they had not forgotten. Mr. Congreve must have overlooked the politician when he penned his famous line about the fury of a woman scorned.

The office of Surrogate had become vacant, and there were those who thought that my father was the ideal man for the job. He had one of the largest probate practices in the county and was well versed in the law of decedents' estates. No outstanding candidate had appeared against him, and nomination on the Republican Ticket was tantamount to election in Ontario County. Everything looked decidedly rosy when the County Committee went into executive session. My father, full of confidence, was pacing the corridor outside, smoking a cigar. He must have been stunned when he saw the slate that had been agreed upon—for the nomination went to a dark horse from the other end of the county who was, no doubt, equally stunned when his name came out of the hat.

My father felt that he had been lured into a trap. He had been given to understand that he had the nomination in the bag until they thought it was too late for him to put up a fight, and then they handed him a blank. If there had been anything but the revenge motive back of the refusal he would probably have swallowed the bitter pill and hoped for better luck next time. But the thought of working for years side by side with men who were harboring a secret grudge against him and just waiting for a chance to get even so enraged him that he could not resist the desire to drag them and their methods out into the open. If a fight was what they did not want—he felt that it was the one thing to give them, and give it to them he did.

Of course he did not win the nomination. He did not expect to. In after years he used to refer to the battle as a punitive and educational expedition. But he gave his opponents so terrific a hammering over their petty politics that the Democrats came around and said that if he wanted to carry the fight to the polls he could have the nomination on their ticket. He was too loyal a party man to accept, and as soon as the primary campaign was over he was ready to lay off and help elect the Republican ticket.

His punitive and educational expedition was not wasted, however, for the next time the office of Surrogate became vacant the same men who had previously refused him the nomination now brought it to him on a silver salver surrounded by olive branches; but my father was undergoing a period of ill-health at this time and was unable to accept. Later on he received an appointment as an attorney for one of the state commissions which added an "Honorable" to his name, but it came at a time when he was so mellow and full of years that the title brought him more amusement than vainglory.

He held this office for some six years, and though he never again became a candidate for an elective office his interest in politics stayed with him to the last. Any campaign, village, town, county, state, or national, was grist to his mill. An election to him was like the sound of an alarm to a fire horse, and he was off on a run to arouse the electorate and help get out the vote no matter what the issue.

During every important campaign our house was the mecca for visiting politicians and spellbinders. Always during the state and national elections there would be large rallies with out-of-town speakers, and some years there were torchlight parades with coal oil torches and oilcloth capes and hats designed in some gay combination of red, white, and blue. Whenever there were visiting speakers my father would introduce them to the citizens in the opera house, and if there was a large enough overflow crowd in the streets he would slip outside to address them from the front porch of the Inn and try to hold them until the big guns could finish their indoor bombardment and come outside for an informal street rally.

A crowd always had a peculiar effect on my father—it never failed to fill him with a desire to make a speech. He was not a long-winded man. He derived none of the pleasure that lecturers and preachers seem to get from seeing listeners writhe in their seats. If his audience showed the slightest sign of uneasiness he would quickly change the subject, and if this did not hold them he would draw his remarks to an early close. But the mere presence of a crowd was like a heady draught to him, and whenever he saw two or three persons gathered together he could not help looking for a suitable rostrum.

During the fight over the Westfall estate a referee was appointed to take some testimony on the ground. While the hearings were going on my father used to bring visiting lawyers home to supper with him nearly every night. Ordinarily my mother was forewarned of these guests, but one night without any notice at all my father came walking in with a tall, dignified man whom he introduced as Senator Saxton.

We were all a little curious to know why the Senator should be in town, for there had been no hearing in the Westfall case that day. It soon developed that the visitor had ambitions to run for Lieutenant Governor, and he had come to my father for advice as to the best way to approach the political powers of our county who were not at the time on good terms with the county chairman of the Senator's own county.

I noticed that my mother had run up distress signals the moment she had caught sight of Senator Saxton, and I suspected I knew the reason why. She had planned as the main dish for dinner that night a favorite of ours which, in a spirit of good, clean fun, we used to call "dead dog."

"Dead dog" was prepared by taking a large thin slice of meat—probably flank steak—and rolling it around a mass of well-seasoned stuffing about the size of a football. Roasted

169

in a hot oven with a liberal basting, this dish would come out brown and glistening. On a large platter, surrounded by a halo of potatoes browned in the pan, it may not have made food for the gods, but it certainly pleased the palates of the hungry horde who used to gather around our table.

My mother was somewhat on the formal side when it came to a company dinner. She liked to serve a whole baked ham or a roast of beef the size of a hatbox, for there was always a good market for whatever was left. She was greatly embarrassed—mortified to death was the way she put it afterward—to be caught with nothing but a "dead dog" in the house. I distinctly remember how greatly I enjoyed her discomfiture; that is the kind of child I was. I enjoyed every moment of it—and still do.

We were really in fine fettle for a party. Seeing my mother bustling around getting out her best linen and the solid silver tableware and opening her choicest pickles and preserves was very heartening to us. We all knew that she could have slain my father for his thoughtlessness—and would probably dress him down after the guest had gone. Her flutterings, together with the prospect of hearing my father get bawled out, had us all a-twitter long before we sat down at the table.

By ones and twos we came drifting into the library to be presented to the Senator. We were always cautioned against descending on a guest in a body. Such a procedure was thought to be too overwhelming, and we tried to make our entrances at intervals of a minute or two which would give the guest a chance to assimilate us in small doses. Once we had been presented we were at liberty to group ourselves around the room in any way we chose, but we were not supposed to leave the room until we all went in to dinner together.

On this particular occasion none of us wanted to leave the room. We could hardly have been dragged away with a team of oxen. We recognized that the situation contained the elements of a crisis, and we wanted to miss no part of it.

When I entered the room my father was standing with his back to his desk, the leaf of which had been folded up to form the inclined plane against which he was leaning. The Senator was standing a short distance away, facing him. They had just finished a glass of sherry, and the empty glasses were standing on the mantel. My mother, a confirmed dry, never shared in these potations. Indeed, she used to disregard them and pretend that they had not actually occurred in her house. As I came into the room my father stopped what he was saying and murmured my name.

The Senator smiled at me. "Hello, young man. Another boy, eh?"

"There are two more around here somewhere," my father said. "You'll see them presently."

I went over and shook hands with the guest as I had been taught to do, and as the two men went on with their talk I drifted to the other end of the room, where my brothers and sisters had congregated. New hardwood floors had just been laid in the library and dining room, which, in addition to being very handsome, were highly polished, and the Senator was asking if we were not finding them very slippery.

My father shook his head. The rugs had skated around a bit at first, he said, but we had soon become used to that. He poked with his toe at the small rug on which he was standing. It was not, he added, as sure-footed as walking on carpets, though he felt certain there would be no difficulty after the wax had worked into the wood a little more.

They drifted into the subject of politics and started a very lively discussion of some of the iniquities of Governor David B. Hill, who was one of my father's pet aversions. My father was laying out Mr. Hill with great enthusiasm when,

171

to emphasize some point he was making, he struck the extended palm of his left hand with the fist of his right. At the peculiar angle at which he was standing, leaning back against the desk, the force of the blow was just enough to dislodge the small rug beneath his feet. It shot out suddenly from under him, and in a trice my dignified father had landed on the floor in a sitting posture, with a thump that shook the house.

We all saw him going, and while he was still in the air we started as one to emit a shout of laughter. But the laughter died on our lips when he went calmly on with what he was saying as if nothing out of the ordinary had happened.

Attracted by the thump and possibly by the strange gurgle of our throttled mirth, my mother suddenly appeared in the double doorway leading to the dining room. By this time my father was standing exactly as he had stood before, talking just as earnestly and whacking his right fist into his left hand just as emphatically. The rug, however, was in a heap on the other side of the room.

As she paused in the doorway, my mother had indicated by a movement of her head that she wished to speak privately with my oldest sister. My sister retired with her into the dining room, and when she came back a few moments later she passed on to the rest of us a confidential message that we were to ask for no more than a single helping of the "dead dog." The animal seemed to have shrunk in cooking, and my mother did not want it to appear as if there were not enough.

Among ourselves we made wry faces. The doctrine of "family hold back," though of infrequent application in our household, was not unknown, and the danger of shortage made the situation more exciting and gave additional interest to the spectacle of our mother putting into a "dead dog" dinner all the elegance she could muster for the future Lieutenant Governor of the state. This was going to be fun, anyway.

172

In serving "dead dog," slices are cut from the end of the loaf with a sharp knife. My father was a fine carver, and the rings he served were as perfect as if cut off by a buzz saw. As was his custom, he had served my mother first and then the guest of honor. After that he went down through the family according to age, beginning with the eldest child. Since my eldest brother was away at the time the family bread line began with my eldest sister. And just as my father was getting ready to serve her she said to him in a low and unobtrusive tone:

"If that's for me, father, I don't care for any of the meat."

My father lowered his carving knife and gave her a sharp look. "No meat?" Had his ears deceived him?

"Just vegetables, please. I don't care for any meat tonight."

Something wrong here. One of the best appetites in the family refusing her favorite dish. He would have to look into that later. The plate of vegetables had just been handed to the maid waiting on table when my second sister spoke up.

"I don't care for any meat either."

My father straightened up. "What's the trouble here?"

My second sister blushed copiously. "I just don't want any meat."

By this time I could see that my mother was flashing signals like a Very light, and it became quite obvious to us younger fry at the foot of the table that the orders had been garbled before reaching us. We nodded among ourselves, however. By keeping our ears open we had found out what to do.

When the third sister refused to have any meat my father, in addition to being baffled, began to be angry. He suspected that some kind of strike or protest was in the air, and he thought it very ill-timed on our part to attempt it while so prominent a guest was in our midst. He had hoped that it might be something that would end with the girls, but

173

when he came to the boys' section in the lower seats he received the same answer.

"No, thank you," my next older brother replied. "Just vegetables."

By this time my mother's face was flaming red. She, too, had hoped against hope that only the girls had their signals crossed and that the four boys coming through with healthy appetites might still save the day. But the same answer went on down the line, even to the smallest boy.

"No meat, please. Just vegetables."

As the baby of the family came through and made the count unanimous, my mother, instead of flying into a rage or falling into a swoon, burst into a gale of laughter such as I had never seen her enjoy before. She laughed and shook until the tears streamed down her cheeks. It was minutes before she was composed enough to explain, and when she did explain she told the whole story—including our name for the dish.

When Senator Saxton grasped what had been going on, he laughed louder and longer than anybody.

He was Lieutenant Governor under Governor Levi P. Morton the next time I saw him. My father and I met him in the railroad station at Syracuse. He was surrounded by men in silk hats and frock coats and was shaking hands with my father when suddenly his eye fell on me. His face lighted up, and he was laughing softly as he bent over and asked me in a low tone if I had eaten any "dead dog" lately.

"I'll come to see you again," he said gaily, "if you'll promise to have 'dead dog' for dinner."

"I'll promise the 'dead dog' if Dad will do his tumbling act," I said.

My father gave me a blank look. "Now what do you mean by that?"

Just then the Lieutenant Governor turned to speak to a newcomer, but I could tell by the look in his eye that *he* needed no explanation.

174

15. The Lawyer Goes to Church

B Y THE time Jerry Billings had served a third of his term my father had begun to weigh in his mind the possibilities of obtaining executive clemency. His first move was to feel out the people around town with the idea that if he found the proper sentiment he would circulate a petition among them that would show the Governor that since the wave of hysteria had passed, the complexion of the public mind had changed entirely.

His efforts in this direction, however, did not go very far. He found people less vindictive than before but none the less positive of Jerry's guilt and well satisfied to know that he was being "justly punished." The idea of a petition was forthwith abandoned, but since my father was compelled to go to Albany to argue an appeal in the Westfall estate, he thought he might as well kill two birds with one stone by making an application to the Governor, even without a petition. He had no difficulty in getting a hearing, and in the absence of a petition he prepared a massive brief on the insufficiency of the circumstantial evidence on which Jerry's conviction was based.

This brief, together with a complete copy of the record, was sent to the Governor for preliminary study before the application was heard. His Excellency listened attentively to what my father had to say and asked some questions which showed a good understanding of the issue—but he denied the application. He had made it a rule, he said, not to interfere with findings of fact by a jury in the absence of very exceptional circumstances, which, to his mind, did not exist in this case.

So Jerry had to serve out his term, less the commutation that he would receive for good behavior. My father felt quite downcast over the decision, though he said very little about it at home. He had not let Jerry know that he was going to make the application for executive clemency, since he was fearful that he did not have quite enough to make a success of it and he did not want Jerry to build up false hopes. But through some obscure channel of communication in the underworld Jerry learned of it and wrote my father, thanking him for the effort. This was my father's first acquaintance with the prison "grapevine."

Letters passed between my father and Jerry at irregular intervals. If Jerry felt like writing, he wrote, and my father always responded very promptly, answering any questions that Jerry might have asked and giving all the news and gossip of the town that he thought Jerry would find of interest. At first there was a grim note in Jerry's letters, a sullen surrender of the body, though not of the will; but after a few months the routine seemed to have subdued him, and his letters sounded much more calm. Eventually they became resigned, even cheerful. Indeed, it seemed to my father that Jerry was much more agreeable in prison than he had ever been outside. And when, after some five years behind the bars, Jerry wrote that he was learning the trade of meatcutter so that he could have a good occupation after his release—my father thought that the letter came as close to expressing enthusiasm as Jerry would ever come.

My father pondered over that letter for days. What contingency of imprisonment was remolding the man? Was

176

it the discipline? Could it be the fact that he was reading and studying more than he had? Might it not be the companionship of other men? My father never could quite decide what it was, though he now felt reasonably sure that the misanthropic exterior had been no more than a defensive mask and that the real man was showing through the letters.

Quite naturally Jerry's spirits rose as the time for his release approached. He was writing more often now, and my father noticed that his letters had lost the labored air of his earlier efforts. Indeed, the last letter that he wrote in prison—written only a month before his release—sounded to my father like the mellowed words of a philosopher. My father shook his head over this letter, too. He wondered if there had been a spiritual change deep down inside the man that could allow him to forgive society for the injustice of a totally undeserved term in prison. Or was it just that the prospect of freedom was so filling his soul that no room was left at the moment for resentment and bitterness?

The exact date of Jerry's release had not been mentioned in any of his letters, and my father had an idea that perhaps Jerry did not know when it was to be. This was a mistake; Jerry knew, but he kept it very much to himself—and early one morning when my father walked out into his garden he found Jerry at work there as if he had never been away.

"We need a new spading fork," Jerry growled, without looking up, as my father went toward him. "I thought I told you that once before."

"What in thunder—!" gasped my father.

Jerry had had his joke, and now he burst out laughing, threw down the spading fork, and grasped my father's outstretched hand. It was the first time my father had ever heard Jerry laugh.

"When did you get back?"

"Late train last night."

"But—but where'd you spend the night?"

Jerry laughed again. "At my place. You had it locked up so tight I had to break in."

"It was a new lock," said my father. "The old one rusted away." He handed the key to Jerry. "Why didn't you come down and get this last night?"

"Oh, I got in a window all right. The inside looks nice. Who painted it for you?"

"Frank Navis. I had Frank down here doing some painting for me, and there was a little paint left over. I thought I might as well put it there as let it dry up."

"Much obliged to you. It looks fine. And that new stove is a dandy. Bet there wasn't much left of the old one."

"No, it was pretty well rusted away. Have you seen anybody to talk to yet?"

Jerry grinned. "Have I! Dan Flynn spotted me before I was halfway off the train. He let go of a trunk he was hauling and stuck out his paw and shook hands with me. And then he dragged me inside the depot so I could talk with Amos and the rest of the boys. I had a regular reception there for about an hour. I kinda expected some of 'em to be offish—but they wasn't."

"Good," said my father. "That's fine." Of course, he never told Jerry that he had arranged that reception in advance through the warm-hearted baggageman, who let it be known around the station that he'd "bust anybody's neck who don't treat the bhoy dacent."

My father gave Jerry a few days to get his place in order and his garden planted and then set him up in a small meat market of his own. The market was a success from the start. Nobody seemed to hold it against Jerry that he had been the involuntary ward of the state. And Jerry was not at all ashamed of it. He spoke of his prison life as men speak of their experiences in the army and had no qualms about discussing it with anybody and everybody who showed the slightest interest in the subject. People had long since

178

outgrown their bitterness against him. The general attitude of mind was that he had paid his debt to society and that society ought to be willing to live and let live.

Nor did Jerry show any bitterness. He never berated the people of the State of New York for sending an innocent man to jail. His position was that his conviction was nothing more than a stupid mistake of the law that might have happened to anybody. Shucks, he wasn't the only innocent man who had ever been sent to jail on circumstantial evidence. So long as the courts allowed that kind of proof there was bound to be a mistake now and then. It was not individuals who were to blame—it was the system. And anyhow, the time he had spent in Auburn was not entirely lost, he said, since he had learned a good trade there. Now he was going to show people how well he had learned it.

Jerry fell naturally into the niche that had been found for him. The market was turned entirely over to him, and from the day it opened its doors my father kept his hands off. He thought that Jerry needed the responsibility. But though he was now a meatcutter by trade, Jerry was still a tiller of the soil at heart. His garden flourished, and soon my father noticed that along with his meat Jerry was selling home-grown vegetables. At the end of the year Jerry proudly came around and made a small payment on the indebtedness.

My father was very much pleased. So was Jerry. Jerry would have liked to give my father a present of some kind, but he did not know what to give him or how to go about giving it. Then Jerry thought of a good way out of his dilemma—he could give a present to the children. That would show his good will and would cause my father no embarrassment. Shortly after Jerry had reached this conclusion he saw my brother and me admiring the carcass of a little black and white pig that lay sprawled—porkwise—in the window of his market. That gave him an idea—and the next day he made us a present of a live pig just like it. He even helped us to build a pen for it in a fence corner behind the barn.

My father was very much upset when he saw it. If anybody but Jerry had given it to us I am sure he would have made us send it back. Indeed, there were some very serious head shakings before my father could bring himself to say that we could keep the little fellow until slaughtering time in the fall—positively no longer—and there was an ironclad agreement that we boys must take full charge of the care and feeding of the pig. Of course we made the promise, though we did not realize what we were getting into, for even a small pig requires an endless amount of waiting on.

We had only one other pet at the time, a little spaniel that had come to the door one stormy night and scratched for admittance. She was obviously a dog of uncertain antecedents, but she had good brains and good manners, and after looking us over for a day or two she decided to adopt us and was given the name of Belle.

An advertisement was inserted in the Lost and Found column of the paper, and though we trembled with apprehension for the next few days no claimant appeared, and Belle was declared to be treasure trove. She was a dog who took her responsibilities seriously, and whenever a child cried in the night Belle was first at the crib side. Every weekday she accompanied my father to the office, but once she had seen him in the door she would turn and retrace her steps as if she felt she were needed at home.

For some reason known only to herself Belle would never leave the premises on Sunday. She would watch with apparent unconcern as the family started for church and lie on the veranda until our return. Only once did she violate this voluntary blue law of hers, and then it was really not her fault. The violation occurred on a very hot Sunday late in August while all the family were away at church.

My father, though a believer, was not a deeply religious man. When thoroughly aroused he could swear with some distinction. He went to church for two reasons, because he had formed the habit and because it was the thing to do. Nobody was considered quite respectable at that time unless he had sound church connections. Which church did not matter, but it must be some church. Most of the well-to-do people in town went to the Presbyterian church. My mother had been brought up a Presbyterian, so in spite of my father's Episcopal upbringing we went to the Presbyterian church. It was undoubtedly good business, and surely it was convenient, for the Presbyterian church was only half a block from our house.

My father never would go to prayer meeting, and my mother, who knew that he could be pushed just so far and no farther, did not try to make him go. He never made a public prayer in his life, and though my mother was willing to overlook this she was adamant about certain devotions in the home. She always insisted upon his saying grace before meals, believing it positively indecent to eat unblessed food. My father used two neat little formulas, one for ordinary days, beginning, "Sanctify, O Lord, this provision of thy bounty," and another, a little more elegant, reserved for Christmas, Easter, Thanksgiving, and my mother's birthday. We also had family prayers once a week. These took place in the library immediately after breakfast on Sunday morning. My father would read a selection from the Bible, after which each member of the family, beginning with the oldest person present and going straight down the line, was supposed to recite a verse from the Bible. We used to get these verses on short notice from a Scriptural Scroll which hung on the wall of the dining room. And one of the tricks the older children used to play on us younger fry was to appropriate the verse that one of us had chosen and leave the victim to fall back on some other verse he happened to remember—if any.

After the verses we all knelt while my father offered a prayer, and I must say that he never failed to offer a good one. There was nothing cringing about it and nothing smug. A word of appreciation for past favors and a respectful petition for guidance during the days to come. In a way his prayers sounded very much like his legal papers. There were no holes in them and no superfluous words. As soon as the prayer was over we scurried off to our rooms to get ready for church.

It would be impossible to overemphasize the importance of church attendance to our family. It was in a way the most momentous social event of the week. I might not have a good pair of rubber boots to wear in the woods or around the creek, but I was never without a good pair of shoes to wear to church. My father was an important man in the church, but his importance was on the lay side. He was a liberal contributor, a wise counselor on fund raising and improvements, and he always took care of any legal difficulties that arose. Ecclesiastical affairs he very willingly left to others. But in matter of attendance for himself and his family he yielded the palm to no man.

Getting the family off to church was an undertaking in comparison with which getting the children off to school was as nothing. School clothes were designed for service rather than looks. They had to be whole and durable, but they did not necessarily have to be either new or modish. Clothes for church were quite another matter; they must be our newest and best. We all had new clothes for Easter, but never for the Fourth of July. Going "on the carpet" for inspection on a school day was very tame in comparison with the Sunday morning inspection. I don't know that I ever got by without being sent back to rewash an ear or repolish the heel of a shoe. Once, to the unholy delight of my brothers, I was sent back for the fourth time to brush some stubborn lint from the rear of my trousers.

We started for school individually, whenever we were ready; but we all went in a body to church. The church bell used to give a warning signal at ten o'clock. When this bell struck we were supposed to start for the library to begin the inspection. This allowed twenty minutes for the adjustment of claims, rearrangement of equipment, and the location and examination of hats and wraps. While all this was going on my father stood there, watch in hand. He could not have been more exacting or particular if he had been starting an army for the battlefield.

Promptly at twenty minutes after ten we walked out of the house and formed on the sidewalk, my father in his silk hat and Prince Albert coat, my mother in an unfrivolous costume of some subdued color not unseemly for divine worship. My father always wore gloves and carried a silver-headed cane. My mother wore gloves that always seemed too tight for her; she was proud of her small hands. Behind them we children fell into double file, usually with the older ones ahead, the younger bringing up the rear.

For years we occupied pews 61 and 62 on the left side of the center aisle—a single pew would not accommodate us all —and we never failed to create a stir when we went down the aisle. The effect must have been something like that of the arrival of a wedding party. Usually my mother and father occupied pew 61, which was just about in the middle of the church, the smaller children between them, and my father on the aisle seat with his silk hat underneath and his hands resting on his cane. That cane used to reach out like an avenging hand and hook profane playthings from our grasp if they appeared to be taking too much of our attention from the services. The older children were allowed to sit in pew 62, which was just behind 61. This was a great privilege. Personally, I got more of a thrill out of the first

183

time I sat there than out of my first long pants. Nearly the worst thing that could happen to a member of our family was to be demoted from 62 to 61. I regret to say that this happened to me on two occasions that I can recall—once when the silver-headed cane hooked a cigarette picture of Della Fox from my nerveless fingers and another time when I inadvertantly spilled a dime novel out of an open hymnal that I was holding before me.

I was in 61 on the occasion of Belle's great heresy in deserting the home grounds on Sunday. When we left for church she had come with us to the front gate and had then gone back and stretched herself on the porch. I remember that part very plainly, for I could not help wishing that I were in her place. I could not see why I had to be destined to be dragged to a stuffy old church for a stuffy old sermon. It seemed to me that Belle did not appreciate her good fortune or she would not have looked so sadly after us as we started along the street.

We had been in church for about an hour. The preliminaries were over, and old Dr. Portman was deep in his sermon. That is, I suppose he was deep in it; he had been droning on for fully half an hour. I found it hard to keep myself amused during the sixty or seventy minutes usually consumed by the sermon. Some days I would go through the hymnal and try to make a new rhyme for every line, preferably a humorous or indecorous rhyme. I was looking around for a good rhyme for some word when my eyes came to rest on my father's boots—he wore boots in those days, as most professional men did. I do not remember whether they suggested a rhyme or not, for something happened which took my mind off his boots. It was the sudden appearance of Belle in church!

Her eyes were large with excitement, and there was a look of deep anxiety in the wrinkles of her face. She was crouching slightly and looking up into my father's face.

184

Another dog would have barked, but Belle did not make a sound. My father saw her almost as soon as I did. He glanced quickly at my mother and then at the dog. They both realized instantly that something must be amiss at home. My father's nod seemed to say, "Stay where you are —I'll handle this." And he hastily picked up his silk hat and stepped into the aisle—only to be confronted by the black-and-white pig, which stopped in its tracks, obviously glad to see somebody that it knew.

My father made a dash at the pig, waving both his silk hat and his stick in an effort to frighten it out of the church. The pig was undoubtedly scared by these hostile motions, but instead of going out of the church it bolted suddenly into a pew occupied by several old ladies. Subdued exclamations, and some not so subdued, escaped from the occupants of the pew, who came flocking into the aisle in great confusion. The pig came with them, and, seeing its escape to the rear cut off by the appearance of two formidable ushers, it dodged into a seat on the other side of the aisle and quickly routed out the people who were sitting there. As it came out of this seat my father landed on it with the cane and so frightened the pig that it set up a terrific squealing.

By this time the people in church who were not standing in their seats and peering back were standing on them. Everyone was trying to locate the runner in the midst of a badly broken field. Dr. Portman did not come down out of his pulpit, since he did not fancy himself in the role of pig catcher. For a time he stood and watched the excitement, and then he slowly folded his sermon and put it in his pocket. When he finally signaled to the organist for the doxology he was too late. The organ boy had joined the chase, and there was nobody to pump air into the bellows.

The terrorized beast finally ran into the arms of a farmer who knew how to take hold of a pig, and squealing hysterically, the little porker was carried out of the church and

185

dumped on the lawn. My brothers and I drove it home, with the aid of all the boys in the neighborhood, but it did take us so long that we were not able to get back in time for Sunday school.

That afternoon Jerry Billings came and, after tying the pig's feet together with a rope, wheeled the beast off in a wheelbarrow. I never knew quite what happened to the pig, but none of us ever saw it again. Belle had taken no part in the chase. When my father reached home—with his silk hat looking as if he had slept in it—she was lying quietly on the veranda. She got up and licked his hand, and my father could not help smiling, even though he was considerably upset.

"Are you trying to tell me," he said to her, "that you appreciate that I did the best I could under all the circumstances?"

16. Gossip and Slander

NOBODY knows better than the country lawyer how little personal privacy is to be found in the small town. For that you must go to the city, where you may live for years in the same house with people and not even know their names—or care. In the country you do care about your neighbors. You want to know who they are and what they are up to.

Gossip is as much a part of country life as the air we breathe, the stars above, the green earth we tread, and the waters under the earth. The word "gossip" is in somewhat bad odor today, but that was not always so. In the beginning the word was "god sibb," denoting a spiritual relationship, such as that of a sponsor in baptism. In Chaucer's day "gossip" denoted a familiar friend, a companion. "My gossip . . . her name was Alisoun." It may have denoted something even closer than a familiar friend. But today, in rural life, the gossip is about on a par with the slanderer. When you call a person *that* you'd better smile.

Much of the gossip floating around the country town is kindly. It is no more than news, and it is not meant to be anything else. The eagerness of newspapers to establish a news beat is no more than the enlargement and incorporation of the idea of being the first to pass on an interesting item about a neighbor. My father used to say that gossip was the boon and the bane of the country lawyer's existence. Without it he could not possibly have known many of the things that it was necessary for him to know; much of the evidence in his cases first came to him in the form of gossip. The successful contest of a will, for example, is almost invariably built on gossip, and, similarly, it is nearly impossible to find the evidence to sustain a contested will without falling back on gossip.

There is some basis of fact behind most of the gossip in a country town, though the lawyer is about the only one who knows how much the fact amounts to, for he is the only one who knows both sides.

"Is that just an ordinary lie, or is it a true lie?" I heard my father ask a man who had brought him an item about a lie that was going around.

The power of the spoken word in the country town was something that my father both feared and respected. He used to tell a story about a man whose standing in the community was completely undermined by a story that, though harmless, was so good that it was repeated over and over again.

The victim was an inoffensive little fellow who had probably killed more men than Jesse James and Billy the Kid combined—for he had been a sharpshooter in the Civil War and by all odds the best one in a regiment of crack shots. He could still obliterate the bull's-eye of a target at a hundred paces, though he was so shy that if a rabbit had turned on him he would probably have dropped his gun and run for his life. His name was Johnny Wright. He was a tinsmith, and a good one. For years he worked as the tinker in a hardware store. When the owner died and he had to do something else he opened up a hardware store of his own. It was a little one-man establishment located next door to a rather ornate saloon run by a gentleman named Tug Wilson.

Tug was a rough-shod fellow who had accumulated a number of enemies, among them a group of rowdies called the O'Brien boys, who lived in Longville, a small though tough community about nine miles away. The O'Brien boys had long been wanting to avenge some grievance against Tug Wilson, but it was not until Tug had refurbished his saloon and installed some large and decorative mirrors there that they saw their chance. They sent word to Tug that they would come down some night and toss a few bricks through his mirrors for him. When he received this warning, Tug came to my father in a panic and asked if there was not something that he could do to stall off the raid.

"Is your glass insured?" asked my father.

"Insured? Against fire, you mean?"

"Against breakage, accidental or otherwise."

Tug shook his head. "Didn't know it could be done. Graves down to Geneva handles my insurance. I'll see him about it today. But, Judge, ain't there any way I can stop those skunks from coming down here and smashing up my place?"

"Do you want to tackle the job of having them arrested and put under bond to keep the peace?" asked my father.

Tug shook his small pointed head. "Is that the only way?"

"It's the only way I know of," said my father, who thought that the threats did not sound very serious. "You don't really think they'll attack your place—after sending you notice?"

"Sure they will."

Tug was right about it. They came the next Saturday night. Two of them entered the swinging front doors at the same moment that the other two entered at the back. All were well armed with rocks and brickbats. The proprietor himself was behind the bar when the barrage began. They could easily have struck him down. But they had no desire to injure him; all they wanted to do was to wreck the place, and after their first salvo there was not an unbroken mirror left.

At the first crash of glass Tug Wilson dropped to the floor behind the bar, where he remained until the battle was over. But the bartender, a hard-looking individual with a cauliflower ear, was made of sterner stuff. He had learned his trade on the old Bowery, where, to survive at all, a man must take care of himself. The initial crash that had sent the proprietor to the floor automatically put the bartender into action. He began to throw bottles—first at the heads of the attacking party—and afterward at any head that raised itself above the level of the table tops. He had a deadly aim and a large supply of ammunition with which he floored everybody in the room. When, suddenly, he saw still another head poke through the swinging door he promptly took a crack at it.

That was how it happened that when the local constabulary finally arrived at the scene they stumbled upon the prostrate form of Johnny Wright lying among the gory O'Briens and the others who littered the barroom floor. Johnny's skull was fractured, and he was bleeding freely from a six-inch scalp wound. They were just carrying him out when my father, hastily summoned by Tug Wilson, entered the door.

People were greatly surprised to find Johnny Wright's name listed among the casualties in a bloody barroom brawl, but Johnny had a perfect explanation. He had heard the noise of the attack from his store next door and had gone to see what the trouble was.

Everybody who heard or repeated that story knew that it was true. Johnny Wright was not a roistering man. He did not use alcoholic beverages in any form. Nobody doubted his word when he said that he had never before been in that saloon or any other. But the picture of good, sweet, pious, inoffensive little Johnny Wright being found with a broken head among a welter of bloody O'Briens after a barroom fracas was more than anybody could resist—and the story was told and retold until it began to get under the skin of the local temperance society of which Johnny had been secretary and treasurer for many years. The temperance people made no scandal about it, but at the end of the year, when Johnny's term expired, they put in a woman to take his place.

He was also dropped from the board of elders of the Methodist Church. When his name came up for re-election he received only two votes out of the entire congregation—probably his own and his daughter's, people said.

Johnny told my father that he used to wonder about these things. He did not like the idea of being misunderstood, and he did his best to explain to people just how the accident had really happened. He used to tell the story to anybody who would listen. For a while people put up with him as a bore, and then gradually, as the constant repetition of the alibi became a fixation, they began to regard him as being a little cracked, perhaps from that smash on the head.

Old Johnny has been dead these twenty years, and all that people remember about him—just as my father predicted—is that he was somehow mixed up in that raid of the O'Brien boys on Tug Wilson's saloon.

Here was a story that was both true and harmless, but the repetition of it left a picture that was misleading and injurious. Local gossip does not often take on the elements of slander until it passes through the mind of a person who is scheming or malicious. Actual trials for slander are scarce in the rural counties, but rarely a month passed during my father's practice when someone did not come to him with what might have been regarded under a strict interpretation of the law as a cause of action for slander or defamation of character. Almost invariably my father was able to clear up the situation by an explanation of the rural jury's reluctance to interfere with what it considers freedom of speech and by a word of warning to the person accused of uttering the defamatory matter.

But even though slanderous talk did not always end up in court, it often led to other things that did. Perhaps the most prevalent of these was suspicion. Just as a sensationally horrible ripper murder is likely to be followed by other sensational ripper murders, a bit of gossip about the goings-on of a married man was almost certain to arouse the suspicions of a number of women about the doings of their own husbands. "Sympathetic suspicion," my father used to call it. Occasionally these blind suspicions would hit the mark, though usually they accomplished no more than to make the wife a little ridiculous.

One of the most unusual of these cases of groundless suspicion came to my father's attention not through a jealous wife who wanted a divorce but through the robbery of the safe in a wagon factory and a night watchman who wanted an alibi. When he was called upon to account for his presence at the time of the robbery, the watchman told my father, who was investigating the case, that he had temporarily left the factory and was making a call on a house-maid of a family who lived near by. Pressed for details, he gave my father the name of Mrs. Orlow Wilson, the girl's employer, who, he said, had seen him there.

Mrs. Wilson came readily to my father's office in response to a letter, but when she learned his reason for asking her to come she shut up like a clam and said that she had nothing to say. When, however, my father had explained that if the watchman was arrested for the crime he would almost certainly subpoena her into court—whereas, by giving a full explanation in advance, she might be able to clear the man, she gave in and told him her story.

She and her husband had been married for over ten years, she said. They always got along well. Orlow had no bad habits, though he was fond of billiards and poker and was out at night a good deal. In fact, nearly the only evenings when he was at home were those on which they had invited another couple in for a rubber of whist. He was usually home before midnight, and Mrs. Wilson had never dreamed that he was doing anything out of the ordinary until her suspicions were aroused by her best friend, Madge Horton.

It had all come about through the indiscretions of a servant girl that Mrs. Wilson had never spoken to in her life. Her name was Rita Phipps. Rita had become so involved with a married man that the whole town was talking, and Madge had suggested that Mrs. Wilson had better keep an eye on her Sarah, who, she reminded Mrs. Wilson, had formerly been an intimate friend of Rita's.

"And another thing," Madge had added. "Your Sarah is altogether too good-looking to have around the kitchen of any married woman's home. I know I'd never draw an easy breath if she was in *my* kitchen."

Mrs. Wilson had never thought of that before, but after she had gone home and taken a good look at Sarah she began to be a little uneasy herself. Orlow had never, so far as she knew, even looked at Sarah or any other woman. But once the thought had come into her mind she found it hard to get out again. Until this time she had paid little attention to Sarah's comings and goings, but now, without really meaning to, she began to watch her quite closely. But with all her watching she found nothing amiss with her pretty serving maid. It was when she was not watching at all that she made the startling discovery that Sarah was taking a man up the back stairs to her room when she went to bed one night.

Sarah had come into the house just after the clock had struck ten. Mrs. Wilson was already in her room, partly undressed. She never would have known that anybody was

193

with Sarah if she had not stepped into the back hall to tell her something about breakfast. She stood there in the dark waiting for the girl to turn on the light before coming up. There was a switch at the bottom of the stairs and another at the top. But Sarah did not turn on the lights, and Mrs. Wilson was wondering why she had suddenly become so economical about electricity when she heard whispering —and then she realized that Sarah was not alone and that two persons were trying to keep in step as they went up the stairs.

Mrs. Wilson did not see the man—not when she made the discovery, at any rate—but she went into her own closet, which, though in the front part of the house, was next to the wall of Sarah's room, and by putting her ear against the wall she could hear them whispering and giggling in a very suggestive manner.

Her first impulse was to discharge the girl without giving any further reason than, "I guess you know why." But she thought better of the idea and decided that before making up her mind what to do about it she would talk over the situation with Madge to see if Madge had any ideas. Madge certainly had.

In the first place, she thought that she ought to come down and listen through the wall for herself. She wanted Mrs. Wilson to be sure of her ground before taking a leap in the dark. And in her outspoken way she approached another angle about which Mrs. Wilson had hardly dared to think. "By the way," she said, "where was your own perfectly good husband last night?"

"Playing poker with yours."

"But he wasn't! Chauncey said that Orlow promised to come—but didn't show up."

For some moments the two women had sat and looked at each other without a word. Then Madge asked, "How long was it after you heard the visitor go downstairs before Orlow came in?"

"About half an hour."

Madge nodded. "Uh-huh, just about what you'd expect. A good safe allowance. Did you happen to notice what time it was when the caller left?"

"Sarah went down and let him out just before eleven. I remember hearing the clock strike soon after she returned to her room."

"And you haven't said anything about it to Orlow?"

Mrs. Wilson shook her head. "Usually I tell him everything, but this time I didn't. I guess it was because I didn't want him to know the kind of girl Sarah is. You don't really think, do you, Madge—?"

"I don't know what to think. But you better ask Orlow— very casually of course—what he was doing last night. Just ask him whether he won or lost at the poker party."

Mrs. Wilson did ask him after he came home to dinner that night, and he answered casually that he didn't play. He said that he had gone with Bert Van Vranken to look at a litter of Llewellyn pups and that by the time they had returned and played a couple of games of billiards it was too late for poker. And anyway, he added, he had not been feeling very lucky lately.

This explanation satisfied Mrs. Wilson, but Madge thought it very thin. She said the situation would bear watching. And the next time that Sarah entertained her gentleman friend both Madge and Mrs. Wilson were listening in the dark as the lovers came up the stairs. When, after an interval of an hour, Sarah went softly down to let her lover out, the two women posted themselves at a rear window from which they saw a man go skulking out across the garden. It was too dark to recognize his features. All they could make out was that the visitor was not a tall man. Orlow Wilson was not a tall man. They were still standing at the window looking out into the darkness of the garden when they heard the clock strike eleven.

Mrs. Wilson had looked at the clock as her husband's footstep sounded on the porch. It was eleven-thirty to the dot. She thought he looked guilty as he came in the door. She would have liked to accuse him on the spot, but Madge had advised against it. A man could lie out of any accusation, she said. The only way to bring him to time was to catch him red-handed. Mrs. Wilson had suggested that they might switch on the light at the head of the stairs the next time they heard the lovers coming up, but Madge had said that this would not prove anything. He would say they were hunting for burglars or had heard a noise up there or something of that sort. There must be no halfway measures, Madge said. If he was guilty he must be caught in the act in the presence of a witness.

"But how can we catch them in the act?" said Mrs. Wilson. "I always hear them turn the key in the door."

"Well—isn't there a closet in Sarah's room?"

There was, and the next time Sarah entertained her visitor Madge and Mrs. Wilson were hidden in the closet long before it was time for the guilty pair to come. At last, however, they heard Sarah coming up the stairs, and they could tell from the sound that somebody was with her. Then they heard the bedroom door softly close and the click of the key in the lock. They gave Sarah and her visitor plenty of time to undress and get into bed. Then they suddenly rushed out and switched on the light. For days Mrs. Wilson had been nerving herself up for this moment, and as her fingers closed on the switch she was muttering through clenched teeth, "I'll give you the surprise of your life—!"

But as the light flashed on she gasped and drew back. The man in the bed was not her husband! The startled face she beheld peering up out of the bedclothes was that of the night watchman of the wagon factory over on the

196

back street, a low fellow who was constantly becoming involved in new scandals before he could live down the old ones.

"You sure did," he mumbled. Then, when he had seen the expression on her face, he added, "But I guess I wasn't any more surprised than you were. You must have been looking for somebody else."

"I most certainly was—" The words escaped before she could stop them.

She put out her hand to steady herself, and he must have thought that she was going to switch off the lights, for he said:

"Just a minute—" He ran his hand under the pillow and drew out a great, ugly revolver. Mrs. Wilson shrank back. "Oh, you needn't be afraid," he said. "I'm not going to shoot. I was just looking for my watch. I thought as long as the lights were on I might as well see what time it is. I have to be back to punch the buttons at eleven."

The robbery had taken place between ten and eleven, and the constabulary were already in charge when the night watchman came puffing up shortly before eleven.

"What about the alibi?" the president of the wagon company asked my father the next day.

"It's absolutely watertight," my father replied. "He was at Mrs. Wilson's house calling on her maid—just as he said. Mrs. Wilson and Mrs. Horton both saw him there—and they both heard him say that he must soon be getting back to the factory so that he could push the eleven o'clock buttons."

17. Diversity of Practice

PECIALIZING is something that the country lawyer knows very little about. He may prefer a certain type of practice. He may become an authority on this or that, just as my father became an authority on probate practice and the law of real estate, but if he is going to make his living from the law he will have to be ready to handle almost anything that comes along. An average day in my father's office would run something like this.

When he reached the office in the morning he would find two farmers waiting outside the door. Perhaps they would want a lease of a farm on shares. To draw this, with the use of a printed blank form, would take only half an hour if they were agreed as to terms. If they were still bargaining he would seat them in the private office and go about his other work while they were threshing out the details. Meanwhile, another client would drop in to change his will, or to sign the surety bond of an administrator *de bonis non*. By the time farmers were through with their lease my father might have handled three or four other transactions. The next caller might want to know what his prospects were for collecting damages for personal injuries inflicted by an assailant who had mistaken him in the darkness for another man. As the battered claimant went out another farmer would come in and retain my father to handle a claim against the railroad company for killing a valuable cow which had strayed on the right of way through a hole where the fence had been burned from sparks of an engine ten days before. My father would jot down the particulars, and as he was on his way home to lunch a produce buyer would hand him a sheaf of papers and ask whether he was entitled to redress against the telegraph company for delivery of a telegram to the wrong party, the cause of the spoilage of a carload of potatoes on the siding.

After lunch a land owner would come in to inquire what his rights were to a driveway which he had been using for twenty-five years and which was his only means of access to a lot purchased from the man who had just boarded up the driveway and posted a No Trespassing sign. Then a grocer who had bought a new horse for his delivery wagon would come stamping in, full of fight because the animal, which had been warranted to be sound, had turned out to be blind in one eye.

And so it would go on all day long—one kind of thing after another. Questions arising under contracts, torts, decedents' estates, domestic relations, negotiable instruments, bailments, fraud and deceit, justifiable error, trespass, ejectment, injunction, mandamus, partition, foreclosure, defamation of character, false arrest, breach of promise to marry, desertion, corporations, partnership, gifts, guaranties, and covenants running with the land. The range of my father's practice covered the entire field of human emotions and human possessions, human behavior and human frailty.

Many of the questions that came to him could be settled with a word. Others required hours of research. Then there was the vast machinery of procedure by which the process of the law is put into application. The summons and complaint, the answer, the framing of issues, the complicated

199

series of notices by which a cause is brought on for trial; the location and interview of witnesses, the preparation and entry of the verdict or judgment of the court; getting the process of the court into the hands of the sheriff or constable to the end that the judgment may be enforced—all this comes within the task of the lawyer. Nothing is automatic. There is not a step from the inception of the suit to the payment of the judgment that does not require the personal work of a lawyer.

The diversity of legal knowledge with which the country lawyer must be equipped if he is to make even a decent living out of his practice is the most staggering blow that the young practitioner has to face. Fortunately for him he seldom realizes what he is up against. Everything is new to him when he first hangs out his shingle, and the questions come one at a time. If at this stage of his development prevision were vouchsafed to him, the average young lawyer in the country would split up his shingle for kindling wood and find a job as apprentice to a plumber or some other task which could be mastered without such an endless amount of headache.

With his vastly wider field, the city lawyer can pick and choose. If he likes corporation work he need take nothing but corporation work, and if he is good at it or has sound enough connections there will always be plenty for him to do. The country lawyer, on the other hand, must take every kind of case that comes along—or go over the hill to the poorhouse.

By the time that I had been admitted to the bar I already had an inkling, from a study of the entries in my father's old law registers, of the diversity of work that lay ahead, but along with this was the comfort of having my father's files and precedents to guide me. I did get a vast amount of help from these old files and precedents, but I was not long in learning that no two cases are ever exactly alike. Once, however, when a small shoe dealer who had overbought for the fall and was unable to move his stock because of unseasonably fine weather, came to me to make an assignment for the benefit of creditors, I had a dim recollection that he had done the same thing some years before while I was away in school. When I went back into the files I found that my father had seen this same man through four similar assignments in his forty years of merchandising. Here were precedents aplenty. All I had to do was change the names. I even used as assignee a man who had served in the same capacity twice before.

All the business establishments in town were small, and, with a few exceptions, they frequently changed hands. As soon as one businessman had made a failure in business another stepped into his shoes, often opening the identical kind of business in which his predecessor had failed.

There was a nice location for a grocery next to Jim Hoyt's bank. It was a large store, with a good cellar and entrances on both Main and Church Streets. T. J. Manley, one of the town's substantial citizens had made a competency there when there were fewer stores in town and was now living on the income on his accumulations. A series of unsuccessful grocery ventures had followed in T. J.'s wake. Then one day Jim Hoyt, the banker, had come into my father's office with fat, pink-cheeked, three-hundred-pound Jimmie Lovejoy in tow. Jimmie had been a clerk for T. J. Manley and had sold the banker the idea that he knew the Manley formula for success. The banker said he was going to set Jimmie up in business and wanted articles of partnership drawn, with himself as the silent partner.

The details were soon arranged and the store opened with a flourish. It seemed to my father that it was doing a good business, but at the end of the year the banker withdrew his support, and once more the place was vacant. When my father asked Jim Hoyt what the trouble was the banker drew down the corners of his mouth.

"Jimmie's a good feller round a grocery store. Folks like him. Keeps things lookin' good. Tends to his books—but he's the eatin'est feller I ever see. Had that store a year, and in all that time I don't believe his jaws was ever still for five minutes. Always chewin' on somep'm—crackers, cheese, dried beef, candy, cookies—anything he could get his hands on. Wasn't partic'lar so long as it was somep'm he could eat. Any store that had him for a customer oughta get rich."

My father smiled. "You mean he ate himself out a job?"

The banker nodded. "If I'd give him time enough he'd of ate himself into bankruptcy. But we have to make one hand wash the other, you know—so I had to shut down on him."

Jimmie was not out of a job long. He went on the road selling groceries for one of the houses he used to buy from. Since he had to travel out of Syracuse he moved his family there to live, and whenever he came to town after this he used to stop at the Inn.

Old Tick looked glum the first time Jimmie registered there. "Ain't no money in a guest of that size," he muttered. "Eat you out of house and home, and then break every goddarned piece of furniture he sets down on." The innkeeper should have known what he was talking about, for he weighed only fifty pounds less than Jimmie.

It was while Jimmie was staying at the Inn that he saw the handbill which led him straight to a fortune. It was posted in the lobby.

PANCAKE SOCIAL
All You Can Eat—With
Plenty of Butter and Real Maple Syrup
ONLY 25¢
Monday Oct. 17   6 to 9 P.M.
Hook & Ladder Parlors
Auspices Ladies Relief Corps
EVERYBODY COME

202

Jimmie came into my father's office with the bill in his hand. "We want you to come over and be the judge. I'm gonna tackle Old Tick's record."

My father glanced at the bill. "How many can you eat, Jimmie?"

"Don't know. Never counted. But Old Tick et forty. That's the record—so far. I oughta be able to beat that."

"It sounds like a lot of pancakes to me," said my father.

Jimmie shook his head. "Just a starter."

"All right," said my father. "I'll act as judge. When does the contest begin?"

"As soon as the shebang opens—six o'clock. I don't want 'em to run out of syrup—or makin's neither."

Mrs. Ross Remsen, who was locally famous as a cook, presided at the pancake griddle. Her cakes were uniform in size, about four inches across, and beautifully browned. Jimmie coasted over the first forty without any trouble at all. After that he slowed down a little, though he was still able to keep up with Mrs. Remsen. By the time he had eaten fifty he began to talk more and eat less. Plates of pancakes which were now coming faster than he could eat them began to accumulate on the table. And presently the sight of so many uneaten pancakes got in its deadly work. He stalled along until he had reached sixty. Then he slowly laid down his knife and fork.

"I guess that will be about all," he said.

"Then you can't eat any more than sixty?" asked my father judicially.

"I couldn't eat another pancake if it had a ten-dollar bill pinned on the top of it." Jimmie licked his lips listlessly. "I've had enough."

So my father awarded him the record at sixty pancakes.

The story got into the papers, and the maker of a prepared pancake flour offered Jimmie a job in his sales promotion department. The company put his picture in all its

advertising, and Jimmie ate pancakes in the store windows of every state in the union. The campaign met with extraordinary success, and Jimmie was taken into the firm. When he died he was a vice-president and a very rich man. As soon as Jimmie became rich he began to reduce, and the last time he dropped in to see my father he was as proud of being under 250 pounds as he had formerly been of weighing over 300. Jimmie was always a great storyteller, and one of his best stories was how he had eaten himself out of a grocery store and into a fortune.

Even after Jimmie Lovejoy went out of the grocery business, somewhat under a cloud, the T. J. Manley tradition survived. Wiseacres were still nodding their heads and telling what a lot of money Manley had made there. It was no old-timer, however, who succeeded Jimmie. The next firm to try its luck was composed of two earnest young men who had clerked in other grocery stores and saved their money. When my father drew the articles of partnership for C. F.

Winrock and George Herman they told him that they would be able to open their doors without a dollar of debt.

My father heard no more about their finances until they had been in business for nearly three years, and then Jim Hoyt came to him and asked if there was any way he could get the $2,000 they owed him before they folded up. My father spoke to each partner privately and asked him to come to the office alone for a discussion of the situation.

Winrock was the first to come in. He was a man who stood up very straight and talked very fast. His eyes never seemed to come to rest at any one point but were always in motion. My father reminded him that when they had gone into business the firm was out of debt, and now at the end of three years they were owing the bank alone more than $2,000, with drafts arriving daily from various grocery houses which the bank was unwilling to pay without some adequate security.

Winrock nodded. "Yes, I know all about it. I guess it's the end."

"You mean you can't pay anything?"

"Not a nickel. We're broke."

My father looked puzzled. "But where did the money go? You boys are both hard workers. You both attend to business. You don't live extravagantly."

Winrock pursed his lips and said that he could explain if he wanted to; and after my father had led him on for a time, he did explain. For the first year they had both worked hard, he said. But at the end of the year they found that they had cleared less money than either of them had made as a clerk. Of course, they figured that it was the first year, and they thought they would do better in the future; but at the end of the second year they were no better off. The partners had cleared just about as much as they had paid their clerk— and still they had done a good business, just about as much as two men could conveniently handle with the aid of one clerk. They had both taken their family groceries out of stock at cost, but there had been a big turnover—enough, Winrock thought, to have ensured each partner a very decent return.

According to Winrock's reasoning there was only one answer—he was being robbed by his partner. Winrock had thought about it half the night after they had struck their balance. He couldn't see it any other way. Of course, he did not want a scandal about it. He did not want any trouble. All he wanted was what was rightly his; and he made up his mind that night that he was going to take it when and where he could most conveniently get it. He did not consider that it would be stealing, for he would be taking only what rightfully belonged to him.

This was told to my father in the strictest confidence. Winrock said he had had no intention of preferring charges against his partner because he felt that he had in a way nullified the harm that his partner had tried to do him.

Later in the day George Herman came to see my father. He did not stand up so straight as Winrock. His shoulders usually sagged except when he was playing his cornet in the band. Nor was he as outspoken as Winrock. It was some little time before my father could get him to admit that he had any idea where the money had gone, and then Herman felt out the situation by remarking that his wife had been suspicious for some time that Winrock knew more about that than he was willing to admit. By a little questioning my father found that her suspicions had been aroused at the end of the second year. Herman said that he had been a little suspicious himself. And finally he admitted that he could see only one way to come out whole when his own partner was robbing him. Of course he couldn't prove anything, but he came to the conclusion that the best thing for him to do was to look out for himself.

So the third year found the business in the anomalous position in which each partner was robbing the other at every opportunity. The cash receipts fell off appallingly. The only time that there was any amount of cash in the drawer was when the clerk alone was left in charge. Both partners soon became aware of the shortage of cash, though neither dared to mention the fact, since each suspected his own defalcations to be the cause of the shortage. Drafts began to arrive at the bank more and more frequently, and Jim Hoyt would come charging into the store, waving the colored slips of paper in their faces.

For a while the partners were able to argue him into honoring the drafts, but after he had shut down on their credit the wholesale houses would sell them nothing except C.O.D. The business did not last long after that. The banker took the fixtures and what was left of the stock and began to look around for a bright young man to put in this exceptional location where T. J. Manley had made a fortune.

My father respected the confidence in which the inside story of this firm had come to him. He never told the banker the real facts behind the failure. Indeed, he never told either partner what the other had confessed to him. Each went to the end of his days thinking that by his own shrewdness he had kept the other from making a dupe of him.

Jim Hoyt did not always fare so badly as in this case. His usual method was to say a very positive "no" when asked to honor an overdraft, though he very often changed his mind before closing time. However, he did not hesitate to use strong-arm methods if the occasion seemed to require bull-dozing, though he was never quite as ruthless as in the case of Ellen Caldwell.

My father had heard rumors of an affair between the two but had paid little attention to the talk. Ellen was a rather colorless individual in her middle thirties, a good enough dressmaker, he imagined, though hardly seductive in type. The town had thought of her as just another old maid dressmaker who did not have what it took to win herself a husband. That would pretty well have described my father's opinion of her when, one morning, Lon Judson came into his office and motioned with his head toward my father's private room. My father followed Lon inside and closed the door.

"Well, Lon," he said, "what's on your mind? You look agitated."

"I am agitated. Good and damned agitated. I want to know if it ain't blackmail or somep'm for a creditor to insist that a man's wife has gotta have her sewin' done by a certain dressmaker—or he'll demand payment."

"Is the claim due?"

"Well, yes—maybe it is. Past due, you might say, but he's been takin' interest on it every ninety days."

"And you mean to imply that an extension of time will not be granted unless the wife will patronize a certain seamstress?"

"That's about the size of it," said Lon.

My father shook his head. "I don't see anything criminal about it."

"But you'll admit that it's damn peculiar. You gotta admit that. Old Jim called me in as I was passin' the bank this morning, and he says, 'Lon,' he says, 'where does your wife get her dressmakin' done?'

" 'Don't get no dressmakin' done,' I says. 'Can't afford it.'

" 'That so?' he says. 'She could up to a week or so ago.'

" 'That's *her* business,' I says.

" 'Uh-huh,' he says. 'Well, bankin's mine, and I'll be obliged if you'll let me have the money on them notes.'

" 'What!' I says. 'You want me to pay 'em now—with the coal business the way it is?'

208

" 'One hand has got to wash the other,' he says.

" 'But money's scarce,' I told him.

" 'You're right it's scarce,' he says, 'and if you're in such bad shape your wife can't even afford to have a little sewin' done—I guess we better be lookin' out for what's comin' to me,' he says.

"Of course I could see what he was drivin' at all right. You've heard all this slang that's goin' around about Jim and Ellen bein' ketched in the act by Jim's wife? And I'll admit that my wife did take some sewin' away from Ellen. I grant you that. But she tells me all the ladies in the missionary society agreed not to give Ellen no more of their sewin' to do, and my wife's a vice-president, you know."

"But how does the missionary society happen to be involved in a question of public morals?" asked my father. "I thought they were interested primarily in getting clothes on to the heathen."

"Well, don't you see, Jim's wife is the president—and the missionary society was sorta instrumental in her ketchin' Jim in the act, you might say. She had Ellen to her house doin' some sewin'. They was usin' an upstairs bedroom for a sewin' room. Well, she come away and left Ellen there to do some work while she was to the missionary meetin', and along come the feller from Jim's farm with a crock of butter and some chickens for Sunday dinner, and Ellen didn't know what to do about 'em, so she told the feller to drive on to the bank and ask Jim. Well, sir, when Jim heared that Ellen was there in the house alone he said he'd go down and tend to the things himself—and he did. He tended to somep'm else, too, up there in the sewin' room, and that's when Jim's wife come in and ketched 'em. Boy, was she mad! She ordered Ellen right out of the house and throwed her coat and hat after her."

"But how did Mrs. Hoyt happen to go home at just that time?"

209

"She just ran over for a minute to see how Ellen was gettin' along, and when she didn't come back a couple of her friends from the society went over to see what the trouble was—and she told them what had happened. Well, sir, they come back and told the society and by nightfall the story was all over town. Now Mrs. Hoyt thinks the affair had been goin' on for some time, but she ain't sure just when it started."

"And you think the affair is still going on?"

Lon exploded. "Do I *think!* After what he said to me this morning?"

"Can you raise the money anywhere else?" asked my father.

Lon slowly shook his head. "Not a chance."

"Then," said my father, "you'd better advise your wife to forget her scruples and let Ellen finish that dress."

One by one the ladies of the missionary society went back to Ellen Caldwell for their dressmaking. At first they went as inconspicuously as possible—but they went. What they may have said to their respective husbands about it is neither here nor there; for the husbands only grunted and said it couldn't be helped. But the members of the missionary society were not the only ones. Every man in town who expected to get any accommodation at the bank began to send his women folks to Ellen. Jim Hoyt actually bore down on only two persons, Lon Judson and Frank Hulse, whose account was several hundred dollars overdrawn at the time. But the story got around, and it was just as effective as if Jim had taken each prospective borrower into his private office for a little talk. And because the women had to go they saved their pride by pretending that they preferred to go, that there was no other dressmaker in town who could compare with Ellen Caldwell.

It was not long before Ellen had so much business that she found it necessary to hire a helper. By the end of the year she had three assistants. Ellen never went out to work any more; all the work had to be brought to her. She kept very much to herself and saved her money. My father heard plenty of ugly talk when Jim's bank failed and the books showed that, though she usually had a generous balance, there was practically no money in her checking account when the bank closed its doors.

Not long after the collapse of the bank Ellen came to my father to have some papers drawn. She had sold her dress-making business to two women from out of town and was moving to California. Jim Hoyt's enemies started the rumor that he was planning to join her there after the bank failure had blown over; but Jim's breakdown and sudden death put an end to that story. Ellen made quite a fortune in Southern California real estate, which was then just beginning to attract capital from the East. She died intestate, and all her property went to her brother Egbert. That is, it would have gone to Egbert except for the fact that he was deeply religious and regarded it as tainted money. My father, who was handling Ellen's estate, could never persuade him to touch a dollar of it.

Egbert did not smoke or drink. He did not even eat peanuts or chew gum, both of which he regarded as wasteful and therefore sinful. He called himself a man of humility and peace. His one extravagance was praying in public. He could, as a matter of fact, make a very good prayer. A wealth of ecclesiastical words seemed always on the tip of his tongue, and he always seemed a little put out with the Lord for being so lenient with sinners. Egbert's chief trouble was that once he had started to pray he had great difficulty in stopping.

How well I remember those red-letter Sundays when Egbert would rise in his seat to take heated exception to some statement of the minister and defiantly hold the floor until the congregation took matters in their own hands by "singing Egbert down."

When Ellen's estate came up for settlement Egbert refused to waive citation. In fact, he returned the papers my father sent him, with a blistering letter to the effect that it was a sin even to settle the estate of so wicked a woman. The process servers regarded Egbert as slightly insane and begged to be excused from serving papers on him; they were afraid he might go berserk and kill somebody. So my father put a citation in the hands of his secretary one day with instructions to hand it to Egbert when my father gave her the sign. Egbert used to pass the office daily, and when my father saw him coming along the street he stepped to the door and called to him. As soon as Egbert was inside the office my father started an argument by stating that an inanimate object was incapable of being infected with sin or taint by a living person, no matter how wicked that person might have been. When he had Egbert well warmed up my father turned to his secretary and told her to hand Mr. Caldwell the paper she had on her desk. She held it out, and Egbert took it in his hand.

"See anything tainted about that?" demanded my father.

"Taint is something that only the eyes of God can see," said Egbert. He examined the paper, and when he saw what it was he dropped it like a hot coal. But by that time the service was complete, so my father did not detain him.

Egbert's children—and he had had several big strapping boys—belonged to a more tolerant generation. They made no claims of being men of humility and peace. If they prayed at all they did it in the strictest privacy. They smoked when they felt like it, and they never hesitated to take a drink. After Egbert's death they quite willingly accepted the money left by their Aunt Ellen, and not only did they spend it in going to sinful horse races and prize fights but they used a portion of it to pay for a fairly handsome memorial window to their father which they presented to the church that he had attended with such militant devotion during his lifetime.

212

18. The Law Loses Some of Its Dignity

FROM his earliest youth my father had been inculcated with great respect for the dignity of the law. Two of his uncles were jurists, and he thought of the profession in terms of beaver hats, skirted coats, and serious faces hidden behind ambuscades of beard. His first move after his admission to the bar was to buy himself a beaver hat. His next was to start a beard.

Taken by itself, either of these acts might have been trifling and unimportant; but, as it happened, both turned out to be significant, for they were, in a way, prophetic. Never again did my father so far neglect his dignity as to face the world beardless; and many, many years were to elapse before he would be seen in public in any form of headgear less pretentious than a beaver hat. Time and a peculiar combination of circumstances finally induced him to adopt a soft felt hat, but his attitude about wearing a beard remained impregnable for a lifetime.

The beard seems to have reached the crest of its popularity in this country during the Civil War. At the end of the war nearly every officer of importance on either side of the conflict had a full beard. Even President Lincoln had fallen into line. There were a few exceptions if we are to believe Mr. Currier and Mr. Ives, but beards were the rule. During the postwar years beards as well as business went through a period of reconstruction. My father's beard ebbed and flowed with the tides of fashion. At one time he wore his mustache waxed and curved like a Texas Longhorn. At another he had a bushy pair of "mutton chops." Perhaps the most extreme of his facial decorations was a pair of long, lacy Dundreary whiskers which came to his shoulders. How he kept these out of his food at the table and from hanging down his back on a windy day is still a mystery. But beards were imperative at the time, and a man would put up with a great deal to have a proper one.

A picture taken in the nineties shows him with a full beard in the General Grant tradition, and from that time on no razor steel ever again touched any part of his face. There was a short period when he parted his beard in the middle to keep company with Governor Hughes, but he soon tired of this and began to trim his facial coverage in the manner accredited to Sir Anthony Vandyke. With slight variations of length and taper he wore it this way the rest of his life.

At the time when my father began his practice the tall hat was still the accepted badge of quality. It was, however, no longer made of beaver, for these industrious animals were already on the way to extinction. Silk and felt were taking the place of fur, though the shape of the gentleman's headgear continued to follow the time-honored lines that had been in vogue for centuries among the English gentility. But an age of informality was in the making, and as time went on the tall hat began to lose some of its popularity.

The tall hat was a troublesome article to wear, and the ordinary citizen must have been glad to be done with it. The professional man, however, to whom dignity was a valuable asset, did not yield to the trend quite so easily as his nonprofessional brother. The tall hat was as much a part of the doctor's stock in trade as his little black bag filled with strange-smelling phials. It was as inseparable from the lawyer as his "green bag" or his brief case of today. And it was as indispensable to the cleric's calling as his vestments or his shiny black suit. The town bankers, too, clung to their tall hats long after the nonprofessional gentry had let theirs fall into disrepair and had replaced them with soft hats and derbies.

My father had been in practice for twenty years before he was seen in public in an informal hat. He would have surrendered to the tendency of the times much sooner had it not been for my mother. Progressive as she was about many things, she was a bit of a Hard-shell on the question of wearing a tall hat. She still thought it one of the niceties of life, one of the marks of distinction that set the professional man apart from those in the ordinary walks of life. Probably nobody in town so thoroughly endorsed her views as Art Robbins.

Art Robbins was a horse breeder. That is, he would, for a consideration, provide the father for a colt. His stallion, Clydesdale Boy, was standing at stud that summer in the barns at Woodpecker Inn. Every day Art Robbins would drive the magnificent fellow up and down the streets for exercise. His neck arched, his great hairy legs churning, his huge hoofs pounding the roadway, Clydesdale Boy went up and down the streets several times a day. Sometimes he would rear slowly on his hind legs, his eyes rolling, his forefeet pawing the air. But that usually occurred when he wanted to impress some passing mare.

"Down, boy! Down!" Art Robbins would say to him. "You're makin' a holy show of yourself."

"He's a regular circus horse," people used to say to Art Robbins, and that is probably what put the idea in Art Robbins' head; for one day he came over to my father's office and asked if he could have one of my father's old stovepipe hats. My father gave him several—and that afternoon when Clydesdale Boy went up and down the street his driver, in a tall though battered silk hat, felt as impressive as a ringmaster.

People thought at first that it was just a caper of Art's; that he would wear the hat for a day or two and then, after the joke had worn off a bit, toss it aside and forget it. But it did not work out that way. Whenever Clydesdale Boy went up and down the street, his neck arched, his great hairy legs churning, his huge hoofs pounding the roadway, Art Robbins would be seen in the sulky behind him wearing a stovepipe hat.

The joke grew stale. The Lincoln hat wore out, and a Benjamin Harrison hat took its place. What had been a grotesquerie became a commonplace. Everywhere you went you would see the great breeding stallion driven by the man in a silk hat. If you were walking along the street you would hear the clatter of hoofs—and there they were. My father's supply of old hats ran out, and Art began to get hats from other sources. It was mostly the doctors and the bankers who supplied him, for the clerics themselves wore their hats down to the last thread. There is no monotony so complete and so boring as that of an oft-repeated joke.

"There goes that Robbins man again," my mother would say irritably as Clydesdale Boy went prancing past the house. "I almost wish I had never given him those old silk hats."

My father had heard her say it more than once. He was accordingly surprised one day when he came home to lunch to have my mother remark that she had another hat for Art Robbins.

"What one is it?" asked my father.

"The one you've been wearing."

"But what's the matter with that hat? I bought it only a little while ago."

216

My mother smiled uncomfortably. "Well, to tell you the truth, my dear, that hat had an accident this morning."

"What kind of an accident?"

"Annie set it on that chair in the corner while she was dusting the hatrack—and somebody sat down on it."

"What a place to put a tall hat!"

"Yes, it is a dark corner. Nobody could be blamed for not seeing it there."

"I suppose that means I'll have to get another one."

My mother nodded. "Yes, you'll have to get a new hat—that's something I want to talk to you about."

"But what is there to be said? I'll just drop Whillock a line and ask him to send me another. He's got my size, and he'll know what to send."

My mother looked thoughtful. "I wonder if he will know what to send. I've been thinking about it all morning. Don't you think it's about time for you to make a change?"

"A change?" My father gave her a puzzled look.

"Why—I think—I think I must be tired of seeing you in a tall hat."

This had long been a matter of mild dissent between them, and now to have her come suddenly around to his way of thinking struck my father as a little strange, though he thought it discreet not to say so.

"What would you suggest?" he asked.

"Had you ever thought of wearing a flat-top derby like the one Judge Foote had on the last time we saw him?"

My father cocked an eye at her. "For a formal hat?"

She was careful not to force the point. "Don't you think it would be suitable?"

"Um-m-m—might be. I'm going up Saturday for the Special Term. I'll drop into Whillock's and try on a few."

"Well, don't let him sell you another tall hat—at least not for the present."

My father did not press her for reasons; he was too skilled an examiner to keep on asking questions after getting the right answer. He wore the new flat-top derby to church on Sunday. The following week Dr. Richards was there in one very much like it. When my father asked him about it the doctor smiled and said it was his wife's idea. Soon there was not a tall hat to be seen at church on Sunday morning—which meant to my father that other wives had had the same idea, whatever it was. Then one day he happened to be on the street as Art Robbins, with a battered stovepipe cocked over one ear, drove past with Clydesdale Boy—and

218

suddenly he knew the answer, which he explained to me in these words:

"No woman wants people to be reminded of a breeding stallion every time they see her husband with a tall hat on."

My father never forgot the critical way in which the old innkeeper had squinted at the new flat-top derby the first time he saw it.

"It's intentional, is it?" Old Tick had asked. "You didn't just fergit yourself and come away without your stovepipe by mistake?"

Nobody could remember having seen Old Tick with any kind of hat on. And now nobody ever would, for Old Tick was dead.

My father smiled reminiscently as he recalled the old fellow's oft-repeated quip that he weighed 256 pounds in his stocking feet. This would have been easy to prove or disprove had there been a set of scales in the hotel, since Old Tick had never been known to wear a pair of shoes. He shuffled around in dingy carpet slippers. Cobb, the porter, said that this was so that he could spy on people, though this was probably not true; for, like most extremely fat men, Old Tick had trouble with his feet.

And never, in all the years he had lived in town, could anybody remember having seen him with a coat on. He always went about in his shirt sleeves. His pants and vest were invariably of dark blue, and all his clothes looked as if they had come from the same bolt—which for many years they did. Johnny Watson, the tailor, had Old Tick's measure, and all he had to do when a new suit was needed was to let out the waistline of his pattern an inch or two and snip enough from the bolt of blue broadcloth for pants and vest. Old Tick never ordered a new coat. When he died no coat could be found to fit him, and he was buried as he had lived —in his shirt sleeves.

Old Tick came to town from what he used to call "back East," meaning a little town in the Mohawk Valley probably not more than a hundred miles away. He had arrived several years before my father and had taken over the management of the Inn. And there he continued as proprietor for nearly four decades before he was carried out in a made-to-measure casket with extra heavy handles.

During all the years that Old Tick was running the Inn my father had never known him to go any farther out of the house than the front veranda. There, on a fine day in summer, he might have been seen, leaning over the rail, gossiping with passers-by, or dozing in his chair, which was extra stout and extra wide. Old Tick was not a good hotel clerk, though it must be admitted that he looked the part of innkeeper to perfection. He was too crochety and too inquisitive to be a good clerk. No couple who came to register at his hotel could get past him without a wedding ring on the proper finger of the woman's left hand or the production of their "marriage lines." He had what amounted almost to an obsession that every couple who came to his hotel had come for immoral purposes. He presumed them to be guilty until they could prove themselves innocent. And nearly always the question would be discussed at the top of Old Tick's high, squeaky voice before a lobby well filled with hangers-on.

Next to immorality he loathed illegibility of handwriting. "Why the hell don't you l'arn to write your name so's a body can read it?" was perhaps his most frequent comment after a prospective guest had signed the register. "Anyone would think you was tryin' to keep folks from findin' out who you really be."

But for all his cantankerous ways Old Tick became a famous figure in the western part of the state, and guests were sent to him by Powers in Rochester and Yates in Syracuse. This may have been because of Mrs. Tickner's justly celebrated meals or possibly because of the very high quality of the liquor served at the bar. Certainly it was not because of any marked affability on the part of the proprietor.

My father always admired Old Tick for his punctuality. There was never any deviation about the hours at which the dining room was open to the public. No matter if there was a complete breakdown in the kitchen—when the appointed time arrived for a meal to be served the gong was sure to sound, and as its crashing echoes died away the doors of the dining room would swing open. The old landlord was equally punctual about closing the dining room.

"One hour is time enough for any man to get a full meal of victuals," he used to say. "I can eat all I can hold in considerable less than that. Could prob'ly do it in under forty minutes if I had a mind to. And I ain't gonna have Idy standin' over that hot stove more'n a hour at a time for no man's money. No sir, I ain't, by—" Old Tick was famous for his colorful flights of profanity.

He did yield a point, however, on Sunday mornings, for the dining room doors were open on the Lord's Day until eight-thirty.

"You needn't think piety's got nuthin' to do with it, though," he used to say. "Some folks has a pretty good time on Saturday nights, and they're apt to wake up on Sunday feelin' a little sluggish. When I sell a man a headache I want to give him plenty of time to enjoy it."

In spite of Old Tick's punctuality it was well known that Mrs. Tickner was not so exacting. She was a motherly soul who could never refuse food to anyone who came tapping at the kitchen door, no matter what the hour. She even had a way of keeping a jar of doughnuts and one of sugar cookies on the kitchen table at night for the folks who couldn't sleep "without a little somep'm on their stomach."

Every morning, as soon as the papers had been brought over from the six-fifty-seven train, Old Tick used to perch

221

behind his desk and read aloud for the benefit of himself and any sitters who might be around that early exciting bits from the morning paper. When talking, Old Tick was likely to speak rapidly and run his words together; but when he read he went slowly, pronouncing—or as often mispronouncing—every syllable of each word with meticulous care. Suddenly he would stop, raise his spectacles, and consult his large silver timepiece. "Just a minute," he would mutter. "Gotta close them goddam doors." Newspaper in hand, he would shuffle out and close them. Then he would shuffle back and take up where he had left off—even if it was in the middle of a word.

Summer and winter, there was always the pleasant smell of stale beer around the place. It seemed to float through the halls, to hang in the faded wallpaper, and to lie in the squares of black-and-white stone of which the office floor was made. This floor was at one time the epitome of elegance in the flooring of a public house. People came from the surrounding towns just to see it. But with the passing of time the black squares had worn away much faster than the white, leaving the floor in a state of baffling unevenness, which, beyond a doubt, accounted for the rolling gait of many of the patrons of the place who undertook to walk from the door of the barroom across the office and out onto the street, especially at night, when the light from the oil lamps was somewhat dim.

Always a wheezy breather, Old Tick became more and more wheezy with the passing of the years. Late at night, after the bar had been closed and the lights were out, his loud snoring could be plainly heard by persons passing in the street. As he grew older and fatter and flabbier and the wheezing in his pipes became more troublesome, he found it impossible to lie down without bringing on a coughing spell. So for the last few years of his life Old Tick slept upright in a bed which was provided with a small vertical

222

mattress along the headboard as well as the horizontal mattress on the stout springs.

"Put me down, Cobb," he gasped to the porter who was sitting with him one day. "I don't wanta die a-settin' up on my bottom."

But putting Old Tick down was no small matter, and Cobb had to run for help. He reached the bottom of the stairs just as my father came in the door, and together they hurried back to the sickroom, where they found the old man apparently breathing his last.

"Too late, Cobb—" he wheezed. "always too late—I shoulda sent somebody else—" His eyelids fluttered. His head dropped down on his fat breast. The wheezing gradually ceased.

"I'm afraid he's gone," said my father. "Still, I think you'd better go for the doctor."

"All right," said Cobb, "but mebbe we better straighten him out first."

Suddenly Old Tick's eyes popped open. "What time is it—?" he gasped.

"Close to noon," said Cobb.

"How close?"

"Two or three minutes."

"Well, what the hell y'hangin' round here for? Go downstairs and get that cymbal!"

"But the doc tole me to keep you quiet."

"He did, hey? Well, what the hell does he know about runnin' a hotel? Do as I tell you and fetch that cymbal damn quick! Mighty man—" His voice trailed off.

My father bent over him. "You can't be banging cymbals," he said. "You're a sick man."

"Think I'm gonna peg out, do you? Well, mebbe I am— but that can wait. I want the cymbal."

Cobb hurried down and brought it. "Here it is," he said.

223

"Now hold the dang thing up where I can hit it—and gimme that stick."

Cobb put the stick in his hand, but Old Tick was weakening fast. He could hardly grasp it.

"What time—is it—now—?"

Cobb held up the big silver watch. "Thirty seconds to go."

"Tell me—when the second hand—is straight up—if I can last that long—"

"I'll tell you, all right."

The watch ticked on, but the landlord's hand was sagging. My father shook his head. The old fellow wasn't going to make it. The seconds dragged like hours, and at last the second hand stood straight up—but by this time the old man's hand lay inert on the bedclothes. "Too late," muttered Cobb, "but I said I'd call it, and I will—*Now*—!"

The hand on the bed flew upright. "Wham-m-m-m—m—m—m—!"

Crashing echoes reverberated through the empty corridors and died away up among the rafters of the loft. Old Tick was punctual to the last. He died on the stroke of twelve.

With great difficulty Cobb and my father lowered the huge body and laid it out flat on its back. There had been no rattling in the throat, but neither of them had thought of that, and Cobb was just closing the lids over the staring eyes when the throat muscles collapsed and the air came rushing out of the giant lungs with a whistling scream not unlike the sound of a blown-out tire. Cobb was startled nearly, if not entirely, out of his wits. Indeed, he never completely recovered from the shock of that last deflating breath of his late employer. People used to say that so long as Cobb lived he never failed to go white at the sound of a blowout.

Mrs. Tickner had died a year or so before her husband, and with his passing the Inn entered upon a period of transient management. It changed hands quite regularly, though it never again was a commercial success until the coming of the automobile had brought a paved highway past the door and an obsequious foreigner began to advertise chicken and spaghetti dinners at all hours of the day and night.

Cobb told my father confidentially some years after Old Tick's death that in the stillness of the night the shuffling of the old man's slippered feet could still be heard on occasion. He said that once when a gay party was making merry in the dining room at an hour when all respectable persons ought to have been asleep in their beds—the doors were suddenly slammed shut by a fat old man in his shirt sleeves. At least that is what one of the diners told him, though the others had insisted that it must have been the wind.

19. Choosing His Clients

IN COUNTRY practice the young lawyer is likely to
take every case that comes along, for he feels that he
needs the experience and the publicity, to say nothing
of the money. The well-established lawyer, however, is
bound by no such necessity and feels free to pick and choose.
This he does according to his likes and dislikes, his ethics, his
preferences, his abilities, and a dozen other controlling
factors. Lawyers who have no taste for criminal practice
will avoid all causes involving a crime. Others will eschew
matrimonial cases, not because of any disapprobation of
divorce but because of the ill repute with which shady
divorce lawyers have branded the administration of the
domestic relations law.

During his early practice my father took nearly every
case that was offered, but as he became better established
he began to refuse the types of work that he did not like to
handle or the kind of client he did not care to represent.
Occasionally a scheming lawyer, in the hope that he may
be retained by the rich litigant, will refuse to take the case
of his poorer opponent. My father was never thrifty enough
for anything of that kind. I do not believe that he was ever
swayed by so practical a motive. If he disliked a man or
distrusted him, he would not take his business on any terms;

and on the other hand, if a litigant happened to be his friend or had ever done him a favor, my father would handle his case for him even if he knew that he would never receive a penny for the most arduous services.

Nothing so enraged my father as seeing the law used as an instrument of injustice, and he would accept the case of the veriest old vagabond against the mightiest if he thought there was any chance to uncover what he called "facial piety" on the part of the higher ups. He took particular delight in unmasking anything that had even a faint aroma of persecution, an attitude which first and last must have cost him no small amount of business. The case of old John Bement will illustrate the point.

John Bement was a miller, such a miller perhaps as Geoffrey Chaucer may have had in mind when he penned *The Miller's Tale*. John was bent and slow-footed. He was probably ruptured in three or four places, though he could still shoulder a sack of middlings, or handle a barrel of flour with the best. Like every miller, John wore the traditional white hat. His long beard was a pasty white, and his clothes were so caked with the dust of pulverized grain that they cracked open in places. But he was a good miller as millers go and as honest as his employer would allow him to be. If John had been content to be nothing but a miller he would never have been under suspicion at all. But he had what he thought was a gift—perhaps it was—and he meant to make use of it.

Early on Sunday morning he would be seen wandering around the woods and stream banks gathering roots, "yarbs," and simples in their seasons. From these he distilled juices and extracted essences which he compounded according to secret prescriptions of his own. The results were reputed to be good for this or that ailment. On his shelves there were luck draughts and love potions. Most of his concoctions were harmless, and some may even have had

227

medicinal virtue, though their curative value was not what created the demand for them. It was the mysterious something imparted by John himself that gave his remedies favor among the simple folk of the town. People used to say that he possessed the power of magic.

My father had heard rumors about the old fellow, of course, but he had never paid much attention to them until one of the local doctors came to him and complained that the old miller was practicing as a witch doctor. The doctor said that he had reported the case to the county medical society and the society had authorized him to engage my father to make an investigation, with the idea of a prosecution on behalf of the society if he could find anything to base it on.

The thought of a witch doctor in those days of enlightenment greatly appealed to my father, and he said he would look into the case. A day or two later he dropped into the mill, ostensibly to order some cracked wheat for his chickens. He was fortunate enough to find John alone and had little difficulty in getting the old fellow into a discussion of the native wild flowers—about which the alleged witch doctor was very well informed—and eventually led the way to the subject of herbs and their uses. He easily unearthed enough to have warranted an investigation that might have cost the county medical association from three to five hundred dollars in counsel fees and possibly have extracted a stiff fine from the old witch doctor or perhaps even a sojourn in jail.

But that was not my father's way. He found John to be a rather heart-warming old fellow, and instead of making an example of him and earning a good fee for himself, he explained to the witch doctor just what he should and should not do to keep within the law.

"Remember, now," my father said as he was leaving, "you can sell your roots and herbs and your concoctions and love philters to anyone who wants to buy, but you must not diagnose, and you must not prescribe."

Old John nodded. "I understand," he said, "and I'll be careful to do just as you say—but it will be all right for me to treat my specialties, won't it?"

"What are your specialties?"

"Warts, wens, corns, and bunions."

My father smiled. "I guess that will be all right. So you're a specialist on warts?"

"Yes, sir! I certainly can handle 'em."

"What do you think of this one?" My father raised his hand and displayed a growth near the base of his thumb.

The old miller peered at it through flour-laden eyebrows. "Toad wart. Looks like an old-timer."

"Been there for twenty years."

"I'll guarantee to cure that for two bits."

"What's your treatment?"

"Ain't no treatment—I just blow 'em off."

"All right, go ahead." My father handed him a quarter.

The witch doctor steadied the hand and blew a mighty blast of breath over it.

For a minute or two my father stood and watched the wart. Then he said, "Well, it's still there."

"Sure it is. I don't claim to do no miracles."

"How long will it take?" asked my father.

"Oh—ten days or two weeks. You just go 'way and forget all about it, and the fust thing you know it'll be gone."

My father did go away, and he did forget all about it until a fortnight later when the doctor came up to him on the street and asked him if he had done anything about the old witch doctor.

"I certainly have," said my father. "I've been all over it with him, and I've talked with a number of his alleged patients. He sells an occasional bunch of herbs, but he does not diagnose and does not prescribe. He deals mostly with warts, wens, corns, bunions, love potions, and luck charms. I guess none of those interferes with your practice, does it?"

The doctor snorted indignantly. "I should say not!"

"By the way, I consulted him when I was there." My father began to look over his hands in search of his wart.

"Consulted him?"

"Yes, about my wart. He guaranteed to cure it in from ten to fourteen days."

"And accepted a fee?" asked the doctor eagerly.

"He certainly did."

"Splendid!" cried the doctor. "Now we've got the old rascal on a charge of fraud! He had no right to guarantee a cure."

"I'm afraid not." My father shook his head.

"Of course we've got him," the doctor insisted. "Why not?"

My father held out his hands for the doctor's inspection. "Because the wart is gone. You can look for yourself."

The doctor deflated and walked indignantly away—and that was the last ever heard about prosecuting old John Bement as a witch doctor. John never knew what a narrow escape he had had, but he did know that my father was interested in wild flowers, and every week or two John would bring him a rare specimen that he had found on one of his Sunday morning rambles.

Another old vagabond came into my father's life through his affection for a little gray mare my father bought for a carriage horse. That is, she was gray when we got her, though she turned to a snowy white within the next year or two. Her name was Daisy, and the name of her gentleman admirer was Sim Cranford.

Sim was a lump of an old man left over from the days of Victor Hugo. He was bent and grizzled. His huge head was set squarely on the front of his chest, and his misshapen hands hung sprawling almost to his knees. A bulbous nose

230

spread out like an awning above an impenetrable jungle of beard. His eyes were at the same time bleary and disdainful, and one had a drooping lid. Sim may have had a gay youth, but he was well along in years before he came to town, and I don't know of anyone who ever saw him smile. His huge, protruding jaw and pendulous lower lip were never made for mirth, and though Sim was guilty of an occasional witticism it was always of the kind that bites.

It was about two weeks after we bought Daisy that my father chanced to meet Charley Scott, the man from whom he had bought her. Charley asked how my father liked the horse, and my father said she was very satisfactory.

"Has old Sim shown up yet?" asked Charley.

"Who is Sim?"

"Sim Cranford—he sorta goes with the horse."

My father shook his head. "Haven't seen anything of him yet."

Charley grinned knowingly. "Well, you will. He got to my house about three days after the horse did. Found him in the barn one morning cleaning her off.

" 'What you doing here?' I says to him.

" 'Can't you see?' he says.

" 'Why, yes, but that don't seem to help much.'

" 'Don't, hey?' he says, and went right on cleaning her.

"I'd been in town the night before and had a few drinks. I remembered seeing old Sim somewhere, but I still didn't think I was tight enough to hire him and not know it. So I says to him, 'Who said an'thing to you about going to work here?'

" 'Nobody,' he says. 'Guess I can clean the mare if I want to, can't I? Don't look to me as if she's been cleaned since you got her.'

" 'Go ahead and clean her, if you get any fun out of it,' I says, 'because that's all the pay you'll ever get.'

231

"'Who said an'thing about pay?' he says. 'I've took care of this mare ever since she was dropped, and if I wanta put a little elbow grease on her coat I guess you ain't gonna care, be you?'

"'Suit yourself,' I says, 'so long as you understand they's no pay in it.'

"'Lookit the stain on her flank,' he says. 'Ain't you got no straw?'

"'She gets as much beddin' as the rest of 'em,' I says.

"'Oughta have three times as much,' he says. 'Where's the soap?'

"I let a yell outa me. 'Soap for a *horse!*' I says. I took a team and went out in the field to work. When I come in at noon he was hoeing in the garden. I told my wife to set a place for him at the table, and he stayed right there with us until I sold the horse."

"How long was that?" asked my father.

"Oh, coupla years. I used to buy a little tobacco for him every week, and I'd take him into town with me about twice a month. If I gave him a dollar he'd get drunk and be outa commission for a day or two, though no matter how bad he was he never failed to take care of Daisy. Well, I got so I'd give him about a quarter. That would buy him a few beers, and still he couldn't get drunk on it. Lived in the barn. And you never saw such a garden as we had when he was around. He was contented there as long as I had Daisy—but two days after I sold her he was gone. Ain't seen him since. I run across Howard Gerow one day—you know I bought Daisy from Howard. I asked him if he'd seen an'thing of Sim lately, and he said no, not since he sold the horse to me. Sim come to Howard with the horse, just as he did to me. Showed up when he bought her— disappeared when he sold her."

"Where did Howard get her?" asked my father.

232

"Got her from Dan Chase. Same thing there. Old Dan was a hard nut to crack. He ordered Sim off the place every day for about two weeks, and then he give up and let him stay. He was there when Dan died. The women folks would have been glad to have him stay, and he did stay until they sold Daisy, and then he left without a word."

"Where did Dan get Daisy?"

"From Clarence Jones. Sim was workin' for Clarence when Daisy was foaled—and the old feller's been with her ever since."

"Except the last two weeks," said my father.

"And I wouldn't be too damn sure about that last two weeks if I was you," said Charley with a laugh, "I don't believe the two of 'em was ever separated that long."

When my father came home that night he strolled out and looked around the garden. Then he inspected the interior of the barn carefully. After that he came into the house and called me into the library, where he was already detaining one of my brothers, who, with my aid, was supposed to take care of the place. I was suspicious the minute he began to tell us how well the garden looked. I don't think my brother was suspicious until my father began to compliment us on the appearance of the barn. We were taking this with what we thought was fitting modesty when he suddenly asked how we came to wash the carriage without being told. We stammered and said we thought it needed washing, but by this time we must have looked like a pair of condemned felons.

"There's something I want to ask you," my father said slowly. "Did you boys do all this work yourselves?"

My brother looked helplessly at me. He knew that I didn't think him a very accomplished liar, and this was his way of telling me that I'd have to carry on.

"Wh-what do you mean by that?" I asked.

"Did you do the work alone—or has somebody been helping you?"

I was swallowing hard. "Well, I—I guess we did have a little help."

"Sim Cranford?"

We nodded.

"Where have you kept him?"

"In the barn. He sleeps up in the hay."

"What do you pay him?"

"Nothing—just buy him a plug of tobacco once in a while."

"But what does he eat?"

"Oh, we take a few leftovers out to him."

"Then Ann knows about it?"

We hastened to exonerate our friend, the cook. "It wasn't her fault. We made her promise not to tell."

"I've learned an awful lot from old Sim, Dad," said my brother. "He knows more about horses than anybody you ever saw. He knows just how a horse thinks."

"He's a good gardener, too," I put in.

My father shook his head. "He'll have to go. We can't keep him around here."

"Then you'll hafta sell Daisy," pleaded my brother. "Sim belongs with her."

"He'll have to go," said my father sternly.

"You'll hafta tell Sim," I said. "He'll never believe us."

"Well, he'll believe me."

My father went stalking out to the barn. He was not stalking when he came back half an hour later. His own love of horses gave him a complete understanding of Sim's affection for Daisy. He did not need Sim. He much preferred to have us do the work—but he did not send Sim away. Instead he had a coachman's room finished off in a corner of the carriage barn. There was a stove to keep the place warm in winter, and there was a comfortable bed—though

I was never sure whether Sim slept in it or not. But in any event that is where he lived out his span. Daisy survived him. She was well along in the twenties when my father pensioned her for life and sent her out to a farm where there were green pastures, plenty of shade trees, and a brook of running water. Nor did Daisy's carcass go to the bone man when she died, to be ground up for fertilizer. She was decently buried, and her grave was marked with a stone.

IN MEMORY OF

DAISY

A HORSE THAT WAS KIND AND TRUE

AND OF

SIMEON CRANFORD

HER FAITHFUL FRIEND

20. Making a Will

I T WAS my father's idea that the real character of a man never comes so close to the surface as when he sits down to make his will. It was, he used to say, about the only time that the ordinary mortal tries to look at his family as from the grave; and usually it was the first time that a man thought of his property not as something to keep and protect but as something that must be given away.

The initial impulses of a man making a will are usually based on love and affection. If he must give his estate away he wants to give it to somebody he loves. After a little, however, he finds the thought of fairness tugging at his elbow, and he begins to consider what is right and just. There is no ethical or legal or actual reason why a testator should treat all his children equally. It is true that in the absence of a will the law treats with equality all those of like degree of relationship, but that is simply because the law has no way of knowing what the decedent's preference may have been.

Without a doubt this law has had a great deal to do with building in the mind of the man of property a belief or impression that every child has a right to be treated like every other child. And very probably the sonorous phraseology of the foxy old scrivener who used to draw the early wills did a great deal to confirm this belief or impression.

236

The words "share and share alike" may not add one jot or one tittle to the validity or meaning of a phrase ordering a bequest to be "divided among my children equally," but the phrase is nevertheless something that has rung in the ears of the man of property for centuries.

Persons who have liked to make an agreeable impression through life are likely to make an agreeable will, slighting nobody and overlooking nobody. They want people to think as well of them after they are gone as they did while they were walking the earth. The stingy man is inclined to give his property in little dabs here and there or to tie it up so that the recipients cannot control it and he can feel that he still has a grip on it. One parsimonious man my father used to tell of never could bring himself to the point of signing a will even after it was drawn, so painful was the mere idea of giving away his property.

Occasionally an old shellback would come along who wanted to carry a quarrel beyond the grave and cut off the offending son or daughter with six cents. And though it was my father's definite intention to let a testator dispose of his property according to his own inclinations, he would sometimes try to argue a man out of what appeared to be an unjust or spiteful act of disinheritance. "You can't change these things after you are dead and gone," he used to say, "and if, in another life, with a little clearer vision and a less prejudiced view, you find that you have made a mistake and are treating your own flesh and blood unjustly, you are not going to feel quite as well satisfied as you would if you could say, 'Well, at least I gave him the benefit of the doubt.'"

Sometimes his arguments prevailed, but just as often they didn't. He spent some time trying to induce Kate Vandenburg not to make what he considered a frivolous will, but Kate was adamant.

237

"I haven't got much," she said, "and I ain't got a relative in the world that I want to leave it to. And if I take a notion to leave it in such a way as to embarrass that son-of-a-gun—there ain't nobody can stop me. You've already told me it wouldn't be illegal, and if you won't write it the way I want it, there's plenty who will."

"Well, Kate," said my father, "after all, it's your money, and you can dispose of it any way you want to. But you came to me for advice and I'm going to give it to you."

He did at some length, and when he had finished Kate yawned.

"All right," she said. "Now go ahead and draw that will the way I told you to."

In a way Kate was a pariah. She lived alone in a little house on a back street. She had no occupation, no pension, no visible means of support. Kate lived well and always paid her bills. If she had begged for her bread and lived in penury she would probably have been considered perfectly respectable. But Kate was no beggar. Everybody in town knew what she was, though of course some of the men knew better than others.

Kate had come from a good family—that is, an old and rather large family that was pretty well scattered over the township. The younger generation used to make obscene jokes about Kate, and one of them, just for fun, named his little brindle bitch after her. That was a joke that everybody enjoyed, even Kate, for when she heard about it she snickered and said, "That's the first member of the *family* to be named after me." Everybody enjoyed that, too.

Most of the Vandenburgs were tall and good-looking, but Kate was short and chunky. She wore gold-rimmed spectacles and went around looking much more like somebody's grandmother than everybody's pal. She was thrifty and had money in the bank, and though she never went to church she never missed a horse race or a ball game.

238

The better element in the town had disapproved of Kate for years. From time to time they talked of running her out of town, but she did not seem to mind. Perhaps she did not even know of the talk. Or perhaps she realized that so long as they kept on talking they would never do anything about it. Then one of those periodic waves of reform swept over the town. The old guard were thrown out and a new administration installed, with Dan Richman at the head. As the new Village President, Dan proposed to clean up the town. He said that Kate must go.

"Go?" said Kate when she heard of it. "Where to?"

Anywhere, she was told. It did not really matter where so long as she got out of town.

Kate laughed. "I was here when Dan Richman was still diggin' cellars for a livin' and long before he outsmarted his partner and got control of the wheel works that's killin' off the trees and smokin' up all the houses in the neighborhood. He'd better not start anything he can't finish."

"Won't go, eh?" said Dan when he heard of this. "I'll show her. I gave her a chance to save her face and move quietly away. Now I won't show her any mercy. I'll have her declared a public nuisance. I'll get the signature of every resident of her neighborhood, and I'll *run* her out of town!"

Kate laughed when she heard of the threat. "You tell Dan to let me see them signatures when he gets 'em," was all that she said.

Dan was able to get only one signature in the entire block, and that was from a woman who was socially ambitious and anxious to ingratiate herself with the circle in which the Richmans moved. The others shook their heads. "Never saw nuthin' wrong," they said. That was all Dan could get out of them. They did not tell him that Kate had let it be known that all who signed the petition would have to appear in court in a smutty slander case later on. The reformer scratched his funny three-cornered head and kept trying. During the entire two years that he was president he kept on trying in one way or another to get rid of that darkened house on the little back street. But it was right there when Dan was finally beaten and a less fanatic faction came back into power again.

Kate made no comment about the election, and when somebody asked her what she thought of it she said she didn't pay much attention to such things. But when the new board of trustees came in nothing more was heard about running her out of town. She lived there unmolested for the rest of her life, which, after all, was not so very long. She was caught in the rain while driving home from the

240

races and came down with a heavy cold that developed into pneumonia, from which she died.

The Vandenburg family turned out handsomely. They filled the house with flowers—when they found that there was money in the bank to pay for such things—and took full charge of the funeral arrangements. For three nights the lights burned brightly in the little house all night long, and then Kate was buried in one of the family plots—quite naturally, the one in the old and dilapidated Pinewood Cemetery.

My father did not produce the will until after the funeral, and then he handed it to the town clerk who had been named as executor. From the will it appeared that Kate had left her entire estate—a matter of some $2,000—in trust for the comfort, care, benefit, and burial of her only namesake in the family, the little brindle bitch. And after the death of her aforementioned namesake, the residue of her estate, real and personal, with all accretions and accumulations, was given, devised, and bequeathed to one who had long been a valued friend, Dan Richman, who, while Village President, had treated her with kindness and consideration.

Of course, Dan indignantly declined the bequest. He said he had never spoken to the woman in his life and that under no circumstances did he care to become the residuary legatee of a dog. The orphan asylum named as alternate legatee had no such scruples.

There was something more than the revenge motive behind Kate Vandenburg's will. My father always thought that it was a final flash of defiance in the face of a disapproving world as well as an unquenchable desire to get a good laugh. Kate had always been known as a wit, and her sharp retorts to tradesmen who tried to bandy words with her were locally famous. She told my father that if she could get a good laugh at the expense of Dan Richman it would be worth the money, even if he should pocket his pride and accept the legacy, which Kate more than half expected him to do.

Another local humorist who tried to leave a legacy of mirth was Willum Pruyn, who had for many years been one of the town's leading victualers and costermongers. He was a prominent Mason, an Odd Fellow, a Pythian, a Knight of the Maccabees, and a member of every other lodge within reach. He was a popular raconteur and after-dinner speaker. In his younger days he had been famous for his practical jokes. It was he who planted a wax dummy in an abandoned well behind the barn of the Inn. Then late one night, after leaving a pool of beef blood on the sidewalk, with a clearly defined trail of drops leading to the well, Willum had aroused the town by a fusillade of pistol shots on the main street.

Citizens had leaped out of their beds and come running but had found nothing amiss until the next morning, when the early risers discovered the pool of blood and the trail of drops leading to the old well. The fire bell and Old Tick's cymbal had turned out the entire population, still uneasy from the shots of the night before. There was a gasp of horror when the grappling hooks brought up the body—but it was followed by a howl of laughter when the victim was recognized as a dummy purloined from I. Goldwasser's clothing store the night before.

This was Willum's answer to the present of a jar of beef blood from the butcher next door, who said in a spirit of japery that some young blood was needed around there.

Willum was in quite another mood, however, when he came to my father to have his will drawn. For once in his life he was serious. The death of an old crony had brought him face to face with reality, he said, and he thought he had better attend to property matters before the old gentleman with the scythe got around to him. He had no close relatives, and to the two distant cousins who were the objects of his bounty he left $5,000 apiece, these two legacies to constitute the first charge against his estate. Thereafter he went on and very generously left $2,000 to each of the lodges of which he was a member. He left $1,000 to the town and $1,000 to the village. Another thousand was to be divided between the two fire companies for new equipment. He left $1,000 to each of the churches and finally ended his benefactions with $500 each to the village band and the local baseball team. All the rest, residue, and remainder of his estate was to be used to erect a suitable memorial to himself, the nature and location of which were to be determined by the executor and the village board.

My father had always supposed that Willum was in comfortable circumstances, but he had never realized the extent of his property. He went ahead and prepared the will, which was executed and witnessed without any of the buffoonery that usually characterized Willum's doings. The buffoonery came after Willum's death, which occurred some two or three years later. The newspapers had given his public-spirited generosity a large spread, and the executor and the village board were already quarreling over the memorial when an appraisal of the estate disclosed a total amount that was not quite enough to pay in full the legacies to his two distant cousins. All the rest of it was just one of Willum's practical jokes.

It is not at all unusual for the contemplation of death to bring people to the point of making plans for their own obsequies. Very frequently testators give detailed instructions as to their funerals, specifying the kind and cost of the casket, the name of the undertaker, and often describing the monument and even the inscription to be cut on it. But it is not often that the one to be funeralized selects the bearers and even invites them to serve. That, however, is what happened in the case of Gra Richardson.

243

As a child I could always tell when a new baby was coming to our house; for a few days before it arrived Gra Richardson would move in on us. She did not come so much in the capacity of nurse as that of disciplinarian. She was a tall woman, bony and angular. Her hair and eyes were coal black, and she had a stern jaw and a sharp tongue. We children never talked back to her—we didn't dare. As a child I had little if any fondness for her, though later on I acquired a respect and eventually a real affection for the grim old puritan. In spite of her sharp tongue and her sardonic sense of humor, she was a fine woman—and one of the few that I ever obeyed unprotestingly.

As indestructible as the old lady seemed, time did finally make an impression on her, and at seventy-five she retired from active service. She no longer made a business of greeting the new arrivals and furnishing private policing for confinement cases but turned her talents to the upbringing of the children of a few selected clients. It was a strange household, with no two persons bearing the same surname, but it was a well-ordered house, even after the rheumatism bore down on Gra Richardson and she had to walk with a *T*-shaped cane on which she leaned quite heavily. During the last few years of her life Gra Richardson could not get around the house at all without her wheel chair. Then she used to post herself in the bow window of her little red house just across from the railroad station and watch people come and go. As a result of her observations from her window she knew more about other people's affairs than any able-bodied person in town, and though most of her items were based solely on conjecture, told in her racy idiom, they were well worth listening to.

Only a short time before her eighty-fifth birthday she saw me getting off the train one day and beckoned to me to come over. We bantered a while, as we usually did, and then suddenly she said, "I called you over here to ask you to do me a favor. Will you promise before I tell you what it is?"

I smiled. "Well, I suppose it's a little risky—but I'll take the chance."

"I want to know if you'll be a bearer at my funeral."

I was stunned for a moment, but I pulled myself together and finally managed to say, "When is it to be?"

"Don't know yet, but when you're my age it's likely to be 'most any time."

"I'll promise on one condition."

"What is it?"

"That if you live longer than I do you'll send lilies of the valley to my funeral."

"I'll agree to that," she said. Then she leaned over and looked out of the window and some twenty-seven years into the past. "I never thought when I saw you come into this world that I'd be sittin' here today askin' you to help carry me to my last restin' place. You were a red little devil, and you had black curly hair on your head, same as you have now. I recollect your ma was worried about you because you didn't squawk. You never was much of a squawker. I didn't think you'd turn out to be a lawyer—you were too quiet."

"Squawking is only a small part of a lawyer's business."

"Guess that's right. You made more mischief than any two or three young ones I ever saw. But that ain't why I'm askin' you to be one of my bearers. I got a reason and a good one. Did you go to Colonel Stevens' funeral?"

I nodded.

"Well, do you remember who the bearers were? Probably not. They were all old men—but maybe you do recollect how they staggered when they carried the casket down the church steps and out to the hearse? Come near fallin' down with it; and I made up my mind then and there that I wa'n't goin' to be carried to my grave by a lot of dodderin' old men my own age. I'll be laid out in this room right here, and that ain't goin' to be an easy door to get a casket out of—with the stairs and the bannister rail and all. There'll be you and George and Will, and I'm goin' to ask Rob Thompson the next time I see him. I ain't made up my mind about the rest, but you can be sure they'll be young and reliable." She stopped and caught her breath. "I can count on you, can I?"

"Give you my word—but I hope you won't be in any hurry about setting the date."

"Too busy to be bothered, I suppose." She flashed a smile, showing her large teeth, firm and yellow as those of a horse. "Well, there's only one thing I want to caution you about—don't step on the flower beds beside the walk when you're carryin' me out. It's hard to make things grow along that walk."

The young men she had selected were four years older when they carried her out of her little red house. We found, as she had predicted, that the door was a hard one to get a casket out of. So hard, indeed, that after struggling for a few moments we followed the undertaker's suggestion to go around through the dining room and out the side door. And it may be said for the young men that not one of them staggered or stumbled or stepped on a flower bed as they carried her out.

Sometimes the plans made in contemplation of death would occupy a person for many years. John Carruth, who always thought of himself as the thriftiest man in town—other people called him the stingiest—spent his entire life "accumulating an estate" to leave to his children, since his own father had left him penniless. His accumulations were never "property" for any of his family to enjoy during his lifetime but an "estate" that would come into being only after his decease.

246

John's family never had enough to eat or enough to wear. They took no recreation; that cost money. They got along without ice in the summer and with very little coal in the winter. His wife died in her thirties of pernicious anemia. The oldest boy developed tuberculosis and had to go to the Adirondacks. His sister went along to take care of him because housekeeping was cheaper than staying at a hotel or sanitorium. She caught the germ from her brother, and they both died. The other son came down with a peculiar softening of the bones ascribed by the doctors to malnutrition. And when, after his last child's decease, John came in to change his will he was very bitter.

"Here I work and slave all my life to accumulate an estate to leave to my children, and before I can leave it to 'em they all up and die on me."

"Yes, John," said my father. "There's only one way I know of to beat that kind of hard luck."

"Well, what is it?"

"You could have spent a little more of it for their benefit while they were still alive."

"Um-m-m—I see what you mean," said John. And then he sat down and made a will giving his entire estate to some relatives in Canada that he had never seen.

My father drew nine wills for one man. He was a quarrelsome little fellow who owned a very desirable farm of thirty acres. His eight children were all grown up and living away from home. When his wife died old Teddy asked one of the sons to live at home and work the place. It was the youngest son, Tim, who had been married only a short time. Tim agreed to come and make a home for his father if Teddy would leave the place to him. Teddy agreed. My father drew the will, but after a year or two Tim and his wife moved out; they couldn't get along with the old man. Then one day Teddy came in to change his will. He said his son,

Hank, was going to take the farm on the same terms, that he should have had Hank in the first place.

Hank lasted about a year, and then there was another new will. This time it was Elmer who was taking over. The next time it was Lizzie, his daughter, and her husband. And so on, straight through the family. Then Teddy got a housekeeper and tried working the farm for himself, and he made a will leaving the place to her.

When Teddy died, all these wills came piling into my father's office for the purpose of finding out which one really was his last will and testament. Some other papers were brought in, too, and from them my father learned that the property had never belonged to Teddy but had been taken in his wife's name.

So the children inherited the place, share and share alike, and then they had a lovely squabble about the best way to dispose of it.

21. Miscellaneous Matters

ONE of my father's serious purposes in life was to be methodical. He always did things just so. He had an orderly mind, and he tried to bring up his children to have orderly minds, though nature did not always cooperate with him on this point. He wanted the house to run like clockwork, and to quite an extent it did. He was as implacable as an army bugler about routing the family out in the morning and about having breakfast served whether anybody was at the table or not; but he was equally implacable about getting his children into bed.

Children under eight years of age were bundled off to bed immediately after supper. Children from eight to twelve were allowed to stay up until nine o'clock. Ten was the retiring hour for everybody over twelve except my father. He would sit up and work or read until all hours. At one time or another all of us used to read in bed on the sly, and when my sisters were old enough to have beaux there were some pretty wordy battles over the ten o'clock rule. My father used to say that ten o'clock was late enough for any young cub to sit around mooning. He insisted that two and a half hours of mooning was all anybody could be reasonably expected to stand—callers used to come at seven-thirty in those days.

Of course the young couple at our house did not have two and a half hours alone. The earlier part of their mooning was done under difficulties at best, for until nine o'clock there were sure to be eavesdroppers lingering behind curtains or under the furniture. One of the first things my sisters did after ushering in a caller was to search the room, and they seldom failed to uncover one or more of us. Since there were three sisters, the callers used to come in droves. There was a good deal of sitting and talking, but there was plenty of music and dancing, too. Singing around the piano was a favorite diversion. On moonlight nights in the winter the older children were allowed to go coasting on Frisbie's Hill, which was a fast half-mile run; or they would go skating on Howe's Pond—but in either case they had to be home by ten o'clock.

Instead of scaring the swains away, this ten o'clock rule attracted them. They thought they were getting very select company. On some of the evenings at home they would play table games, tiddlywinks or, occasionally, euchre, though for five years playing cards were banned from our house because my mother happened upon a card game in the room of one of my older brothers on Sunday afternoon. In later life—I can't help smiling as I write it—I often played bridge with my mother on a Sunday and she thought nothing of it, since cards were no longer regarded as an instrument of the devil and were, indeed, being used to raise funds for the support of the church activities. My father had nothing to do with this interdiction. It was one of my mother's ideas. And my father was the one who finally brought it to an end after finding some of us boys playing pedro behind the barn one day.

There was a time when my father used to ring a going-home bell at ten o'clock, but the girls finally put an end to that. They also succeeded in pushing the time up to ten-thirty on Friday and Saturday nights and eventually, to eleven. Of course, if they were giving a party they were allowed to stay up until one o'clock. Sometimes I found it hard to tell the difference between a party and just an ordinary lot of callers. My usual test was to look over the refreshments. If it was an ordinary occasion they would serve nothing but apples and hickory nuts or popcorn, and there would be the fun of cracking the nuts and popping the corn over the kitchen stove. But if it was a real party there would be cake and ice cream or perhaps a candy pull, and the small fry would be allowed to stay up an extra hour or two. We never served coffee at any of these young folks' parties—it was supposed to muddy the complexion of budding young ladies, and, besides, it didn't agree with my mother.

All three of my sisters had beautiful complexions. You could distinguish a complexion in those days when making up was still a sin, or at least a scandal, and cosmetics had not yet become a part of the financial structure of the nation. I remember how enraged my sisters used to be while visiting their cousins in New York to be openly admired in the shops and on the streets as "pretty rosy-cheeked girls from the country."

Although in regard to his schedule my father was compelled to give ground in the front part of the house, it still prevailed stringently in the culinary wing. The kitchen door was locked at ten o'clock, and any maid who stayed out later than that was out of luck. We once had a very comely maid named Sadie, who had a host of admirers. One or another was waiting nightly at the door to take her out for the air, but Sadie found it very difficult to get back before ten, and one night, just to emphasize the importance of punctuality, my father locked Sadie out and went to bed, leaving two of my sisters entertaining beaux in the parlor. He had just turned out the light and was getting himself settled in bed when Sadie began to knock on the door and call under his window. She had seen the light as she came along the street and felt sure that he could not have gone to sleep.

At first my father refused to get up. He argued that one of my sisters would hear the rumpus and answer the door. But my sisters were too much engaged, and since Sadie was too good a girl to lose my mother insisted that he must go down the back stairs and let her in. He gave in reluctantly and began to grope around for his dressing gown. He could not find it, and after a little he muttered testily that he would go just as he was.

"What—in your nightshirt?" my mother protested.

"Well, why not? I can turn the key and dodge back to the stairs. She won't see me."

He did turn the key and dodge back, but in his haste he could not seem to find the doorknob. As he felt around the paneled wall of the kitchen, he heard Sadie come in the door. A moment later he heard the metal lid of the match-box drop and realized that she had a match in her hand. At just that moment his fingers felt the knob and closed on it. In all haste he opened the door and stepped through, thinking that he was in the passage leading to the back stairs; but in his haste and the darkness he had opened the cellar door by mistake—and he had taken only a single stride before he stepped off into space.

Our cellar stairs had twelve steps, and near the bottom they passed between two brick pillars which had been built to steady the floor above for dancing. On both sides our cellarway was lined with shelves used for the storage of various articles. Jams and jellies were on the top shelves. Glass jars of preserved fruits and vegetables came next. Then came a vast array of pickles in glass and spiced fruits in crocks. On the lower shelf were the clothes wringer, the wash tub, and various other laundering implements.

When my father felt himself going, he threw out his arms and grabbed at anything he could get hold of to stay his flight; but try as he would he could not get a grip on anything stable. Jams and jellies accompanied him through the air. Mustard pickles and catchup followed and eventually landed upon his unprotected head like the gentle rain from heaven. In a final effort to save himself he got his arm around a large crock of spiced peaches—but even the spiced peaches could not stay his flight.

He fell true to the mark and missed both pillars, a feat that few of the glass jars were able to duplicate; but for some little time after he had struck the cellar floor and lain there inert and dazed the articles that he had dislodged came tumbling after him. There was the sharp jingle of glass, the clean-cut bark of exploding jars, the dull though reliable thud of crockery, and finally the long, thunderous rumble of the wash boiler as it rolled slowly down, step by step. After that came an ominous silence.

Still holding the unlighted match in her fingers, Sadie stood petrified in the kitchen. She had no idea what could have happened until from the depths of the cellar my father's voice rose up like a voice crying in the wilderness:

"Where in hell am I!"

There was no direct answer to this query, but from the head of the cellar stairs the still, small voice of Sadie asked timorously, "Are you hurt, Mr. Partridge?"

"How the hell do I know? I'm all covered with something that I think is blood—bring a light."

My oldest sister, who had been sitting in the back parlor with a beau from Hobart College, caught her young man by the hand. "That was father!" she cried. "He's fallen down the cellar stairs—and he may be terribly hurt!"

Another sister who was sitting in the front parlor with a beau home from Columbia on a vacation, alarmed and mystified by the ill-omened medley of sounds, sprang to her feet and followed. The four reached the kitchen just as Sadie, lamp in hand, was approaching the cellar doorway. But before she could reach it my father stepped out into the kitchen.

His nightshirt was still on him, though by this time it was so decorated as to resemble the batik ceremonial robe of a Malay chieftain, and his person was pickled, jammed, jellied, and preserved from head to foot. As he came into the light my father drew a hand quickly across his face and said in a tone of relief:

"It isn't blood—it's tomato catchup—I can taste it." Then he turned to Sadie and said sternly, "This is what comes of your being late. I hope you'll make an effort to be on time after this." And he turned and marched off upstairs without even saying good night.

When, the next morning, I heard what had happened I was crushed. It was almost more than I could bear to think that the one time when my father fell downstairs in the grand manner I had to sleep through it.

With a son in college, a daughter in boarding school, another daughter clamoring to go, and five younger children scattered through the grades of the public school, my father must have felt his nose against the grindstone; and still he never said much about it. We all understood that the older ones should be taken care of first, and the rest of us would have to wait until our turns came. And that was the way it worked out, all the way down to the youngest. The interval between children was about two years, on the average. The younger ones grumbled somewhat at having so many things handed down to them, but it was encouraging for them to know that when they went away to school they would have the preference.

It was a long pull, requiring careful management, but by speeding the advancement here and retarding it there the long-time plan succeeded without developing a peak load heavy enough to sink it, though there must have been some anxious moments. As the older ones finished their education and went on to something else the burden lightened, and what must at times have been a terrific economic pressure decreased. As the years passed my father, though at the top of his mental powers, began to lose some of his physical drive. He no longer tried cases for the excitement and thrill of the trial. He soothed and dissuaded the most aggressive and belligerent of his clients; he brought the parties together and arbitrated their differences if possible. Gradually his interest in the theory of law deepened and his insistence on its technical application relaxed. Justice had always been more important to him than the law, and as time went on it became more and more important. It would be impossible to tell the number of causes settled in his office without recourse to suit, since no entry was ordinarily made in the register unless papers were served; but it must have constituted a very large proportion of his business.

Trying to keep up with the children in school and college convinced my father that his education was in need of brushing up, especially in the field of science, and he bought what was said to be a complete scientific library in some sixty-odd volumes containing the complete works of Huxley, Spencer, Tyndall, and a dozen others. For some years he read these books diligently when he was not working far into the night on some legal question, but he never was able to negotiate them all, for after his death a gleeful fundamentalist whom he had several times demolished in arguments at a time when evolution and the belief in a supreme being were supposed to be irreconcilable found one or two of them with uncut pages.

With the acquisition of this scientific library my father's vocabulary became even more overwhelming. Since many of the unfamiliar words were not to be found in his old dictionaries, he had to buy new ones, and he took particular

255

delight in displaying some of these verbal discoveries in court.

At this period of his life he was in complete harmony with the county leaders of the Republican Party and occupied a seat high up in their councils. He never missed a party convention, state, senatorial, judicial, county, or town. To him the convention was the place where political parties were made or unmade. "If you don't nominate the best men, you certainly can't elect the best," he used to say. "Forget geography and pay more attention to ability if you want the party to thrive." He was always enthusiastic about getting out the vote, though he felt that the real issues were decided at the convention, because by the time that you got to the ballot box you had only two men to pick from, whereas at the convention you could make your selection from the entire political party. I once heard him liken the ballot box to a baby's rattle. "The baby thinks it's important," he said, "because it's the place where the most noise comes from."

My father never allowed politics to interfere with his friendships, however, and all through the county he had almost as many friends in one party as in the other. People of all shades of political opinion were among his intimates, and though he used to joke with them and tell them how badly they were going to be beaten, he never entered into acrimonious debates with them—and the Democrats as well as the Republicans used to bring their campaign papers and reports to him to be sure that they complied with the law and were properly filled out and executed.

He was everybody's friend, and a stiff person could always unbend with my father. Country life often begets shyness, and so adroit a listener had my father become that he could draw out the most bashful person without the mental anguish from which shy people usually suffer when making disclosures of an intimate or confidential nature. Shy people interested my father, and I once found tucked away in his files an amusing compilation of notes about shy persons he had known. The material was undoubtedly intended as spade work for some literary purpose—probably a novel after the pattern of Dickens, to whose works he was greatly devoted.

The first of his experiences with shy persons was with an old lady who was brought to his office once every three months to sign her pension papers. In between these infrequent visits to town the old lady seldom saw anybody but her son and her daughter-in-law, and by the time she had reached my father's office she would be so flustered with excitement that she was unable to sign her name until she had taken an hour or two to compose herself. Every fifteen or twenty minutes she would grasp a pen and try a few practice signatures to see if her nerves were sufficiently steady. At that time the pension department was exasperatingly insistent upon the legibility of signatures to pension vouchers, and several times hers had been sent back to be signed over again. One day old Mrs. Scott sat around the office for more than four hours before she could produce a signature that my father considered legible enough to pass the lynx-eyed pension examiner.

Another of his bashful discoveries was a medical doctor named Frank Hall. The word "medical" is used because so many of Doc Hall's patients had originated in the barnyard that a great many people thought his professional equipment was that of a veterinarian only. People used to say that if a farmer stopped to get medicine for a sick hog, the doctor would answer the bell; but if a man came in all bundled up to get medical aid for himself the doctor would hide under the bed and pretend that he was not at home.

The story was that soon after Doc Hall was admitted to practice he ran into an epidemic of diphtheria and lost a great many cases—so many, in fact, that he never recovered

257

his self-confidence after the shock. From that time on his faith in himself kept slipping until he was practically useless in any case more serious than a hard cold. He would thump a patient expertly with his knuckle and ask him to say "Ah-h-h," and then would shake his head and retire from the sickroom and suggest to the family that he be allowed to call another doctor into consultation without delay. Once in a confinement case the baby arrived before the consultant, and if it had not been for the presence in the kitchen of a farm woman who had been through several confinements of her own he would probably have lost both mother and child. For instead of attending to the things that very much needed attention he kept running to the window to see if his reinforcements were in sight.

Still he managed somehow to make a living while building up the practice of other doctors at the expense of his own. Few people realized what a good doctor he was, but in defending himself from serious cases he had made himself a master of preventive medicine. He was well along in years and was himself sick in bed when my father was called to the house to draw his will.

"It's a shame to bother you," Doc Hall said as my father sat down beside the bed. "Not much to leave, but what there is I want to go to my wife. She's had a lot to put up with. I haven't amounted to much as a doctor, but she's stuck to me through thick and thin. I guess I shouldn't have been a doctor in the first place—didn't have guts enough. I'm good enough on minor ailments, but the minute a patient begins to get really sick I begin to imagine things, and I want somebody to share the responsibility with me. If the patient lives, he doesn't bother to call me the next time —just goes straight to the consultant."

My father nodded and went on with his writing.

"I always lose my nerve in an emergency," the doctor continued. "I never went through to the end of a seri-

258

ous case yet—but *this* time I'm going to see it through single-handed."

My father glanced up. "What case do you mean?"

"My own case."

My father read the will over to him. Witnesses were called in, and it was properly executed in accordance with the provisions of the rather fussy statute. When my father was ready to leave, he stepped over and shook the old doctor's hand.

"You're sure you don't want me to send Dr. Hazzard to have a look at you?" he said with a smile, for he did not really think the old doctor was very sick.

Doc Hall shook his head. "No sir!" he said quite positively. "I'm going to see this case through if it's the last thing I ever do."

And it was. They buried him within the week.

Another timid man was Leman Parks. The story about Leman always appealed to my father because, as he said, the shy little fellow lived and died without doing anything memorable and was lying in his coffin with his hands folded and a cluster of cala lilies at his head when he became the most talked about person in town. The only reason that my father went to his funeral was that he was afraid there would not be many people there. Leman lived some five miles in the country, and as my father drove along the road on the day of the funeral he picked up Elon Shepard, one of Leman's neighbors, dressed in his best clothes and obviously headed for the same place.

"Couldn't really spare the time to go," Elon explained as they drove along. "Hayin' just now, and you can't tell how long the good weather's goin' to last. But Leme was such a retirin' little feller that hardly anybody knew him, and I was afraid there might not be enough folks to the funeral to make much of a showin'. Me and the wife has been helpin' a little with the 'rangements. I was over last night doin' a few odd jobs and helpin' to get a place ready for the quartette to set."

"The quartette?" my father asked. "What do you mean?"

"Yeah, a singin' quartette. They ain't got no instrument in the house, you see, and they wanted some music. A quartette don't need no instrument, you know."

As they drove up to the Parks place they could see that they needn't have worried about the attendance, for teams were tied to the fence all up and down the road. My father was seated in the parlor when he saw Elon helping the undertaker carry in the bench for the quartette. They placed it beside the stairway in the hall so that the singers could be heard in both rooms. Shortly afterward Elon slid into a chair beside my father.

"Just varnished that bench last night," he whispered. "Had to leave it out till the last minute so's it would get dry enough to use—but it did."

That was just the trouble—it didn't. Elon had not counted on the body heat that would be generated by sitting on a wooden bench on a hot day. And when the quartette rose to sing my father was astonished to see the bench rise with them. For a few moments they endeavored by inconspicuous movements to disconnect it from the seats of their pants without attracting attention, and then they lost their patience and tried to wrench it loose by main strength. The undertaker rushed to their assistance, and at his suggestion they remained seated during the remainder of their singing.

In his notes my father mentions the look of tension on their faces as they sang "Lead Kindly Light," though he observed that the tension was entirely absent when they rendered their last hymn. He was certain that there was nothing accidental about this selection. He could see it coming long before they struck their opening chord, and he felt sure that it would be just what it was, "Abide with Me."

260

But at any rate, by supper time that night shy little Leman Parks was the most talked about man in town.

Of all my father's collection of shy men I think Billy Bob Rivers was his favorite. Billy Bob started out in business as a photographer, but he was so shy and embarrassed whenever he took a picture that his suffering actually made the sitter uncomfortable. Indeed, Billy Bob was too shy even to get his sitters into an advantageous pose, and once he had put his head under the black cloth he found it almost impossible to take it out again.

Billy Bob, who must have been a very ingenious fellow, built his own camera, even to the grinding of the lens. The first camera was cabinet size, and while he was waiting for his clientele to build up he made himself an eight-by-ten and ground the lens for that. The grinding of the lens was something that just suited him—he could do it all by himself. When the larger camera was finished and he was still not overwhelmed by persons who wished to have their pictures taken, he began to grind himself a four-inch lens for a telescope.

The townspeople nudged each other significantly when he mounted his telescope in a fence corner of his little place half a mile out of town and, one clear night in June, surveyed the starry dome of heaven. They used to twit him about his spyglass, as they called it, and about his "Red House Observatory." They asked him humorous questions about the man in the moon, very much, one imagines, as the neighbors used to taunt Alec Bell about the telephone and the Wright boys about their flying machine. But Billy Bob took their japery good-naturedly. And when one day his name appeared in the headlines of the city papers the shoe was on the other foot; for Billy Bob Rivers had discovered a comet.

In spite of this, however, the neighbors thought that Billy Bob could be of more practical value to the world by spending a few days trimming his apple trees than he could by discovering a comet every night in the week. What good were comets anyway?

This view was not shared by the younger generation, who had acquired a deep interest in stargazing. On every clear night, and even on nights that were hazy, young couples could be seen strolling down in Billy Bob's direction with the commendable intention of studying the heavens. The astronomer seemed surprised when the parents of some of these young visitors asked him if so many callers did not interfere with his work. "Not at all," he said. "The nights are lonely, and I'm only too glad to have them for company."

It was not until years later, after Billy Bob had ceased to be "the Professor" and had become "the Doctor" that he remarked to my father that few of these youthful callers ever came any nearer than the orchard fence.

"They seemed to be able to behold the wonders of nature much more clearly from underneath the shadows of those old apple trees," he said; "and without doubt they made discoveries every night that would have amazed and delighted me had I been able to make them for myself."

The story of Billy Bob's success is too well known to require retelling here: how he discovered with his spyglass more comets than the astronomers at Yerkes and Mt. Wilson together and how he was given the chair of Astronomy at Hobart College. People used to wonder how he could fill that chair and do his night work, too; but that was simple. His astronomy course occupied only an hour a week, and there were seldom more than three or four students in his classes. Success had robbed Billy Bob of much of his shyness. though not all, for on the quizzes it was *he* who answered the questions rather than risk embarrassing his students by stumping them.

22. The Layman Looks at the Law

IN THE city, where people are herded in this direction
and that in great masses and submit without question
to all manner of indignity merely because others accept
it without protest, legal rights do not amount to much.
The rush-hour subway packers at Times Square who seize
women and shove them through half-open doors of cars,
pushing gleefully at any protruding portions of their
anatomy which threaten to obstruct the closing of the door,
simply could not exist outside the large city.

Law, in the city, is as distant from the individual as the
stars. With the exception of the few called for jury duty and
the element who make their living out of sharp practices of
one sort or another, the only New Yorker who ever sees the
inside of a courthouse is the unfortunate individual in quest
of a divorce or in possession of a ticket for traffic violation.

The situation is quite different in the country. There the
law is a real and living entity. Find me a countryman who
has never seen a lawsuit and I will show you a blind man.
Outside the city the common man regards the law very
much as he regards the Army and Navy. It is a medium
through which he can protect his rights and redress his
wrongs. Who ever heard a city man threaten to "have the
law" on anybody? He may threaten to call a policeman or

to sock you on the jaw; but he would not have the slightest idea how to go about it if he wanted to get legal redress.

On the other hand, the machinery of the law is as familiar to the countryman as the machinery for cutting hay. He knows a lawyer to go to—perhaps half a dozen. He is probably acquainted with the judge. And it is quite likely that he understands a thing or two about the legal aspects of the question at issue because of his familiarity with a similar case in which one of his neighbors had been involved. In the country a man goes to his lawyer as freely as he goes to his doctor. He has property rights and personal rights in which he takes a certain dignified pride, and he does not propose to have them trampled upon.

The law is as readily available to the common people of the country as the post office or the mail order house, and the purposes for which they invoke it are almost as diverse as their demands on the latter two pillars of rural tranquility. The reasons for which people go to law are as varied and individual as the people themselves.

My father had one client who would start a lawsuit with as little provocation as he would begin a game of checkers. His cases would rarely reach the higher courts, since so small an amount was involved, though my father did have a spirited legal tilt in the Supreme Court with a telephone company which was rash enough to run its line along the highway crossing his farm without first concluding its arrangements with him. He was not a disagreeable man; quite the contrary. He did not particularly enjoy an argument and would not continue one to any great lengths. His attitude was that the justice court was meant to handle such matters. Old John Haynes would state his contention as clearly as he could, and he would listen to what the other side had to say.

"All right," he would remark when his opponent was through speaking. "If that's your position we'll have to take it to court and see which of us is on the right side."

There was no ill will on his part, no hard feeling. Taking a dispute to court was less annoying to him than wrangling, and when the case was settled the decision would be final. There would be no recriminations and no calling of names. If he was beaten, he paid the costs as cheerfully as if he had been rolling the bones for drinks. In addition to farming, John sold agricultural implements and ran a small coal yard at the Junction. He usually had five or six men in his employ and was frequently taking men on and letting them go according to the demands of his business.

He was an exacting employer, and when he gave a man instructions he intended to have them carried out. His implement business furnished him with an occasional trial, for he was quite insistent about having purchasers make their payments according to agreement, though he always tried to make it clear to defendants that legal action was no indication of personal ill will.

Usually, when a client came in with a grievance, my father would try to effect a settlement without starting suit, though this rule did not apply to John Haynes. If John had a ghost of a chance to win there was a lawsuit—that is, unless the other fellow lost his nerve and backed out. And no man ever served a summons on John Haynes without having a lawsuit on his hands.

Another early client of my father's with a flair for litigation was Gus Worden, an itinerant farm hand who worked around at one place or another all summer and then in the fall had a lawsuit with nearly every one of his employers over the unpaid balance; or perhaps it would be over an assault committed in ejecting him from the premises. Gus was an old hand at the business and never had a dispute with an employer unless there were witnesses around. Unlike John Haynes, who went to law because of the convenience, Gus went to law largely for the enjoyment of the thing. He fairly basked in the sunshine of his own importance during a trial. The only trouble with him was that in the expansive mood brought on by so much publicity he found it very hard to keep sober until the end of the trial. From time to time he would slip out through the crowd and get a drink, and during one of his cases he became so inebriated that my father had to have him detained outside the courtroom until after the case had gone to the jury.

But Gus Worden was not the only one who went into litigation for the pleasure of it. The periodical appearances of Don Weldon's wife, Maribel, in justice court were almost entirely of a social nature. Indeed, her lawsuits constituted about the only social life the Weldon family had, and Maribel made the most of them.

Maribel was a pretty woman in her middle thirties at the time of the particular case I have in mind, which was her last appearance in any court so far as I can now remember— except the divorce court, and that was some years later. She had a beautiful complexion and a pair of big blue eyes with dark, curved lashes. Her figure was beyond reproach. She had a slender waist of almost wasplike proportions with most agreeable curves above and below. The woman was really enough to take the breath away from a rural jury, as my father had learned on the one or two occasions when he had represented the hired man who usually played opposite her in these legal comedy dramas.

The husband was a simple-minded dolt whom she could wind about her finger at will, and though he owned the eighty-acre farm which he had inherited from his father and on which they lived, the lease was always negotiated by Maribel. Indeed, she was the business manager of all farm matters. In these leases the Weldons would always reserve a ten-acre corner containing the homestead, the garden plot, and the orchard. The balance of the farm was let out to a share cropper.

These tenancies invariably came to grief over some sort of woman trouble. Either Maribel couldn't get along with the tenant or else—as was usually the case—she got along with him entirely too well.

My father used to speak jestingly of Maribel's "fatal beauty," though he meant this as no reflection on her eye-filling loveliness. He really thought that in her surroundings and with her methods she was very likely to furnish the motivating force in a homicide. Not that he imagined Don would ever get up spunk enough to slay under any provocation whatever. What he really feared was that some jealous wife would catch her husband in an act of indiscretion with the man-hungry beauty and put a charge of buckshot into

267

one or both of them. He had been predicting something of the sort for years.

No tenant of the Weldon farm was ever known to renew his lease—his wife usually saw to that—and with the likelihood of trouble staring him in the face all the desirable tenant farmers in the locality shied away from the Weldon place, and Maribel was eventually compelled to look elsewhere for her tenant conquests. She placed an advertisement in a Rochester paper and received a promising-looking answer from a man named Horton who lived in Steuben County, too far away to have heard any of the numerous rumors about Maribel and her methods. Two or three letters passed between them which led to arrangements for Horton to come and look over the place.

He came and looked and liked what he saw. After he returned home there were further letters in which terms were

reached and the tenancy agreed upon. Since no formal lease was ever drawn, the contract between the parties rested entirely upon these letters.

Horton, who was a very presentable young man in his middle thirties, was a serious farmer, ambitious to get along. He had a wife entirely satisfactory to him and was not at all interested in the blandishments of Maribel or any other woman. So of course the lease did not work out. Maribel, considering herself scorned, turned on her tenant with annoying and unreasonable demands concerning his farm methods and management and eventually haled him into court for an accounting and damages.

When Horton first began to see the way the wind was blowing, he came in to consult my father and from that time on was guided by advice of counsel. The plaintiff had little to complain of as to the management of the farm, and the differences between them finally settled down to a contest over the terms of the lease. Fortunately Horton had kept all the letters he had received from Maribel, and he had made copies of the letters he had written her. In trying the case, my father had not introduced the letters until he was putting in his defense. It was quite evident that Maribel had told her lawyer that there was a verbal lease, and he was trying the case on that assumption.

The situation must have been very much to Maribel's liking. The hall was packed to suffocation—and it was packed with men. She could not help but realize that all these men had come to watch and admire her, for she was the only woman in the room. She was the center of attraction, and she looked as lovely as a fresh-plucked rose. Her trim figure was glorified by a simple black satin dress, and her ravishing blonde hair showed beneath her saucy black hat like a mist of spun gold. Whenever she raised her eyes she saw men—wherever she looked, nothing but men—

and the men saw nothing but Maribel. Thus far it was one of the most successful lawsuits she had ever put on . . .

"Mrs. Weldon, I show you a letter dated February fifteenth of last year." This was my father speaking. "Is this letter in your handwriting?"

Her attorney, a pompous old fellow from Geneva named Lyman S. Barkin, was quickly on his feet. "One moment!" he rumbled. "Let me see that letter!"

The letter was handed to him. He and Mrs. Weldon ran through it. She was not a very legible writer, and this took time. But the letter was harmless enough, and Barkin finally conceded that it was in her handwriting. My father had it marked and received in evidence, but he did not read it at the time. He laid it on the table and held out another letter for Mrs. Weldon to identify. Barkin demanded the letter, skimmed through it, and again conceded her handwriting. Whereupon my father put the letter in evidence and produced another.

Barkin barely glanced at the third letter. "We concede that the plaintiff wrote it," he said condescendingly, "but I don't see the purpose of putting all this junk in evidence."

"I'll try to explain that a little later," my father said disarmingly and produced another letter.

Barkin did not even glance at this one. He held it up for Mrs. Weldon to see. "Did you write that?"

"Yes, that's my handwriting."

"I offer it in evidence," said my father. "Please mark for identification."

"Received and marked," mumbled the justice.

My father kept the letters in his own hands where nobody would be looking at them and did not take occasion to refer to them again until he was making his summary to the jury. Then he struck them with his hand and declared that they constituted a complete refutation of the plaintiff's claim that the lease was verbal. He took up the letters one by one

270

and read them aloud to the jury. He read the harmless letters first but soon came to one which had some meat in it. In this letter the plaintiff agreed to furnish feed for the stock until new pasturage was available, a promise which she had denied on the witness stand. This was one of the letters that Barkin had not read. He squirmed over it and demanded to see it. As he sat reading it my father took up another letter that Barkin had admitted without reading.

This letter was written shortly after Horton's return to his home after the first inspection of the Weldon farm. It began by discussing some of the questions under consideration, but once these were out of the way Maribel went into personal matters in one of her most kittenish moods. Her detachable flatiron handle, a semicircular wooden grip, had not been seen since the day Horton was there, and she was humorously charging him with being responsible for its disappearance. My father read this part out clearly and distinctly, not only to the jury but to the entire courtroom.

Ed Horton, I want to know what you did with my flatiron handle the day you were here. If you swallowed it I hope it don't stick out in some funny place and make your wife think she's got a freak on her hands . . .

He could read no further for some minutes, so great was the tumult and laughter in the courtroom. Indeed, the room was never again completely in order during the rest of the trial. Barkin tried his best to repair the damage that had been done to his case, but he was unable to get control of the crowd long enough to put in a very serious argument to the jury. The plaintiff's case collapsed completely, and Maribel Weldon, who could face anything but ridicule, held no more of her levees in court.

It was some years after this trial that my father pointed her out to me. By this time neither her face nor her figure would have launched a thousand ships, though I must admit that she was still a pretty woman.

271

The case of Maggie Bibby never reached court. To tell the truth, it was no case at all; but it illustrates so clearly the attitude of some laymen towards the law that I feel it deserves notice.

Maggie's mother had come over with a wave of domestics from the British Isles back in the eighties. She had brought with her by hand a fine old set of dishes that had been her wedding china. The set had descended to Maggie, and it was the delight of her heart. Not a dish had been broken, and with the exception of a nick in one of the dinner plates every piece was as perfect as when it had come from the ovens of the pottery.

For a number of years Maggie had the enjoyment of the china all to herself, and then when she began to take in for laundering the finery of the summer residents, she found among her patrons a number of admirers of the fine old set. Tentative feelers would be put out to see if she would be willing to sell it, but Maggie always refused. She said that it had belonged to her mother, and she could not even think of parting with it.

My mother had offered to buy the set from Maggie when she was working for us as a maid, but Maggie had declined to sell. She had promised, however, that if she should ever seriously consider selling she would give my mother the first refusal. Since this understanding was well known to my father, he was doubly surprised when Maggie came to his office one day with tear-stained eyes and told him that she had sold her china but that it was all a mistake and she wanted him to get it back again for her.

"I might as well tell you the whole thing," she said, well knowing that my father would get it out of her. "Mr. McLouth has been at me all summer to sell him those dishes, but I refused. He offered me thirty dollars to begin with, then forty, then fifty, and finally sixty-two fifty. That was an awful temptation, but at first I refused. Then one day in the

272

window of a china shop in Geneva I saw a set that *looked* exactly like it. It was marked six dollars complete. I went in and asked the man if it was old, but he said certainly not, that it was brand new.

"I looked it over carefully. It was even checked like mine. The man said they had a way of doing that to make them look old. I could hardly tell the difference myself. I kept thinkin' that if it weren't for the one nicked plate nobody could tell them apart. Well, to get on, I bought the set and took it home. I laid my own china away and put the new set on my sideboard. Then I done a terrible thing—I took a kitchen knife and nicked one of the plates. I made up my mind I would tell no *lies* about it but that if anybody wanted to buy that china I would ask a good price.

"That very night Mrs. Carmichael came to the house for her laundry.

" 'Oh, that lovely old china,' she said. 'Aren't you ever going to sell it?'

" 'That?' I turned and looked at it. 'Oh, I don't know. Perhaps I'll sell that sometime—if I can get my price.'

"She began to beg me to name a price, and finally I said fifty dollars, and she went right home and got the money. Of course I made her promise not to show it and not to mention it to a soul or I'd have all my customers mad at me. Well, she promised."

"And she didn't keep her word?" asked my father.

"Oh yes," said Maggie. "Of course she did—but let me explain. I went back to Geneva and got another set for Mr. McLouth. I put it out just the way I did the other."

"And you nicked another plate?"

"I certainly did, and, would you believe it, I sold two more sets before Mr. McLouth came around. One went for fifty and the other for fifty-five."

My father shook his head. "But you must have known that people would compare notes sooner or later."

"Oh, no, they never did. Each sale was strictly confidential. I made every buyer promise never to show a piece in this town. You see, Judge, I sold only to summer visitors who were getting ready to leave. One set went to Cleveland, another to Albany. There was no danger of their telling."

My father looked very disapproving. "What did your husband think about it?"

"Oh, I never told him. It was that confidential. But I finally made a deal with Mr. McLouth. It was the last set the man in Geneva had. Sixty-two fifty I got for it. He offered me a check, but I wouldn't take it. So he said he'd be back with the money the next afternoon, because he was leaving for home on the eight-thirty train that night. I put the dishes out on the sideboard and got everything ready for him the next afternoon. But before he arrived the boy came rushing in from the farm with the horse all in a lather. He says my Katie was in labor and callin' for me. The nursing woman was already in the house and the doctor on the way, but she wanted her mother.

"I threw on my wraps, but I said I must see Mr. McLouth first. But he wasn't at the place where he stayed—he'd gone for a drive. Well, I left word for him to come at seven, when I was sure John would be home from work. Then I went back and pinned a note on the door for John. I told him I was sellin' the china and that Mr. McLouth would call for it at seven. I said the price would be sixty-two fifty, and would he take good care of the money for me? And I told him the news about the comin' of the baby. Well, as it happened, John had had a drink on the way home and it addled him a bit. And when he saw about the baby and about the price for the china he went back to the Inn and had another.

"He hadn't been in the house at all but was settin' on the porch when Mr. McLouth drove up. But bein' a little addled, John didn't go in the front door. He went around the house to go in at the back, and there in the woodshed he come across the bushel basket where I'd put my mother's real dishes to get 'em out of sight.

" 'Ha-ha!' he says. 'She's got 'em all ready for me.' And he took the *real* ones out and gave them to Mr. McLouth—"

Maggie Bibby stopped and wiped the tears out of her eyes. "When I got back and found out what he'd done, I flew at him—and for the first time in our married life the neighbors had to come in and part us."

"But, Maggie," said my father with a hopeless shrug. "What do you expect me to do in a case of this kind?"

Maggie gave him an astonished look. "Why, I've always understood the law would rectify a mistake—and this is a clear case of mistake if there ever was one."

My father shook his head. "The law will rectify a mutual mistake of fact, Maggie; but you can hardly expect it to compel restitution where one party is accidentally honest while attempting to perpetrate a fraud on the other."

"You mean you can't write to Mr. McLouth and tell him he's got to send the dishes back and I'll return his money?"

"We can't make him do it unless he wants to."

Tears flooded Maggie's eyes again. "And I did so want to give my new namesake my mother's set of dishes."

"I'm afraid your new namesake will have to be satisfied with the set now on your sideboard. But," he added maliciously, "she'll never know the difference."

Maggie gasped. "What! You mean I should give my own grandchild a false set of dishes? I wouldn't do such a thing!"

"That sounds more like the Maggie I used to know," said my father. "I don't suppose you'd want me to write and tell Mr. McLouth the whole truth?"

"I'd die of shame."

"How would it be if I should write him that you are heart-broken and are willing to give him one hundred dollars to get the dishes back?"

275

"I'd do it in a minute—I'd give him *all* the money, every cent!"

My father looked very stern. "I thoroughly disapprove of all you have been doing, Maggie, but I'll try to get you out of it if I can."

He wrote Mr. McLouth that Maggie was crushed when she realized that her mother's china was gone and that she would, he was sure, be willing to pay seventy-five dollars plus the cost of shipping and packing to get the dishes back. He was afraid that if he offered any more the canny old Scotsman would be suspicious. If Mr. McLouth suggested one hundred dollars, that would be quite a different matter. But Mr. McLouth answered at once saying that Maggie's offer was a big relief to him because the dishes did not match any of his wife's things, and his wife did not like them anyway. He said he would be glad to return them at cost, plus the packing and shipping charges, of course.

So the dishes came back, though my father did not tell Maggie how pleased Mr. McLouth was to get rid of them. Instead he gave her a lecture on honesty and warned her that if he ever heard of her selling another dish, he would expose her to every person who had ever bought her mother's set of china and advise them all to bring suit against her for fraud and deceit.

In his younger days my father would have taken this lapse in ethics much more to heart. And if it had so happened that the family had known about it we would have had a few well-chosen remarks at every meal about the importance of honesty. My father was a close-mouthed man. A secret was as safe with him as with the Sphinx, but he had a curious belief in the power of repetition, and if he had a point he wanted to drive home he would repeat it until the time came when we would join him in a family chorus. When we began to do that he would usually drop the subject permanently. We used to think that we had cured *him*, but I have since concluded that his reason for dropping the subject was that he felt he had cured *us*.

His repetitious allusions to the "perfect miscarriage of justice" in Jerry's case had resulted from a different motive. These allusions were in protest against a wrong. Then, too, my father had difficulty in adjusting himself to the discovery that an innocent man could be sent to jail. There had been a time when the family had heard enough about this defection of justice to make them a little weary; but it came to me the day of Jerry's funeral that I had not heard my father mention the subject after Jerry's return from prison.

I could see reason enough for dropping the subject. The obvious absence of any feeling of bitterness or resentment on Jerry's part and his dogged determination to make good among the very people who had sent him away were enough to keep my father from risking the revival of any of the old hostility by talking about it.

There never was a funeral in town at all like Jerry's. The services were held in his own little house, which, to everybody's surprise, was jammed with people. In fact, the house was not big enough to hold more than half who had come there, and all through the service there were as many standing in the yard as were inside the house.

After the services at the house were over and the casket had been put in the hearse, two carriages drew up to take the minister and the bearers to the cemetery. Usually, at funerals, there would be anywhere from ten to fifty carriages, including private conveyances, and in one or two of the really important funerals there had been as many as one hundred. I can remember quite clearly sitting on the horse block in front of our house and counting the carriages as they went past in some of the big funerals. The number of carriages was at that time significant. It was supposed to be an indication of the impression made on the community by the deceased. Jerry had no relatives that anybody could learn

277

of, and somehow the two lone carriages behind the hearse brought a surge of pity—or perhaps it was remorse—to the onlookers standing silently by.

Everybody there seemed to have felt it, for when the cortege started to move, a double line of people fell impulsively in behind the carriages and followed them on foot. Hardly a person who was at the service failed to get in line.

Although it was not the first time that people had walked to the cemetery with a body it was the first time that they had ever marched in the street behind the hearse. There were some desertions, of course. Old people, carried away by the emotion of the moment, found that they could not keep up or that it was too far for them. Others may have fallen out, but as the funeral procession passed slowly through the business section there were many additions to the line. It was as if people were trying to make amends for the deep injustice they had done Jerry.

Nothing was said about it. Nothing needed to be said, but the general feeling that day was that Jerry had won his way back to full respectability, that his rehabilitation was complete. I have since wondered whether any of the marchers who toiled slowly up the hill in that double line were reminded of the winter's night when the incendiary had iced that very hill before setting fire to a building on the top of it. Probably not, for nobody was harboring bitterness that day.

23. Amicus Curiae

THERE is a peculiar legal fiction in which a person acts as *amicus curiae*, friend of the court, an unofficial adviser to whom the court may turn for advice when it is beyond its depth. The position of the country lawyer in his community is closely akin to this relationship —only the lawyer is the people's instead of the court's friend. My father was constantly besieged by those who wanted not legal but personal advice on problems that would have tried the ingenuity of a Solomon—and always he gave them the best that was in him.

"If folks were in a *little* trouble," old Al Westgard once told me, "they would get down on their knees and talk it over with God; but if they were in a *lot* of trouble, they'd go straight to your father."

My father never turned anybody away. His "wealth of useless information" often stood him in good stead, and when he was not telling people what they could or could not legally do he was advising them on one or another of the obscure problems of all sorts with which the human animal is forever complicating his life. In an hour's time he would be consulted on some knotty problem of ethics—business acumen—subsoil plowing—insecticide—education—ancient history—water farcy—bumps and scours—though it was

279

perhaps the subject of marital relations that brought him more extracurricular problems than any other. These involved nearly every difficulty that a man or a woman can devise from the simple fact of living together. Only once, however, was he called upon for assistance in the matter of the predetermination of the sexes—and even then he proved to be helpful.

This came up in the case of Fred Hixon and his wife who, in their twenty years or so of married life, had been blessed with ten beautiful children—all of them daughters. It was upon the occasion of the birth of the tenth consecutive woman child that Fred Hixon, on the completion of his rounds as milkman, came heavily into my father's office and handed my father a cigar.

"What's this for, Fred?" asked my father.

"Oh, another little stranger up to our house."

"Girl, of course?"

"That's what they tell me."

For a few moments my father puffed silently on the cigar. "How many does this make?"

"Ten, by God!"

"What—no more than that?"

Fred drew a long breath. "Wasn't when I left home this morning. Listen, Judge—you've got plenty of boys—how do you do it?"

My father smiled. "Why, Fred, I haven't the slightest idea."

"But you're always reading and studying things. I've got a notion you know more medicine than most doctors. Did you ever come across anything in your reading—anything authentic on how to control sex?"

"Control it? What do you mean?"

"Well, take a case like mine. Say for instance, that a family would like to vary the monotony by having an occasional boy. Is there anything they can do about it?"

My father shook his head. "There's been plenty written on the subject of sex determination. Some wonderful theories have been evolved. The only trouble is they won't work."

"But isn't there anything a fellow can do?"

"Science has been working on the subject for years, but the question of the selectivity of the sexes is still a closed book, and when science fails us there is only one place to go."

"Where do you mean?"

"To the necromancers."

"You mean you want me to have my fortune told?"

"Not just that, Fred." My father tilted back in his chair. "You know old John Bement, of course?"

"Sure do. Known him all my life. He's a good man around a mill."

"Did you ever hear that he knows how to weave a magic spell?"

Fred smiled. "I've heard a lot of things about him."

"Did you ever hear of his power to blow away a wart or a corn?"

"I've heard he claimed to do such things."

"Well, it's true. He can do it. He blew away a wart that had been on my hand for years."

Fred scratched his head. "But, Judge, I haven't got any corns just now, and I never had a wart in my life. I don't see just what they've got to do with the case anyhow."

"Well, just be patient, Fred, and you'll see what I'm driving at. Now then, how much money are you willing to spend to be assured that your next heir will be a male?"

"Why, Judge, I'd be willing to spend any reasonable amount—anything up to—let's say up to twenty dollars."

"Fine!" said my father. "Then you do what I say. You go to old John and tell him what you want, and he'll fix you, I'm sure."

Fred looked hard at my father. "You ain't fooling me, are you, Judge?"

My father aimed his cigar ashes at the coal scuttle. "I never was more serious in my life."

"You mean you really think he can do something for me?"

"Of course he can. See what he did to my wart."

Fred slowly nodded his head. "What do you think he would charge?"

"Not over twenty-five cents. That's what it cost me to get rid of my wart."

Fred stood up. "I'm probably the biggest damn fool in this town—but I'm going to try it." He started for the door, but stopped with his hand on the knob. "You won't say anything about this, will you, Judge?"

"Not if you'll promise to keep quiet about my wart."

Fred Hixon laid a box of cigars down on the desk. My father was signing letters with a scratching sound. Fred remembered the big gold pen. He recalled seeing my father writing with it years before. "Some pen," he said as my father dropped it in a bronze tray.

My father laid his hand on the box of cigars. "What's this for, Fred?"

"I guess you earned them, Judge."

"Earned them? What do you mean?"

Fred was grinning broadly. "It's a boy—!"

"Can't be." My father shook his head.

"Why not?" Fred was still grinning.

"Because you're not drunk."

"Never you mind about that," said Fred. "I soon *will* be!"

"But why the *box* of cigars?" asked my father.

"Because you're the one who's really entitled to the credit."

"How so?"

Fred lowered his voice so the girl in the back room could not hear. "If it hadn't been for you I'd never have gone to old John Bement."

My father tilted back in his chair. "Then you did go?"

"Sure I did."

"And it worked?"

"I'm tellin' you it worked!"

"What did it cost you?"

"Two bits, just as you said."

"But—but what did he do—what's his method?"

Fred bent close to my father's ear. "He told me to fetch him a horse chestnut, and I did. He held it in his hand and blew on it, and then he gave it back to me and told me to carry it in my left hip pocket until the next child was born."

"And you did that?" asked my father.

"You better believe I did. I remembered your wart—and I did exactly what he told me to do."

"Funny thing about that wart," said my father.

"Funny?" asked Fred. "How do you mean?"

"I mean," said my father, "that it came back again."

It was not to John Bement that my father went when he wanted to swear off smoking, though the cure he tried was quite as unorthodox. He had been told that the habit could easily be cured by the use of a preparation that was called "Tobac-No." This remarkable remedy came in the form of tablets which were to be chewed whenever the tobacco addict felt the craving to smoke. My father purchased a few boxes of the tablets and set out to effect a cure. To the surprise of both himself and the family he had in two or three weeks completely cured himself of smoking—but in its place he had acquired the habit of chewing those tablets.

This habit annoyed my mother even more than the smoking, and since the Tobac-No habit grew on him and he was devouring several boxes a day she became convinced that there must be some habit-forming drug in the tablets and begged him to resume his smoking. After a hard fight he succeeded in giving up the tablets and getting back to the cigars again.

Always it was cigars. He despised cigarettes. In his younger days he had smoked a pipe, but that was only because he was interested in coloring a meerschaum. When he had finished the job he abandoned pipes forever. He always smoked when he worked, and although he tried to remember the ash tray at home he never gave a thought to his cigar ashes at the office. I used to watch the ash gather on his cigar as he bent over one of his lawbooks. It would get longer and longer—and finally it would drop into the book. Unless it happened to obscure what he was reading he would let it lie there until he was ready to turn the page, and then he would carefully blow it off—on the floor. There was not a lawbook in the office that had not felt a cigar ash on nearly every page; and smell—those books reeked to heaven! I haven't seen them for years, but if one should be hidden and buried among the lawbooks of the Congressional Library I am sure I could scent it out in a very short time.

The speed with which my father could take on a new habit was sometimes a little disconcerting to the family. Let him do a thing a few times, and it would fall into the regular curriculum; and once it was established, nothing but a fight could break it off. My mother once had the porches painted. The large side porch which gave entrance to both the kitchen and the dining room was done first, but this did not interfere with my father's goings and comings, since he had seldom made use of it. When, however, the painters had put a coat of paint on the front porch my mother warned them to set up a sturdy barrier to keep my father out or he would absent-mindedly tramp right through the fresh paint and into the house without realizing what he was doing. The painters followed her instructions and barricaded the front steps with a heavy ladder and a sign warning of fresh paint.

When my father came home and found the barricade he stopped before it as if puzzled. He glanced here and there, looking for a way around. Then the sign caught his eye and registered, and he entered the house by the side porch. During the three or four days that the painters were putting on two coats and allowing the paint to dry thoroughly they kept up the barrier continuously. It was, however, an unnecessary precaution; after the first day my father did not go near the front porch. He took the walk around to the side porch as if he had always been going that way—even after the barrier was removed.

At first my mother thought that he was doing it to allow the paint on the front porch to become thoroughly dried before using it. But when a week had passed and he was still coming in the side door my mother spoke to him about it. She said he needn't come that way any more, for she was sure the paint was dry. He nodded and said all right, but that night when he came home to supper he went right around to the side porch.

"Did you forget about the front porch?" she asked.

He gave her an uncomprehending look. "What about it?"

"It's all dry. You can use it now. You needn't go around to the side porch any more."

"That's right—I did come in that way. I'll try to remember."

For a week she said no more about it, and my father continued to come and go by the side porch. Then one day my mother thought of a way to break him—she had the painter come and put a fresh coat on the steps of the side porch. The painter could not see that they needed it. He was inclined to be a little touchy at what he thought was a reflection on his workmanship and the quality of his paint. But my mother was insistent. She stayed there and saw the steps painted, and she supervised the building of a suitable barricade.

That night when my father came home she watched as he walked around the house and looked in amazement at the barricade. After a moment he bent over and tested the paint with the tip of his finger. When he saw that it was indubitably fresh he retraced his steps and came in by the front door. He inquired about the fresh paint on the steps, and my mother explained that she was not satisfied with that part of the work and had made the painter do them over again. My father never scented a conspiracy. Once or twice he forgot and walked around the house until he came in sight of the barricade; whereupon he turned and came in the

front door. And by the time that the steps were dry enough to satisfy my mother—his habit of coming in the front door had been completely re-established.

When I was admitted to the bar my father made me a present of a very handsome roll-top desk. Just how he happened to select that particular style I never knew. The pigeonholes and drawers of a roll-top are a great improvement in the matter of privacy, but, as every lawyer knows, what a man needs when he draws papers or looks up the authorities is plenty of room. I kept things in that desk, but I never worked at it. Whenever I had any legal work to do— which was nearly all the time—I would spread out over the top of the Elder Woodruff desk or the center table in the back room, which was even larger.

On returning home after taking the bar examination in Rochester, I sat down with my father and told him how I had answered the various questions that I could remember. I noticed that he kept making marks on the back of an envelope and finally asked him what he was doing. He said that he was keeping track of the number of questions I was able to recall. Before I went to bed that night I had recalled more than ninety out of one hundred. The rest of them came to me within the next day or two. He gave me a safe passing margin, which was afterwards confirmed by the board of examiners.

For the next ten years I practiced with my father, sitting across the desk from him and threshing out with him all the vexing questions of procedure which bedevil the early years at the law.

He was not inclined to dandle me on his knee or give me any legal cuddling. He would discuss a case with me for hours at a time, but when it came to trial he would stay away and leave me entirely to my own resources. He did slip into the back of the Town Hall during one of my early cases to hear my summary to the jury, but I did not know of it until long afterward. He accepted any number of cases in justice court and then sent me in to try them, whether I thought I had a chance to win or not. Some of them I did manage to win. Quite a number of them were lost, but he did not seem to think that was very important. John Haynes tried to get us on opposite sides of one of his cases, but I discovered what was in the wind and ran out on him.

We worked together on a number of cases in the probate court, and he had me sit in with him on a few trials in the Supreme Court. In all these cases he allowed me to help select the jury and to examine some of the less important witnesses, though he handled most of the trial himself. A little later on when a rather unimportant case came along, he saw it on the calendar—and then dropped out and left me to handle it as best I could.

I am now willing to confess that I was very nervous to be on my own before a Supreme Court Judge I had never seen before; but my experience in the justice court stood me in good stead, and as soon as we had settled down to the taking of testimony my nervousness left me and I managed to pull through without making any serious blunders.

24. The Little Black Book

SOON after I went into practice with my father he turned over to me the handling of all accounts that came into the office for collection. Until that time I had not thought much about the lawyer's part in inducing people to pay their bills, and I am forced to say that I found collections the most distasteful branch of country practice. For a while my father let me handle things in my own way, but one day when he had looked over the docket of causes I had started in the justice court he shook his head.

"There is no better way to lose a possible client," he said, "than by annoying him over the settlement of a trifling bill that he does not find it convenient to pay."

For an hour he sat and talked to me about the dangers and difficulties that could arise from the mishandling of small claims sent in for collection. The collection fees, as he pointed out, were insignificant, and it was his attitude that no lawyer could afford to handle so hazardous a practice for the fees alone and might better discard it entirely. I was a little puzzled until he explained to me how a collection business could be used to make friends and build up a future practice. If a man honestly wanted to pay a bill my father would sit down with him and try to work out a way that it could be done. Sometimes it would develop that a man had a number of pressing creditors, and my father would try to get them to agree to accept a proportional payment at regular intervals, so that all could be paid at the same time instead of permitting the harshest creditors to get their claims in full while the indulgent ones received nothing.

It was not unusual for him to find a job for a man who was willing to pay his debts but was out of work. In fact, one of the most successful ways my father had of getting rid of the annoyance of collecting small claims was to pay the bill himself and let the debtor work out the amount by doing some unneeded labor around our place. I always knew what it meant when an impecunious fellow appeared at the door and said that my father had sent him down to trim the apple trees or whitewash the henhouse. My father never could resist a hard luck story, especially if the narrator would lay heavy enough stress on having a large number of children to support.

The second branch of legal work to be placed in my hands was the conveyancing. I found this as delightful as the collection work was disagreeable. The drawing of deeds, bonds and mortgages, bills of sale, and leases appealed to me as it probably appeals to every young lawyer. The work is not difficult, and, when one has caught the knack, requires little technical skill. The only drawback in conveyancing in country practice is that so much of the work comes at one time.

Moving day in the country is in the spring instead of the fall. All leases and land contracts are dated for performance on April first. Deals that have been hanging fire for months will be closed on that day. New owners take possession. Former owners move out—perhaps to a new place bought with the money received from the old. Stacks of currency used to pass through our office on April first—farmers rarely used checks, even if they had bank accounts. They preferred to see the money. One year my father and I completed more than twenty transactions on a single closing day, and we must have handled several bushels of currency. The identical thousand-thousand bundles of money came back to us from the bank over and over again.

In some localities the day is referred to as "settlement day," though in our town it was always called "closing day." It was not a good time to move. Usually the frost was coming out of the ground, and the roads were deep with mud. But from the point of view of the farmer it was the most appropriate time of all the year. And as long as a town is small enough to be dependent upon the surrounding agriculture for its trade, the probability is that most of the deeds and mortgages as well as the leases will bear the date of All Fools' Day.

After I was pretty well broken in with the conveyancing, the probate practice began to find its way to my desk. This was my father's own special province, and at first the estates which came to me were small. Gradually, however, as I learned the intricacies of the practice, some of the larger estates were placed in my hands. I had been his partner for two or three years before my father let me handle a mortgage foreclosure from the filing of the *lis pendens* to the referee's sale and the final order of confirmation. Shortly after this I was steered through an action of partition. And in due time I was given my initiation in a proceeding for the withdrawal of funds deposited in the County Treasurer's office, one of the most devious and complicated processes with which the country lawyer is likely to be faced.

It was at about this stage of affairs that the first damage action for personal injuries came into the office. A woman whose husband had been killed at an unprotected railroad crossing was seeking compensation from the company. My father had never taken a case of the kind and was inclined to believe that any lawyer who did was putting himself in the class with the "ambulance chaser," who was at that time operating openly all over the state. I had been thoroughly grounded at law school in the law of negligence and was anxious to try my hand at that branch of the law. I finally took the case on my own initiative and was successful in obtaining a substantial settlement from the railroad company. After that we handled a considerable number of personal injury cases.

Those were pleasant years—working there in the office with my father. There was plenty for both of us to do, and the hours we spent facing each other across the Elder Woodruff desk as we discussed the various aspects of a difficult legal question—or perhaps as we talked politics or debated the advisability of my buying one of the new-fangled horseless carriages that were just beginning to menace the country roads—are a gratifying memory.

Being a horse lover and having no mechanical bent, my father had a natural distaste for the motorcar. That did not, however, prevent me from owning the second car in town, a two-cylinder Rambler with a single door in the back by means of which to get in and out of the "tonneau." This was in 1905, and by 1909 my father had bought one of the first four-cylinder Cadillacs, though he never would learn to drive and always insisted that he liked the horses best.

In his late sixties my father began to take on some excess weight. After he had passed into the seventies he slowed down perceptibly so far as his physical actions were concerned, though his mind was as nimble and his memory as keen as ever. He never retired from practice, though most of the work of the office gradually found its way to my desk. He tried no more litigated cases after he was seventy, but he still handled an occasional matter in the probate court.

His interest in politics was unflagging, and though he no longer canvassed or made speeches, he was often in the chair at the county conventions, especially if there were contests and a riotous meeting was anticipated. He was a firm presiding officer and never allowed a meeting to get out of hand. And he was still the official greeter of the town when distinguished guests were to be received or introduced.

I had been through a severe illness in the winter of 1912, and after a long struggle with typhoid fever I had come limping back to the office in the spring in thoroughly run-down condition. My father had handled as much of the work as he could during my absence, but he was eventually compelled to bring in a young lawyer as an assistant. The assistant, who proved to be a very capable lawyer, stayed on after my return, for I had arranged to go shortly to California for a long period of recuperation. As soon as my hand was again on the helm my father went away for a vacation, realizing that he would have to carry on while I was away at the coast.

Some rearrangement of the office was necessary, and it was while we were moving the Elder Woodruff desk from its place by the window of the front room to a new location in the rear office that I accidentally found the little black note-book, without the aid of which a number of the incidents in this volume would have been incomplete and some of them entirely unknown. In shoving the heavy desk, one of the end panels came loose and fell out on the floor. When I picked it up to replace it I discovered that it was the removable door of a compartment hidden between the backs of the two tiers of drawers. It seemed strange that in all the years I had been around the office, first as a law student and afterward as a partner, I had never run across this secret cubby-hole before. When, long ago, I had found the secret drawer hidden in the molding of this desk, I should have been on the lookout for another, but for some reason I did not think of such a thing.

I still recall the thrill with which I explored the opening and the delight with which I found that my father had discovered it before me and had left some secrets hidden there.

The first thing I drew out was a bottle of Piper Heidseick champagne, woolly with dust. I shared this later with an old friend who is now a teacher in New Haven. On the label was a date which my father had written there nearly thirty years before. Then came a bundle of love letters and a penciled memorandum which showed how near these yellowed missives had come to figuring in a breach of promise suit many years before. With them was a threatening letter which might easily have sent the writer to jail for attempted extortion. In a heavy sealed envelope was a collection of poison-pen letters, a sheaf of admitted writings (including letters, checks, recipes, and a pledge for pew rent to the Presbyterian church), and a confession that had been signed in the presence of two witnesses and sworn to before my father as notary. There were a forged mortgage, some bogus notes, two fraudulent wills, and other memorabilia to delight the heart of a young lawyer.

With all this plunder I almost overlooked a flat object lying in the dust on the floor of the hidden compartment. As my eye did eventually light on it I thought it was a piece of board, and not until I had picked it up and wiped off the dust did I discover that it was a little black-covered notebook. Nothing was written on the dingy cover, and, when I looked inside, the first entry I saw was:

Strange and Unusual Cases
Encountered in my Practice
of Law

It stood out boldly at the top of the first page in the handwriting of my father. From the general character of these notes it was obvious to me that he had meant to use them as the basis for something that he was intending to write. What it was I never found out, because, so far as I know, he never got around to writing it. Some of the entries were dated before I was born. The last were made while I was in college. Other entries were not dated at all. In one place more then four years had elapsed between two entries relating to the same case.

A number of the notes I found quite meaningless—they presupposed certain information that I did not possess. Not a name appeared in the book. All references to persons were made by initial only. The first I was able to identify had long been dead; and when at last I did puzzle out the names of some who were still alive I found them old, respectable, subdued, and quite incapable of the loves and hates and the indiscretions and follies ascribed to them. Of some of the stories I was myself able to supply the ending, though until the finding of the little book I had been quite unaware of the beginning.

Without some other means of identification, the story of H. D. would have meant little to me. The town was full of

Drews, Dixons, Davids, and Dunns, any number of whom had such given names as Henry, Herbert, Harold, and Hugh. But the wife of H. D. was designated as O. D., which simplified matters considerably. There could be only a few candidates for those initials.

Ona—Ora—Octavia—Olive—Olivia—I could think of only one Olivia, and that was Olivia Dilman. So the second letter fitted into place. Then it came to me that Olivia's husband was Hemingway Dilman. There was my H. D.— and the secret was out. Not out, exactly, but at least it was no longer the secret my father had supposed was buried with the Dilmans.

I could remember Hemingway Dilman distinctly. He was the grandfather of one of my schoolmates. I recalled him as a delightful old fellow given to patting children on the head and slipping them a penny or a peppermint drop. He was a very tall man who stood up very straight in spite of his years. His hair was silvery white and curled around the sides and back of his head, and though his eyebrows were gray and fuzzy his eyes were jet black and full of sparkle. He was a handsome old man and must have been a very striking young one.

He was always an important man in town, had been several times a member of the town board, was an officer of both the bank and the church, and always had a hand in anything of importance that was going on. He was one of the most genial men I have ever seen, always very courteous and considerate of his wife. I once said something about that to my father after I had seen Hemingway and Olivia together at his office. He smiled reminiscently and said that it had not always been so. Then he asked me if I had never heard the story of the sudden change that had come over Hemingway. It had, he said, caused quite a little speculation some years before. Some people had even regarded it as a miracle, and still did. It was a curious tale of a tiger turned into a kitten overnight.

Hemingway had long been noted as a martinet in his own family. He was decent and reasonable in all his outside activities, and, though headstrong, was not too difficult in his dealings with his neighbors and the general public. But let him come into his own family circle and he at once turned into a dictator, a czar, an autocrat, a tyrant, a grizzly bear. It rarely happened that any of his commands to his wife and children were questioned; but if they were, the question was quickly squelched with a "simply because I say so."

Hemingway's rudeness to his wife in public made people uncomfortable and caused no end of embarrassment to her friends, who could see no excuse for his being so disagreeable, especially since he was having his own way. His wife's people hated him cordially. And men who had difficult wives used to look at him with envy as he would drawl, "No, my dear, I hardly think we will do any such thing as that; we will do thus and so." That was all. The matter was settled.

The Dilmans had been married some fifteen years before the great transformation occurred, and never once in all that time had Hemingway deferred to his wife's wishes so far as anyone could remember. Then suddenly from a clear sky had come the great about-face. It happened at an ice-cream social that was being given on the church lawn. Hemingway had gathered his two children and was looking around for his wife. He had just remarked to my father and several other men that they were going home. Then he caught sight of her and went up to her.

"Come, Olivia," He laid his hand on her arm as she stood talking to some of her friends. "We'll be going now."

For the first time in her life Olivia paid no attention to the royal decree, nor did she seem to be conscious of the hand on her arm. Other people were conscious of it, however, and began to draw back in anticipation of an explosion that they felt sure was about to ensue. Then suddenly affairs took an unexpected turn when Olivia shook his hand petulantly from her arm.

"Run away, dear." She did not even look at him. "I'm not ready to go yet. I do wish you wouldn't interrupt. I'll find you when I'm ready."

To my father, who stood watching proceedings, Hemingway's face was an interesting study. At first it registered astonishment—quickly followed by a crimson wave of anger and resentment. He drew himself up as if about to deliver a withering blast, then suddenly changed his mind and produced what was meant for a smile. It was not a very successful smile. It was forced and one-sided—but it was enough to mark the turning point in his life.

"N-not ready yet—?" He glanced around the circle of faces and held out his empty hands with a shrug of helplessness. "Sorry I interrupted. There isn't any hurry, really." And he turned and walked away.

Quite naturally the incident caused more talk than anything that had happened in years. But it was, after all, only the beginning. Further developments came rapidly, and it was not long before it had become a commonplace all over town that Olivia had Hemingway eating out of her hand. Never again was there any of the "we'll be going now" sort of thing. Instead it was, "Whenever you are ready, Olivia," or "Would you mind very much, my dear?" And in time it became, "Well, now, I'll have to ask Olivia about that."

Once she got the upper hand Olivia treated her husband with a domineering arrogance that was even more disagreeable than his previous treatment of her. People were glad enough to see the shoe on the other foot, but they were mystified. There was a great deal of speculation about what might or might not have happened to bring so complete a reversal of their positions. There were almost as many theories as there were inhabitants in town, though the speculators were divisible into two general schools: those who regarded the event as an act of divine intercession—who believed that God had softened Hemingway's heart; and those who thought it must be the result of something of a much more earthy origin, though they did not know what.

When I asked my father which side he was on he smiled. "On the side of the angels, of course," he replied. "Best authenticated miracle I ever knew of—saw it myself."

"But didn't people ever find out what was back of it?"

My father shook his head. "Never."

The tale came up for a thorough rediscussion when Olivia died without having surrendered her supremacy. Hemingway, on whom the habit of geniality had by now become firmly fixed, was lost without her. He seemed to miss being trampled on, and within a year or two he followed her to the family burying ground. It had never occurred to me that my father might have had some inside information on the case. His remarks about the miracle had misled me entirely. It was therefore a surprise as well as a delight to find the missing part of the story in the little black book.

Olivia, so the story ran, had come to his office one day and dumfounded him by demanding that he start a suit for divorce against her husband. Divorce, he had told her, was regarded by the state of New York as a pretty serious business and was, as she probably knew, obtainable on only one ground.

"I have that ground," she said.

"This is one of the things," said my father slowly, "which the law is rather reluctant to infer from circumstances. It must be—well, pretty definite evidence."

Olivia nodded. "It is . . . I saw it myself."

For a moment she stared hard at the floor. Then she went on. Hemingway was haying in the west meadow by the creek, a secluded place, far from the house, and since he

299

did not want to take the time to come in for his dinner, she had sent it out to him by a little serving maid. When the serving maid had not come back promptly Olivia had gone in search of her. She had walked out through the orchard but had seen nothing of the girl. She had kept on going and had almost reached the fence which separated the twenty-acre lot from the west meadow when she heard voices. She stopped to listen and could hear the rumble of a man's voice, followed by the giggle of a young girl. The voices came from the adjoining field—and she parted the shrubbery and looked through. She stopped as if unable to tell any more, but my father led her on.

"And you saw them?"

She nodded. "It was Hemingway and the girl. They were —lying on a haycock in the shade of an elm tree."

"Does Hemingway know that you saw this?"

"He ought to—I called to him to stop what he was doing and send the girl back to the house."

"Then what?"

"When she got back to the house I made her sit down and write out a full confession of all that had happened." She laid a folded paper on the table. "Then I hitched up a horse and came directly here."

My father nodded slowly as he read over the paper. "You probably know that a wife can't testify against her husband in a case like this. But we won't go into that just now. I have a better idea, and the evidence in hand is ample for what I have in view." He tapped the confession with his finger. "There is enough here to break Hemingway completely—if you should want to make use of it. You could have him heaved bodily out of the church and dropped from the school board like a hot coal. You could probably have him expelled from the Grange. He'd have to resign as Chairman of the Centennial Committee, and he'd have to give up all idea of ever being nominated for County Clerk or sent as a delegate to the State Convention. You have it in your power to ruin him. But why ruin him? Would you be any better off? And then there are your own children to think about."

"But, Judge—you don't understand."

"Of course I understand."

"But you don't realize how he has ruled and domineered and humiliated me ever since I went into that house as a bride."

"I have a very fair idea of the situation."

"Oh, but I haven't even been able to say that my soul was my own!"

My father smiled. "You can now."

She stared hard at him. "What do you mean?"

"I mean that when Hemingway finds that you have this confession—he'll have to come to your terms."

"But—but what about the girl?"

"You'll have to send her away. I know somebody who is looking for a maid. Fine place for her—several miles away—and no men in the family. Where is she now, by the way?"

"She's outside sitting in the carriage. I didn't dare leave her home."

"Will she do as you say?"

"I think she will. She's terribly frightened."

"Do you know the Cosad sisters on the Orleans road?"

"I know who they are."

"You can take the girl out there. I'll give you a letter to them. They've been looking for a maid. Is she a good servant?"

"Excellent. I hate to lose her, but of course—"

"Yes, of course. Now here's the plan: don't argue with Hemingway. Don't let him stage a grand repentance and get you to forgive him—or you'll be right where you were before. Get one of your sisters to come and stay with you for a while. Shut yourself in your own room and use her as a go-between. Don't speak with Hemingway at all, but have *her* tell him that you refuse to see him until after he has had a talk with me. I'll tell him about the signed confession, and I will make it very plain to him that whether you are to ruin his career or not at some future time will depend entirely upon his own conduct. And another thing—take your time about forgiving him. Don't let him think it's going to be too easy. Let him get down on his knees and do a little begging.

Her face lighted. "Oh, do you think he will?"

"He's got to."

"You really mean that I've got the upper hand?"

"You certainly have. Do you think you can manage anything as important as that?"

"I think I'm as capable of managing it as Hemingway ever was."

My father smiled. "It will be amusing to find that out. And now, if you'll bring that girl in here, I'll throw a scare into her that will last her the rest of her natural life."

25. Resting His Case

ONCE the Dilman mystery was solved I went feverishly at work to identify the principals in some of the other stories in the little book. A number of them I never was able to work out at all, but I found a few of them very easy. There was, for example, the case of "Captain J—, Who Thought He Wanted to Die." I had not gone far into this story before I recognized "Captain J—" as an old friend of my father's named Captain Jenks.

As the Captain approached the sixties, he had decided that he had worked long enough and was nearly ready to retire and take his ease. There were to be no halfway measures about this retirement. He told my father that he did not propose to take a house in town and then work almost as hard as he had before, keeping up the lawn and garden in summer and shoveling coal and snow in winter. When he retired he meant to stop work entirely. So he rented his farm and took permanent quarters at the Inn.

Here the Captain puttered over his farm accounts; or he would go out and play a game or two of billiards with his old cronies while his wife sewed with the ladies of the missionary society or quilted with the ladies of the relief corps. She was busy with these activities at least two afternoons a week, and there were other afternoons when she was occupied with the ladies of other organizations. The Captain and Mrs. Jenks had been living at the Inn less than a year, however, when one afternoon between three and four o'clock the town was thrown into a turmoil by the frenzied beating of Old Tick's big brass gong.

With the thought firmly entrenched in their minds that this gong was sounded only for meals or disasters people began to crane their necks and look toward the Inn. They were certain that something pretty terrible was happening there. The first thought was that the place must be on fire. And when they saw Old Tick in slippers and shirt sleeves come squeezing out the door as fast as his ponderous bulk would allow, his face red and perspiring, his eyes bulging with terror, and his right hand flailing the huge disk of brass with all its power, they dropped whatever they were doing and started for the Inn.

Somebody, just on a chance, began to ring the fire bell, but this only made Old Tick beat the more lustily on his timbrel.

"What's the matter, Tick?" cried those who were first to arrive.

"Jees Cri'!" wheezed Tick as he ceased his belaboring of the gong. "It's the Captain—!" and he trailed off into a string of incoherent profanity.

"Well, what about him? He ain't on fire, is he?"

"Hell, no!" piped the innkeeper shrilly. "He's hung hisself!"

"What's that—*where?*"

"In the attic above the third floor—I heard a noise up there as I was passin' the hatchway—and when I looked up I seen it was open—and then, godamighty—I could see him a-hangin' from a rafter—!"

"Did you cut him down?"

"Hell, no—I'm too big to get up through the doggone hole!"

304

Rescuers went leaping up the stairs and scaled the narrow ladder leading into the loft. And although the Captain kicked out at them to drive them away they succeeded in cutting him down while he was still alive.

I remember the day perfectly. I was about ten years old at the time and was passing the Inn on my way home from school when Old Tick had started his pounding on the gong. With several other boys, I had tried to follow the rescuers into the attic of the Inn to help cut down the Captain's body but had been turned back at the second floor by Cobb, who even then was the officious porter and man of all work around the Inn. I had seen the body carried down, however, and I was only borrowing the words of other people when I repeated the story that the Captain had made the attempt on his life while in a fit of drunken irresponsibility. I felt very important to have been almost a participant in so dramatic an affair and had a great deal to say about it to home, to all of which my father listened without comment.

The Captain had not until this time been known as a drinking man, but the fact remained that neither he nor his wife had denied the drunkenness story; and when, a short time after the attempted hanging, the Jenkses had given up their rooms at the Inn and moved back to the farm, the talk was that Mrs. Jenks was simply taking her husband to a place where the cheering cup would not be quite so much of a temptation. For me as well as the rest of the town the Captain's story was ended. He had had his fling—and had gone back to the farm. And that was that.

It was, for a number of years at any rate; but when I found the little black book I discovered that there was another chapter known only to my father and the principals involved in it. From my father's notes it appeared that as soon as Mrs. Jenks had succeeded in getting rid of the doctor and the various volunteer nurses who had flocked to her assistance the day of the attempted suicide, she had turned the key in the lock and confronted the Captain. What follows is as she told it to my father:

"'I know it wa'n't strong drink,' I said to him. 'Now, Jenks, what was it?'

"He pointed to his throat and pretended he couldn't speak, but I reminded him that he had spoken to the doctor. For a long time he made no answer at all. Then he said in a hoarse whisper, 'Guess I was just tired of livin', that's all.'

"I shook my head. 'You wa'n't tired of livin' this morning. You said you never felt better in your life. Now *what* was it?'

"'Couldn't tell you. Just a impulse, I guess.'

"'Now, Jenks,' I said, 'you never had a impulse in your life. What *was* it?'

"He thought for a while, and then he said, 'Voices told me to do it.'

"'See here, Jenks,' I said, 'you ain't never been one to hear voices. You know that just as well as I do. Somep'm happened to you after I left here at two o'clock—now I want to know what it was.'

"Well, he held out as long as he could, but at last he gave in and told me the truth. One of the servant girls in the Inn had been coming up to his room while I was out tying quilts for the needy, and he had just found out—it was hard for him to say it—that the girl was in a family way. He didn't know what to do, and suicide looked like the easiest way out of it.

"You know without my telling you that I was shaken considerable by his confession, but I was not angry. I took hold of his hand and burst into tears. 'It's as much my fault as yours,' I told him. 'If I could only have given you a child—but it just wasn't possible.'

"I couldn't seem to stop crying—just couldn't help it, and pretty soon he said, 'If you keep that up I'll begin to wish I was back there hangin' to the rafter—I do anyhow. It wa'n't nowise your fault. And if you keep on blamin' yourself—you'll find me there yet.'

"'But why didn't you come to me in the first place?' said I. 'Then there wouldn't be all this talk that's sure to go on.'

"'I couldn't do it, Marthy. All I could think of was keepin' it from you,' he says, 'and the only way I could see to do that—was to put myself out of the way.'

"'But there must be ways such things can be took care of,' I told him.

"'Not in this case,' he says. 'It was too late. She'd just come back from seein' a out-of-town doctor.'

"'But that ain't quite what I mean,' I says. 'I was thinkin' of some other way. It seems so unjust—anybody but me can have a child. Not that Carrie ain't a nice ladylike girl. It's likely she'd make a good mother.'

"'But what other way is there?' he says.

"'Well,' said I, 'I got an idea, but I don't want to talk about it until I go over and see the Judge. I want to know if it would be legal, and all like that.'"

"He raised up both his hands. 'You ain't goin' to tell *him*—?'

"I nodded my head very positively. 'Oh, yes, he's got to know about it. I'll go over and see him right now—and I want you to keep perfectly quiet until I get back. Then I'll tell you all about it. I'm going to lock the door and take the key with me so there won't nobody come pokin' in here and bother you.'"

My father nodded slowly. "I see," he said. "Now what's your idea?"

"My idea is that I want that baby—and I want you to figure out some way to get it for me."

When Mrs. Jenks went back to the Inn she took my father with her. For a time the two were closeted with the Captain. Then Mrs. Jenks went down and asked if she could have one of the maids stay up in her rooms to help with the patient. She selected a rather pretty though plump girl who seemed very nervous at the thought of undertaking this particular job. As my father was going out some time later he stopped to have a word with the proprietor, who was still excited and a little flushed with the stimulant he had taken to steady his nerves.

Old Tick ushered him into the small room back of the office. "Well, Judge, did you git to the bottom of it?" he asked eagerly.

"Yes, I think I did."

"Well what the hell in Jees Cri's name was it?"

"Suicidal dementia superinduced by a severe attack of nostalgia."

Old Tick blinked his eyes wisely. "So that's it, hey? Think it's very serious?"

"Yes, I think it is. There's only one thing to be done—if we don't want him to be trying it again—and that's to get him back on the farm just as soon as we can."

"Jees Cri'! You think he's apt to try it again?"

"I'm afraid so—the first time he gets a chance—if we don't get him away from here."

"Well, godamighty, let's get him outa here in a hurry then!"

"That's what I wanted to see you about. They'll want to be giving up their rooms in a day or two, if that's all right with you."

"Can't make it too quick to suit me. I don't want to find no more bodies hangin' down from *my* rafters. But, hey, Judge, how can he go back to the farm? Hain't it rented to a Dutchman?"

"There won't be any trouble about that. The Dutchman doesn't occupy the farmhouse—he lives in the tenant house."

"Oh, he does, hey?"

"And one thing more," said my father. "Mrs. Jenks would like to take along that maid who's up there helping her. She needs somebody to keep watch of him, and she likes Carrie. Carrie has been taking care of their rooms, you know."

"Carrie's all right. She's a good worker."

"But do you mind letting her go—in view of the emergency?"

"Don't know's I could stop her if she's took it into her head."

A day or two later, with the assistance of Carrie, the Captain was moved back to the farm, and an immediate improvement was noted in his condition. Within a few weeks he had recovered entirely, but Mrs. Jenks was said to be poorly, and Carrie stayed on to take care of her. Not long afterwards the story got around town that the Captain had been in and changed his will so as to make adequate provision for an expected heir. Questioned about it, my father smiled and said to ask the Captain. Somebody did, and the Captain admitted it freely.

"Marthy ain't so young as she once was," he explained. "Fifty-four is a little old for child bearin', but I understand there's cases in the books where women of fifty-seven and sixty and even sixty-five has come through without a hitch."

Well, yes, it was possible, people said. But wasn't it pretty risky?

"Marthy's always been sturdy," the Captain replied. "Never been sick a day in her life. Took her to Rochester to see a specialist, and he says there's no reason why she shouldn't come through with colors a-flyin'."

That was fine, but what local doctor were they having?

"Well, now," the Captain would raise his hat and brush back the scanty gray hair underneath, "Marthy thinks she wants to go back to Pennsylvany for the finish. She was born a Sayre, you know, and the Pennsylvania Sayres are a pretty clannish lot, so I reckon Carrie and me'll be takin' her down there one of these days. Marthy sets powerful store by Carrie. Couldn't get along without her."

It was not long after this that the Captain and Carrie assisted Mrs. Jenks, much bundled up, aboard an evening train. And soon their friends were receiving cards from them containing greetings from Pennsylvania. In the fullness of time the baby was born and Mrs. Jenks came through without any trouble at all. When, some months later, they returned to town Carrie stayed on as nurse girl. Indeed, she practically brought the young one up. The Jenkses had named the baby Eleanor, but they were a little sorry afterwards that they had not named her after Carrie, she was so faithful to the child.

When Eleanor Jenks grew up she was sent away to boarding school and afterward to college, and when the Captain and Mrs. Jenks came to die they left her their not inconsiderable estate—with a curious proviso that gave Carrie the right to stay on the farm and make her home there so long as she lived. People thought this a pretty generous provision, especially since Carrie was no more than a servant in the house, even if she had lived there a good many years and been treated almost like a member of the family. But Eleanor told my father she would not have had it any other way. She said that next to her own mother she loved Carrie better than anybody else on earth.

I saw Eleanor and Carrie together once in my father's office, and after they had gone I remarked that they looked enough alike to be mother and daughter.

"Yes, they do seem to look alike," said my father. "I wonder how much there is to the popular superstition around here that if two people spend a great deal of time together they often get to look alike."

"But how could they?" I asked.

310

The country lawyer at three score and ten.

"Oh, by unconscious imitation. Or perhaps it's just association—people think they look alike because they never see one without the other."

And as we sat talking across the top of the Elder Woodruff desk the little black book containing the true story must even then have been gathering dust in its hiding place only a few inches from my left foot.

The little book had an irresistible attraction for me. I could not seem to take it or leave it alone. If I opened it at all, I would find myself puzzling over its pages for hours at a time. And though I had, as I have intimated, insufficient information to make much sense out of some of the entries, I never opened the book without feeling the challenge of the two pages of newspaper clippings that were pasted in without comment near the end of the book. I felt from the first that there must be a story hidden between the lines of these yellowed bits of newsprint if I could only find the key.

There were six clippings on each page, twelve in all. Not one was over fifteen lines in length. One was less than ten. They had been cut mostly from the Rochester papers. I knew, of course, that they had not been placed there by chance or inadvertence; that was not my father's way. Somehow, somewhere, they would fit into the picture, I was sure of that, though aside from the fact that they all concerned fires of undisclosed origin they seemed to have nothing in common.

Again and again I read them over, looking in vain for some clue that would explain why they had been preserved in that secret record. I studied the brief account of the burning of a large barn on the Leman Pardee farm in the town of Bloomfield. It was a heavy loss, for the barn contained the entire season's harvest . . . I passed on to the burning of a wheel factory belonging to John R. Jessup in Shortsville. The fire had occurred during the installation of some expen-

sive new machinery which had not yet been insured . . .
Another clipping told of a house in the town of Bristol which
had been burned to the ground on Christmas Eve. . . .
The next reported the destruction of a store in Seneca while
the owner was celebrating his wedding anniversary . . .
And there was one that told of the burning of a home after
a death in the family while the corpse was still in the house.

Slowly it dawned on me that fire was not the only thread
running through those clippings; in every one there was an
added element of tragedy. At first I was excited over the
discovery, since it promised a new angle of approach, but
in the end it led me nowhere. I was still without an adequate
explanation of a collection of tragedies—even double ones—
in a book of my father's most private and confidential
records.

My quest had long since passed the stage of idle curiosity.
I was aroused as a man is often aroused by his inability to
solve a simple-appearing puzzle, and I finally decided to
run down the name of each person mentioned in the clippings, to see if my father had previously had dealings with
them or any of them. I picked up a pencil and started to
make a list of the names.

> Leman Pardee
> John R. Jessup
> Peter S. Moore
> Heber Wheelock

I had gone only this far when I happened to think of the
Billings case. Jerry was the only client of the office, so far as
I knew, who had been involved in any mysterious burnings,
and it occurred to me that my father might have clipped
these items for use in one of his innumerable motions on the
appeal of the case. But as soon as I began to check up on the
dates I could see that this was impossible. Jerry had finished
his term in prison and was well on his way back to respect-

ability and rehabilitation before any of these fires had occurred.

However, I thought that I might as well take a look at the records of the Billings case to see if I could find any possible connection. As I opened the big book at the proper page—the list of names fairly leaped up at me. But it was not in a motion on appeal that these names had figured; they were much more closely identified with the case. They were the members of the jury that had convicted Jerry Billings of arson!

Until that moment I had been undecided about the disposition of the little black book. I had considered returning it to its hiding place and saying nothing about it; I had even thought of staging a rediscovery in my father's presence in the hope that he might unravel the parts that I had been unable to figure out for myself. Now, however, I knew that I would have to swallow my pride—or my conscience, if such it was that was giving me a feeling of guilt for having pried into my father's private papers—and ask him the questions that were clamoring for an answer.

What I most wanted to know was when he had discovered Jerry's diabolical scheme to avenge the verdict of the jury. What had aroused his suspicions? How many of the burnings had already occurred? If only a part, what had he done to prevent the completion of the plot against the other jurymen? Did he now believe Jerry guilty of the crime for which he had been punished? Or was it my father's belief that the plan for revenge was something contrived by an innocent man driven by a miscarriage of justice into taking the law into his own hands? What I wanted most of all was to hear the whole story from my father's lips.

That, however, was not to be; for I never discussed any legal matters with my father again. He had expected to return before I started for California, but his journey was

313

delayed by bad weather, and by the time that he had reached home I was well on my way to the coast.

It was not until after my father's death, which occurred quite suddenly, that I learned where the clippings had come from. In settling Jerry Billings' estate, my father had found them among Jerry's private papers.

26. Adjournment Sine Die

I WAS still in California when my father reached his seventy-fifth year. Shortly before his birthday he and my mother had celebrated their forty-ninth wedding anniversary, and the entire family was planning a gala reunion for the fiftieth. Only a few months of their fiftieth year together had passed, however, when my mother fell and injured her back. She never walked again. She had been too gay and active all her life to submit to invalidism with good grace. Her injury and confinement to the house bore heavily on my father. He lost interest in his work, and sometimes he would not go near the office for several days, though he kept some contact with his assistant by telephone.

In the middle of December he came down with a heavy cold which quickly developed into pneumonia. The throat difficulty that had troubled him during his later years became aggravated and acute, and his condition was recognized from the first as very serious. We children came hurrying home from all directions, and though we did what we could to cheer and brighten him he grew steadily weaker.

Three days before Christmas, while the ground was white with shimmering crystals of new-fallen snow and the windows were gaily decorated with holly wreaths and mistletoe, he breathed his last.

Before he died, true patriarch that he was, he summoned each child to his bedside for a final blessing and a farewell—and of course he called for us in the order of our age, beginning with the eldest.

For days after my father's funeral people I hardly knew kept coming into the office to tell me how much my father was going to be missed. So many of them went on to say that nobody would ever be able to take his place that I began to wonder what his place really was. The town in which he had settled was distinctly a horse-and-buggy town. The ten miles of country roads which separated it from the surrounding towns had been as effective as the Great Wall of China in keeping out strange people and new notions. The first breach in the wall had been made by the telephone. Soon afterward the automobile began to bring in the strange people, and the motion picture had furnished the new notions.

At this point in the century the American country town began to lose its flavor, its individuality, its peculiarities of local custom and local idiom. It was no longer the product of its own environment. Outside influences were now directing its growth and development. The great god Regimentation was in the saddle and ready to go.

My father had gone along with the change. He had carried over from the old day into the new, and by virtue of his character and personality had brought a little of the late nineteenth century with him. But what he had brought was intangible—it was something that perished with him like the sound of his voice. The country town of the seventies and eighties, self-contained and self-sustaining, was on the way out. Soon the concrete road would open, and the motorbus would be running every hour on the hour; the weather predictions, market reports, and late news flashes would come booming out of the loud speaker in a steady stream; Cooley's store would be taken over by a chain and given a red front, and instead of being a local club dominated by whimsical, good-hearted old Cooley the place would be designated by a serial number and managed by a board of directors in Hartford, Connecticut.

It was true what they said about nobody's being able to take my father's place—for that place had ceased to exist. The small town was no longer dependent on the country lawyer. All the best of the younger legal talent had begun to drift to the county seat or the larger towns. In the quarter century since my father's death the drift has been pretty well completed. Here and there a shrewd old counselor will still be found among his battered books in a grubby, paper-littered office in an out-of-the-way country town. But the country lawyer, as he existed between the days of Abraham Lincoln and Calvin Coolidge, is no more.